What is Nature?

What is Nature?

Culture, Politics and the non-Human

KATE SOPER

BLACKWELL
Oxford UK & Cambridge USA

Copyright © Kate Soper 1995

The right of Kate Soper to be identified as author
of this work has been asserted in accordance with the
Copyright, Designs and Patents Act 1988.

First published 1995
Reprinted 1998

Blackwell Publishers Ltd
108 Cowley Road
Oxford OX4 1JF
UK

Blackwell Publishers Inc.
350 Main Street
Malden, Massachusetts 02148
USA

British Library Cataloguing in Publication Data

A CIP catalogue record for this book is available from the British Library.

Library of Congress Cataloging-in-Publication Data

Soper Kate.
What is nature? / Kate Soper.
p.   cm.
Includes bibliographical references and index.
ISBN 0–631–18889–4 (alk. paper). — ISBN 0–631–18891–6 (pbk. :
alk. paper)
1.   Philosophy of nature. 2. Nature and nurture. 3. Environmental
ethics. I. Title.
BD581.S67   1995   94–46739
113—dc20   CIP

Copy-edited and typeset in 12 on 14pt Sabon
by Grahame & Grahame Editorial, Brighton
Printed in Great Britain by Athenaeum Press Ltd, Gateshead, Tyne & Wear
This book is printed on acid-free paper

For my parents,
Horace and Julie Sanders
and my sister,
Vivian Sanders

CONTENTS

Acknowledgements   viii

Introduction   1
1 The Discourses of Nature   15
2 Nature, Human and Inhuman   37
3 Nature, Friend and Foe   71
4 Nature and Sexual Politics   119
5 Nature and 'Nature'   149
6 The Space and Time of Nature   180
7 Loving Nature   213
8 Ecology, Nature and Responsibility   249

Index   283

ACKNOWLEDGEMENTS

'Nature' is, of its nature, an uncontainable topic, and this work has inevitably spilt over into areas requiring an altogether more substantial treatment than they receive in this work. A first acknowledgement must therefore go to those authors whose research and writing I have drawn upon but have not accorded the extended discussion they merit. I would be the first to recognize that I have touched on more issues and debates than I have done justice to here, and must apologize for what I know is an over-cursory engagement with some of the material and arguments I here refer to. I would plead only that any synthetic approach of the kind attempted here was, in a sense, bound to relate to more dimensions of its subject matter than it could possibly aspire to accommodate in any adequate fashion. Some may feel that that was a reason to refrain from any such exercise in the first place. I can only hope that there are others who will feel that the project is justified, if only in terms of the thought it provokes about the complexity of our discourses about nature and the variety of tensions to which these are subject.

I must thank Simon Prosser at Blackwell for proposing the project to me in the first place, and for everything he has done to assist its completion. I am also very grateful for the financial assistance provided by the Faculty of Humanities and Teacher Education of the University of North London.

Several people have commented at some length on the whole, or substantial sections, of this book in draft, and have saved me in the process from various misconstructions, lacunae and indiscretions. Such as remain are entirely my own responsibility. I am grateful to Gregory Elliott both for the wisdom of his editorial advice and for his incisive criticism of some aspects of my argument. I must also thank Russell Keat for his valuable recommendations. I am particularly indebted to Ted Benton for the generosity and sagacity of his comments on a draft from some of whose formulations and lines of argument he dissented quite sharply. I would like to thank Steve Kupfer for many inspirational conversations, and for the help he has given me in the writing of certain chapters of this book. I am also grateful to Jonathan Dollimore for his advice and interest at an initial stage in its development.

Earlier drafts of the material which have gone into the making of this book were presented at seminars at the University of Kent, the Architects Association, the Oxford University School of Geography, the Manchester Metropolitan University, the University of Manchester, the University of Southampton and the University of Sussex, and I am grateful to those who facilitated these meetings, and for the critical comments that were offered on my argument in the course of them. I am also grateful for the support of the European Research Group at the University of North London.

I would like to thank Nick Gallie, Leonie Soper, Mark Dorrian, Peter Dickens and Andrew Wright for particular forms of help or encouragement, and Kate O'Donnell, Flick Allen, Keith Pickard, Erick Svarny, Geoff and Nannette Aldred, James Grant, Charlotte Lane, Tom Hammick, Jonathan Rée, Rosemary Ryle, Cora Kaplan, Roy Bhaskar and Hilary Wainwright for their general interest and support. A special thanks for special kinds of support must go to Jude Ryle and Madeleine Ryle.

To Martin Ryle I am above all grateful. He has been unstinting in the time he has devoted to reading and commenting on this book and has given me consistently helpful advice both on its argument and on its textual detail. His support in many other ways has also been more valuable than I can say.

What is Nature?

INTRODUCTION

'Nature', as Raymond Williams has remarked, is one of the most complex words in the language.[1] Yet, as with many other problematic terms, its complexity is concealed by the ease and regularity with which we put it to use in a wide variety of contexts. It is at once both very familiar and extremely elusive: an idea we employ with such ease and regularity that it seems as if we ourselves are privileged with some 'natural' access to its intelligibility; but also an idea which most of us know, in some sense, to be so various and comprehensive in its use as to defy our powers of definition. On the one hand, we are perfectly at home with it, whether the reference is to the 'nature' of rocks or to rocks as a part of 'nature'; to that 'great nature that exists in the works of mighty poets'[2] or to the humbler stuff of 'natural' fibre; to the 'Nature' park or the nature encroaching on our allotment; to the rudeness of 'nature' or to a 'naturalness' of manners. On the other hand, merely to contemplate this range of usage is to sense a loss of grip on what it is that we here have in mind. For the 'nature' of rocks which refers us to their essential qualities is not the 'nature' conceived as the totality of non-human matter to which they are said to belong. Nor, it seems, is the latter quite what the poet is invoking, or the poet's nature the kind of thing we eat for breakfast. Equally, we may ask how we may so readily speak of what is clearly humanly cultivated, whether it be breakfast cereal or our own modes of comportment, as 'natural' while also distinguishing so firmly between what 'we' are and do, and the being and productions of 'nature'; how we speak of both preserved land and wilderness as 'nature', or think of our garden or allotment as both belonging to 'nature' and keeping it at bay.

To attempt to disentangle these various threads of nature discourse is immediately to realize what a vast range of possible topics a work such as this one might be addressing. For nature refers us to the object of study of the natural and biological sciences; to issues in metaphysics concerning the differing modes of being of the natural and the human; and to the environment and its various non-human forms of life. The natural is both distinguished from the human and the cultural, but also the concept through which we pose questions about the more or less natural or artificial quality of our own behaviour and cultural formations; about the existence and quality of human nature; and about the respective roles of nature and culture in the formation of individuals and their social milieu. Nature also carries an immensely complex and contradictory symbolic load; it is the subject of very contrary ideologies; and it has been represented in an enormous variety of differing ways. In recent times, it has come to occupy a central place on the political agenda as a result of ecological crisis, where it figures as a general concept through which we are asked to re-think our current use of resources, our relations to other forms of life, and our place within, and responsibilities towards the eco-system.

Indeed, the debates that have been generated round the idea of nature are so various and complex that the title of this book will seem presumptuous, if not downright absurd. I must therefore dispel some expectations that it may invite, and specify in what sense it is intended. Firstly, this work is not conceived as a historical account of the

idea of nature and does not pretend to offer any comprehensive survey or scholarly engagement at that level.
Nor, secondly, will it be defending a specific philosophy of
nature or elaborating a theoretical position on the various
debates which have been generated around the concept of
nature in social theory and psychology, though it will bear
on those debates, and at times specifically relate to them.
It is not, then, either a contribution to the 'history of
ideas', nor is it primarily focused on questions of ontology,
debates in the philosophy of science or controversies on the
respective roles of 'nature' and 'nurture' in the formation
of human beings and their societies.

My engagement here is essentially with the 'politics' of
the idea of nature, with the social and cultural demarca-
tions which have been drawn through the concept, and
with the ways it is both defended and contested in the
social movements of our times. It is therefore in many
ways much more restricted than my title might suggest.
For though I shall be offering some more general mapping
of Western attitudes to nature, and theories of it, the map
is drawn in the light of the particular forms of attention
being paid to nature at the present time, and with the
specific aim of staging an encounter between two currently
very influential perspectives upon it: that of ecology, on
the one hand, and that of much recent theory and cultural
criticism, on the other. The distinction, broadly speaking,
here is between an approach to nature that has emerged
in response to ecological crisis, is critically targeted on its
human plunder and destruction and politically directed at
correcting that abuse; and an approach that is focused on
the semiotics of 'nature', which would recall us to the
role of the concept in mediating access to the 'reality'
it names, and whose political critique is directed at the
oppressive use of the idea to legitimate social and sexual
hierarchies and cultural norms. The contrast, crudely, is
between discourses which direct us to the 'nature' that

we are destroying, wasting and polluting, and discourses that are focused on the ideological functions of the appeal to 'nature' and on the ways in which relations to the non-human world are always historically mediated, and indeed 'constructed', through specific conceptions of human identity and difference.

   To avoid misunderstanding, I would emphasize that, although this might be broadly construed as a contrast between ecological and postmodernist argument, my essential concern here is with the tension between diverging approaches to nature both of which may have a role to play in shaping a particular political outlook, and which I certainly do not view as neatly dividing between two oppositional political camps. Postmodernism has indeed become loosely associated with a politics, but it seems to me quite misleading to use the term as if it referred to a definitive programme of action rather than to a set of theoretical perspectives which are deployed by their advocates in the interests of a number of specific and often quite differing agendas. Nor can ecology be viewed as constituting a singular political vision since there are widely differing programmes of action which are recommended in the interests of nature conservation. For this reason, I would prefer to speak of a contrast between what might be termed 'nature-endorsing' and 'nature-sceptical' arguments with no presumption being made that these reflect some simple antithesis between a 'green' and a 'postmodernist' politics. Many 'nature-sceptical' discourses do indeed draw on postmodernist theory, but there are others deriving from Marxist, socialist or feminist positions that are highly critical of the postmodernist resistance to any realist or foundationalist metaphysics. It is one thing to challenge various cultural representations of nature, another to represent nature as if it were a convention of culture, and there are many in the Green Movement who reject this conventionalist approach while readily subscribing to critiques of the ideological naturalization of social and sexual relations. But there are also many committed to postmodernist anti-realism who subscribe to the general aims of the ecological movement and view themselves as pursuing emancipatory projects consistent with it. In short, part of the complexity of the issues with which I shall be dealing derives from the fact that very differing discourses or theoretical perspectives on nature may be deployed in support of a shared set of political values.

One relevant instance here is the prescriptive overlap between the more distinctively postmodernist forms of scepticism about nature and ecological critiques of Enlightenment. Both, for example, have put in question Western models of progress and have sought to expose the oppressive dimensions of the faith in scientific rationality and its associated 'humanist' commitments. Many in the Green Movement have denounced the technocratic Prometheanism of the Enlightenment project, and have argued that the 'anthropocentric' privileging of our own species encouraged by its 'humanism' has been distorting of the truth of our relations with nature and resulted in cruel and destructive forms of dominion over it. They have criticized Western 'instrumental rationality' as responsible for abusive and alienating exploitations of the environment and its other life forms, and have argued that its scientistic approach must yield to a more proper sense of our actual dependency on the eco-system and of our organic ties and affinities with the earth and its various species. In these and similar critiques, ecological politics clearly subscribes to key themes of the postmodernist argument, which has equally cast doubt on the emancipatory claims of Enlightenment thinking, and regards its universalist 'humanist' commitments as the vehicle of an ethnocentric and 'imperialising' suppression of cultural difference.

Yet despite these broad affinities at the level of political critique, there is no doubt that the two positions diverge

very considerably in respect of the discourses they offer
on nature, and that to focus on this difference is to
be made aware of the extent of tension between these
seemingly complementary forms of resistance to Western
modernity. For while the ecologists tend to invoke nature
as a domain of intrinsic value, truth or authenticity and are
relatively unconcerned with questions of representation
and conceptuality, postmodernist cultural theory and criticism looks with suspicion on any appeal to the idea as an
attempt to 'eternize' what in reality is merely conventional,
and has invited us to view the order of nature as entirely
linguistically constructed. Derridian deconstruction, for
example, in focusing on the binary dependencies of all
philosophical categories, including that of 'nature', has
called in question the coherence of any appeal to the
latter as if to some reality external to its 'text', and his
theory has prompted numerous cultural readings which
emphasize the instability of the concept of 'nature', and
its failure of any fixed reference. In contrast, moreover, to
the naturalist impulse of much ecological argument, which
has emphasized human affinities with other animals, and
regards a dualist demarcation between the cultural and
the natural as a mistaken and inherently un-eco-friendly
ontology, postmodernist theory has emphasized the irreducibly cultural and symbolic order of human being and
has consistently criticized naturalist explanations of the
being of humanity. Thus Foucault presents the distinction
between the 'natural' and the 'unnatural' (or 'perverse') as
itself the effect of discourse, and rejects the explanatory
force of the reference to a common natural foundation
in the approach to psychology or sexuality. People are
not 'mad' by nature, but as a result of classification;
the discourses of sexuality are in an important sense the
source of so-called 'natural' sexual feeling itself; even
the body must be viewed as the worked-up effect of a
'productive' power and its cultural inscriptions. In all this

argument a culturalist perspective has not only challenged the naturalism and realism of ecological appeals to nature, but in the process has invited us to view the very idea of nature – the idea of that which has standardly been opposed to culture – as itself a cultural formation.

The upshot of this is a kind of communicational impasse between the two perspectives. For while the one party invokes nature in reference to features of ourselves and the world regarded as discourse-independent, the other responds by querying the supposed signified of the signifier: a stance it supports by pointing to the multiple constructions placed upon 'nature' at different historical periods and in different cultural contexts; by deconstructing its dependency on the binary other of the 'human' or the 'cultural'; and by highlighting the ideological service it has performed in a whole range of discourses from the Enlightenment, by way of Social Darwinism through to contemporary naturalism in social and psychological theory. From this latter perspective, the one thing that is not 'natural' is nature herself, and the 'herself' can serve to reinforce the point.

My argument here is thus shaped by the conjuncture at the present time of two perspectives, both of them centrally concerned with questions about nature and appearing to share certain prescriptive positions in common, but driven by quite contrary impulses: the one concerned with the limits of nature, and with our need to value, conserve, and recognize our dependence upon it; the other concerned to remind us of the cultural 'construction' of nature, of its role in policing social and sexual divisions, and of the relativity and ethnocentric quality of our conceptions about it. The query of my title is therefore contextually specific and should be construed more as a gesture towards a problem than as a promise to supply a solution to it. It is intended, that is, as an echo, or index, of the politically contested nature of 'nature' in our own times, and of the ways in which the question of its 'being' is, at least implicitly, at issue in so many of our current discourses about it. But it is also intended to reflect the underlying rationale of the book, which is written in the conviction that both 'nature-endorsing' and 'nature-sceptical' perspectives need to be more conscious of what their respective discourses on nature may be ignoring and politically repressing. Just as a simplistic endorsement of nature can seem insensitive to the emancipatory concerns motivating its rejection, so an exclusive emphasis on discourse and signification can very readily appear evasive of ecological realities and irrelevant to the task of addressing them. Both therefore, one may argue, need to review their theoretical perspectives in the light of the other's political agenda, especially wherever there is a presumption that these are committed to projects which are in principle mutually supportive.[3]

With a view to achieving some reconciliation of these perspectives, I engage at some length with cultural representations of nature, and attempt to give full due to those ways in which it may be said to be a cultural 'construction'. But I defend a realist position as offering the only responsible basis from which to argue for any kind of political change whether in our dealings with nature or anything else. I recognize, that is, that there is no reference to that which is independent of discourse except in discourse, but dissent from any position which appeals to this truth as a basis for denying the extra-discursive reality of nature. I seek to expose the incoherence of an argument that appears so ready to grant this reality to 'culture' and its effects while denying it to 'nature', and argue that, unless we acknowledge the nature which is *not* a cultural formation, we can offer no convincing grounds for challenging the pronouncements of culture on what is or is not 'natural'. Where the nature–culture division is theorized as entirely politically instituted, and hence indefinitely mutable, those seeking to change the 'text' can appeal to nothing more compelling as the grounds for doing so than their particular personal preference or prejudice. But I also argue that such realism requires us to acknowledge the force of certain forms of critique of nature essentialism, and to review the rhetoric of ecological politics in the light of it. Representations of nature, and the concepts we bring to it, can have very definite political effects, many of them having direct bearing on the cause of ecological conservation itself. Just as the ecologists are talking about features of the world which the postmodernists are too loath to recognize, so the Green Movement can afford to be more discriminating in its deployment of the concept of 'nature' and to pay heed to some of the slidings of the signifier that have been highlighted in postmodernist theory. By exploring the tensions between these two perspectives on nature, I would hope both to reveal what I think are simplistic and potentially reactionary dimensions of ecological argument, and in the process to allow nature as spoken to by the ecologists to be taken more seriously by those who would have us attend only to its semiotics.

But if these perspectives and their discourses on nature are particular to our times, they also relate to a history of debates round the idea of nature in Western thought and reflect longstanding equivocations in the use of the term. Since part of my aim is to illuminate contemporary controversies by locating them within this larger framework, the preliminary chapters of the book are devoted to discussions of a more general and historical character. In chapter 1, I open with some reflections of a fairly abstract kind on the concept of nature, focusing on the disjunctures between the use of the term in reference to an order opposed to that of humanity, its use in reference to the totality which comprises both non-human and human orders, and its use in reference to the 'nature' of humanity itself. The exercise is designed to reveal the ways in which

these multiple, and in many ways incompatible, conceptions of nature are at work in contemporary arguments
and have contributed to the tensions between them. In
chapter 2, I emphasize the reliance of all ecological prescription on a prior discrimination between humanity and
nature, and briefly chart the ways in which the distinction
has been drawn in philosophy and social theory. The
focus is on the differing conceptions of ourselves and
the natural world which are reflected in dualist and non-
dualist approaches (the one insisting on the irreducible
difference between the natural and the cultural, the other
viewing the being of humanity as on a continuum with that
of nature). The chapter concludes with some reflections
on the ways in which all Western discourses on nature,
including those most critical of its abuse, carry within them
the ethnocentric legacy of a metaphysical tradition that has
covertly identified the 'human' side of the humanity–nature distinction with 'civilized'/'developed' humanity.

This sets the stage for the more historical survey I offer
in chapter 3 of the ambivalences that have marked our
'civilized' conceptions of, and responses to nature, and the
symbolisms associated with these. I argue that Western
configurations of nature – notably its association with the
'primitive', the 'bestial', the 'corporeal' and the 'feminine'
– reflect a history of ideas about membership of the human
community and ideals of human nature, and thus function as a register or narrative of human self-projections.
Attitudes to nature map the exclusions, devaluations and
revaluations through which Western humanity has constituted and continuously re-thought its own identity. They
also, I suggest, and particularly in the case of the feminization of nature, reflect ambiguities and anxieties of
feeling regarding the use of nature conceived as an external
environment and set of resources.

The implications of the woman-nature association for
ecology are addressed more directly in chapter 4, where

I explore the tensions between ecological 'naturalism' and the 'anti-naturalist' impulses of feminism, gay politics and contemporary theories of the body and sexuality. I suggest that these tensions have a particular interest in the case of feminism given the widely perceived parallels between the oppression of women and the destruction of nature and the complementarity of much feminist and ecological argument. But I also suggest that the question that is posed about 'nature' in this conjuncture between the politics of sexual emancipation and the politics of environmental preservation can only be addressed by way of certain conceptual discriminations that are seldom observed in the respective arguments of either. While I argue that a realist conception of nature is essential to the coherence of contemporary theories of sexuality, I endorse their resistance to naturalist explanations of human behaviour.

The discriminations at issue here are further elaborated in chapter 5, where I argue for the importance of distinguishing between the different concepts of nature which are invoked in ecological argument, and consider their respective implications for political prescriptions about its use. Nature conceived in a realist sense as causal law and process is not the observable nature of aesthetic and moral evaluation, nor is it that which we can be said to 'destroy' or be called upon to conserve. Ecological policies are therefore essentially shaped by the concerns we have for a 'surface' nature conceived as a set of utilities, a source of aesthetic pleasure, or site of 'intrinsic value'. They are also, I argue, shaped by the particular perceptions we bring to the nature–culture, humanity–animality distinctions, though, in considering their role, I take issue with the presumption of much environmental philosophy that an anti-dualist or naturalist position on this is essential to the adoption of eco-friendly policies.

The focus of chapter 6 is on this 'surface' (or, as I term it, 'lay') concept of nature: nature as an observable set of phenomena, and moves from consideration of the criteria through which we distinguish between the more or less 'natural' features or dimensions of our environment, to an engagement with the 'nostalgia' for a lost time-space of 'nature' and ideological representations of rurality. This in turn leads on to some reflections on heritage and environmental preservation and the criticisms it has elicited. I here argue for the adoption of a dialectical approach that would neither deny the mythologizing and patrician dimensions of environmentalism, nor dismiss the preservationist impulse as merely elitist and sentimental.

In chapter 7, I pursue one strand of ecological argument: that which calls on us to preserve nature as a site of aesthetic pleasure and consolation, or as a value in itself, and consider how far the presumption of a common aesthetic (or sensibility to the worth of nature) can be justified in view of the extent to which conceptions of the beauties of nature have been socially conditioned and determined in part through specific – and often politically motivated – representations of landscape and the world of nature. Many of the claims regarding the quality of 'human' responses to nature have been articulated by and on behalf of restricted groups who have been relatively unaware of their own partiality and its sources. This problem, I argue, continues to vex ecological discourses on the feelings elicited by nature and considerably complicates the task of developing a genuinely democratic discourse on environmental preservation.

In chapter 8, I offer a concluding survey of the different reasons that have been offered within the spectrum of ecological politics for preserving and conserving nature, and consider how far they are compatible in their moral appeal. I am critical of any attempt to argue the case for ecology from a position of moral absolutism, and suggest that many of the arguments, rooted in the idea of nature possessing an 'intrinsic' value to which we should always give priority, are ethically confused and potentially reactionary. Generalized accusations of 'human speciesism' invite us to overlook oppressions and divisions within the human community, and are ethically irresponsible if they imply that the cause of nature should be promoted at the cost of a concern with social justice and equity in the distribution of resources. The problem of the destruction of nature has to be located at the level of specific relations of production and consumption and cannot be attributed to some generalized set of human attributes or attitudes. Moreover, insofar as we can speak in general terms here, it is inevitable that our attitudes to nature will be 'anthropocentric' in certain respects since there is no way of conceiving our relations to it other than through the mediation of ideas about ourselves. To suggest that it could be otherwise is to be insensitive to those ways in which the rest of nature is different, and should be respected as being so.

Notes

1 Raymond Williams, *Problems in Materialism and Culture* (Verso, London, 1980), p. 68.
2 William Wordsworth, *The Prelude*, Book Five, 594–5.
3 There will be readers who will reject this formulation as altogether too even-handed. They will object that postmodernist theory is the vehicle of reactionary forms of neo-liberalism which have nothing to offer a green movement committed to radical social change. But as I hope to have indicated my own perspective is rather more complex. I do not dismiss all forms of postmodernist argument as irrelevant to the left, nor do I presume that all those deploying them are apologists of the system whose professed espousal of left-wing values must be viewed as in some sense hypocritical. On the other hand, I would agree that these values cannot be coherently defended by those adopting an anti-foundationalist position and that postmodernist theory is

in this sense deeply inconsistent in claiming adherence to them. This much I would concede to those who would dismiss the emancipatory credentials of the postmodernists. It is no part of my aim here to undermine the fundamental cause of ecological conservation, or to defend any 'postmodernist' posture which would have us focus only on the 'textuality' of 'nature' and its continually shifting signifier.

1

THE DISCOURSES
OF NATURE

In its commonest and most fundamental sense, the term 'nature' refers to everything which is not human and distinguished from the work of humanity.[1] Thus 'nature' is opposed to culture, to history, to convention, to what is artificially worked or produced, in short, to everything which is defining of the order of humanity. I speak of this conception of nature as 'otherness' to humanity as fundamental because, although many would question whether we can in fact draw any such rigid divide, the conceptual distinction remains indispensable. Whether, for example, it is claimed that 'nature' and 'culture' are clearly differentiated realms or that no hard and fast delineation can be made between them, all such thinking is tacitly reliant on the humanity–nature antithesis itself and would have no purchase on our understanding without it. The implications of this are not always as fully appreciated as they might be either by those who would have us view 'nature' as a variable and relative construct of human discourse or by those who emphasize human communality with the 'rest of nature', and I shall have more to say on this in the following chapter. Suffice it to note here that an *a priori* discrimination between humanity and 'nature' is implicit in all discussions of the relations between the two, and thus far it is correct to insist that 'nature' is the idea through which we conceptualize what is 'other' to ourselves.

But for the most part, when 'nature' is used of the non-human, it is in a rather more concrete sense to refer to that part of the environment which we have had no hand in creating. It is used empirically to mark off that part of the material world that is given prior to any human activity, from that which is humanly shaped or contrived. This is the sort of distinction which John Passmore makes central to his work on *Man's Responsibility for Nature*, where he writes he will be using the word 'nature'

> so as to include only that which, setting aside the super-natural, is human neither in itself nor in its origins. This is the sense in which neither Sir Christopher Wren nor St Paul's Cathedral forms part of 'nature' and it may be hard to decide whether an oddly shaped flint or a landscape where the trees are evenly spaced is or is not 'natural'.[2]

Passmore himself admits that this is to use the term in one of its narrower senses; yet it is also, I think, to use it in the sense which corresponds most closely to ordinary intuitions about its essential meaning. The idea of 'nature' as that which we are not, which we are external to, which ceases to be fully 'natural' once we have mixed our labour with it, or which we have destroyed by our interventions, also propels a great deal of thought and writing about 'getting back' to nature, or rescuing it from its human corruption. Ecological writing, for example, very frequently works implicitly with an idea of nature as a kind of pristine otherness to human culture, whose value is depreciated proportionately to its human admixture, and this is an idea promoted by Robert Goodin, in his attempt to supply a 'green theory of value'. What is crucial to a 'green theory of value', argues Goodin, is that it accords value to what is created by natural processes rather than by artificial human ones; and he employs the analogy with fakes and forgeries in art to argue that replications of the environment by developers, even if absolutely exact, will never be the same, or have the same value, precisely because they will not be independent of human process:

> . . . a restored bit of nature is necessarily not as valuable as something similar that has been 'untouched by human hands'. Even if we simply stand back and 'let nature take its course' once again, and even if after several decades most of what we see is the handiwork of nature rather than of humanity, there will almost inevitably still be human residues in its final product. Even if we subsequently 'let nature take its course', *which* course it has taken will typically have been dictated by that human intervention in the causal history. To the extent that that is true, even things that are largely the product of natural regeneration are still to some (perhaps significant) degree the product of human handiwork. And they are, on the green theory of value, that much less valuable for being so.[3]

But persuasive as these approaches may seem, in some ways, there are a number of reasons to question their tendency to elide 'nature' defined as that 'which is human neither in itself nor its origins' with 'nature' defined as that part of the environment which is humanly unaffected. Much, after all, that is 'natural' in the first sense is also affected by us, including, one may argue, the building materials which have gone into the making of St Paul's Cathedral. On the other hand, if 'nature' is identified with that part of the environment that is humanly unaffected, then, as Passmore rightly notes, it is being defined in such a way as to leave us uncertain of its empirical application, at least in respect of the sort of examples he gives: the oddly shaped flint, the landscape where the trees are straight, and so on. The fact that we may not be able concretely to determine what is or is not 'natural' in this sense is no objection, of course, to its conceptualization as that which is unaffected by human hand; but when we consider how much of our environment we most certainly know *not* to be 'natural' in this sense, and how much of the remainder we may be rather doubtful about, we may feel that the conceptual distinction, though logically clear enough, has lost touch with the more ordinary discriminations we make through the idea of 'nature' – as between the built and unbuilt environment, the 'natural' and the 'artificial' colouring, the 'Nature' park and the opera house, and so forth.

If we consider, that is, the force of Marx's remark that: 'the nature which preceded human history no longer exists anywhere (except perhaps on a few Australian coral-islands of recent origin)';[4] and if we then consider the human 'contamination' to which these possible 'exceptions' have been subject since he wrote, then it is difficult not to feel that in thinking of 'nature' as that which is utterly unaffected by human dealings, we are thinking of a kind of being to which rather little on the planet in reality corresponds. Now this, it might be said, is precisely the force of so construing it, namely that it brings so clearly into view its actual disappearance; the extent, that is, to which humanity has destroyed, nay obliterated, 'nature' as a result of its occupation of the planet. This certainly seems to be the kind of prescriptive force that Goodin, and some of those associated with a 'deep ecology' approach, would wish to draw from it, insofar as they present human beings as always desecrating nature howsoever they intervene in it.[5]

But to press this kind of case is inevitably to pose some new conceptual problems. For it is to present humanity as in its very being opposed to nature, and as necessarily destroying, or distraining on its value, even in the most minimal pursuit of its most 'natural' needs. Since merely to walk in 'nature', to pluck the berry, to drink the mountain stream, is, on this theory of value, necessarily to devalue it, the logical conclusion would seem to be that it would have been better by far had the species never existed. But, at this point, we might begin to wonder why the same argument could not apply to other living creatures, albeit they are said, unlike ourselves, to belong to nature, since they, too, make use of its resources, destroy each other, and in that sense corrupt its pristine paradise. In other words, we may ask what it is exactly that makes a human interaction with 'nature' intrinsically devaluing, where that of other species is deemed to be unproblematic – of the order of nature itself. If humanity is thought to be an intrusion upon this 'natural' order, then it is unclear why other creatures should not count as 'intrusions' also, and inanimate 'nature' hence as better off without them. We may begin to wonder what it is exactly that renders even the most primitive of human dwellings an 'artificial' excrescence, but allows the bee-hive or ant-heap to count as part of nature; or, conversely, whether the humanity–nature relationship is not here being conceived along lines that might logically require us to question the 'naturality' of species other than our own. Or to put the point in more political terms: we may suspect that this is an approach to the 'value' of nature that is too inclined to abstract from the impact on the environment of the different historical modes of 'human' interaction with it, and thus to mislocate the source of the problem – which arguably resides not in any inherently 'devaluing' aspect of human activity, but in the specific forms it has taken.

But rather than pursue these issues further here, let me return to the point I earlier raised concerning ordinary parlance about 'nature'. For there is no doubt that any definition of nature as that untouched by human hand is belied by some of the commonest uses of the term. In other words, if we count as 'nature' only that which preceded human history, or is free from the impact of human occupancy of the planet, then it might seem as if we were committed to denying the validity of much of our everyday reference to 'nature': To speak of the 'nature walk' or 'Nature Park'; of 'natural' as opposed to 'artificial' additives; of the 'natural' environment which we love and seek to preserve – all this, it might follow from this approach, is a muddle; and a muddle, it might be further argued, that we ought to seek to correct through an adjustment of language. But tempting as it might seem, in view of the conceptual imprecision of ordinary talk of 'nature', to want to police the term in this way, there are a number of reasons to resist the move. In the first place, talk of the countryside and its 'natural' flora and fauna may be loose, but it still makes discriminations that we would want to observe between different types of space and human uses of it. If ordinary discourse lacks rigour in referring to woodland or fields, the cattle grazing upon them, and so forth, as 'nature', it is still marking an important distinction between the urban and industrial environment. As we shall see in chapter 6, the criteria employed in such distinctions may be difficult to specify, but the distinctions are not of a kind that we can readily dispense with, or that a more stringent use of terminology can necessarily capture more adequately. Or to put the point in more Wittgensteinian terms, it may be a mistaken approach to the meaning of terms to attempt to specify *how* they should be employed as opposed to exploring the *way* in which they are actually used. The philosopher's task, suggested Wittgenstein, was not to prescribe the use of terms in the light of some supposedly 'strict' or essential meaning, but to observe their usage in 'ordinary' language itself; and it is certainly in that spirit that much of my pursuit here of the 'meaning' of nature will be conducted, even if that only serves to expose its theoretical laxity relative to any particular definition we might insist it ought to have. Indeed, there is perhaps something inherently mistaken in the attempt to define what nature is, independently of how it is thought about, talked about and culturally represented. There can be no adequate attempt, that is, to explore 'what nature is' that is not centrally concerned with what it has been *said* to be, however much we might want to challenge that discourse in the light of our theoretical rulings.

Cosmological 'Nature'

These, then, are some of the reasons for questioning the adequacy of any attempt to conceptualize 'nature', even when we are thinking primarily only of the 'natural' environment, as that which is wholly extraneous to, and independent of, human process. Moreover, of course, we do not simply use the term 'nature' to refer to an 'external' spatial domain, from which we and our works are clearly delineated. We also use it in reference to that totality of being of which we in some sense conceive ourselves as forming a part. We have thought, that is, of humanity as being a component of nature even as we have conceptualized nature as absolute otherness to humanity. 'Nature' is in this sense both that which we are not *and* that which we are within.

When the order of 'Nature', for example, was conceived as a Great Chain of Being, as it was in the physico-theology which prevailed from the early Middle Ages through to the late eighteenth century,[6] humanity was thought of very definitely as occupying a place within it, and a rather middling one at that. Based on the Neoplatonist principles of plenitude (the impossibility of a vacuum or 'gap' in being), hierarchy and continuity, the Great Chain of Being perceived the universe as:

composed of an immense, or – by the strict if seldom rigorously applied logic of the principle of continuity – of an infinite, number of links ranging in hierarchical order from the meagerest kind of existents, which barely escape non-existence, through 'every possible' grade up to the *ens perfectissimum* – or, in a somewhat more orthodox version, to the highest possible kind of creature, between which and the Absolute Being the disparity was assumed to be infinite – every one of them differing from that immediately above and that immediately below it by the 'least possible' degree of difference.[7]

Or, as Pope expressed it in his *Essay on Man*:

> Vast Chain of being! which from God began,
> Natures aethereal, human, angel, man,
> Beast, bird, fish, insect, what no eye can see,
> No glass can reach; – On superior pow'rs
> Were we to press, inferior might on ours;
> Or in the full creation leave a void,
> Where, one step broken, the great scale's destroy'd;
> From Nature's chain whatever link you strike,
> Tenth, or ten thousandth, breaks the chain alike.[8]

Pope in the eighteenth century is emphasizing the coherence of the 'natural' cosmos and chaos that would ensue from breaking its 'chain', where as the stress of Mediaeval thought was on the creative and generative power of God's love in divinely willing the fullest of universes.[9] But the essential idea that humanity is within this order of 'Nature', and indeed occupies a fairly modest rung in its hierarchy of being, remains common to both. Humanity is thought of as infinitely inferior to the deity, but also to all those aethereal spirits, angels, possibly more sublime mortals elsewhere in the universe, who people the myriad degrees of difference within the abyss which yawns between man and God. When 'Nature', then, is conceived in cosmological terms as the totality of being, humanity is neither opposed to it nor viewed as separable from it. This is not to deny that there is much in the conception of the Chain that directly encouraged the idea of human lordship over the rest of animal (and vegetable) life. The teleological purposes it attributed to a deity, who had so designed all things and laws of nature as to place them at the service of his human servant, were frequently used to justify a dominion over all those creatures below us in the Chain, and an instrumental use of earthly resources. In the words of a key text of Scholastic philosophy: 'As man is made for the sake of God, namely, that he may serve him, so is the world made for the sake of man, that it may serve him',[10] and this was echoed in many other expressions of a similar complacency over the ensuing centuries. The increasingly ingenious and anthropocentric use of Christian doctrine by English preachers and commentators prior to the Reformation to support an instrumental use of nature has been charted by Keith Thomas, who concludes his survey by suggesting that 'a reader who came fresh to the moral and theological writings of the sixteenth and seventeenth centuries could be forgiven for inferring that their main purpose was to define the special status of man and to justify his rule over other creatures'.[11] In this sense, the idea of the Chain supported those currents of Enlightenment thought which emphasized our difference from, and right to exploit, 'nature', and operated as a kind of theological complement to their secular and temporalized teleology.

All the same, we should note that when conceived as a way of considering the question of 'Man's place in Nature', the cosmology of the Great Chain of Being can by no means be viewed as supplying a straightforwardly anthropocentric answer, and this is particularly true of the inflections it acquired in the age of Enlightenment itself. Descartes, Spinoza and Liebniz had all agreed to the principle that *non omnia hominum causa fieri* ['not everything is created for human ends'],[12] and Locke, Kant, Addison,

Bolingbroke, and many others, were to invoke the idea of the Chain as a reminder of the numerous creatures superior to man, and as a caution against arrogant assumptions of human dominance within 'Nature'. Addison wrote, for example, that the difference of species 'appears, in many instances, small, and would probably appear still less, if we had means of knowing their motives'. Thus, if under one aspect man is associated with the angels and archangels, under another he must 'say to Corruption, Thou art my Father, and to the worm, Thou art my sister'.[13] In similar vein, Bolingbroke argued that superior as man was, he was nonetheless:

> ... connected by his nature, and therefore, by the design of the Author of all Nature, with the whole tribe of animals, and so closely with some of them, that the distance between his intellectual faculties and theirs, which constitutes as really, though not so sensibly as figure, the difference of species, appears, in many instances, small, and would probably appear still less, if we had the means of knowing their motives, as we have of observing their actions.[14]

We may say, then, that, although the Promethean assumptions of human separation from and superiority over 'Nature' do eventually triumph over the idea of our 'middling' rank within its overall cosmology, they were nonetheless continually countered by less confident assumptions, deriving from the Mediaeval theology, about humanity's place within this order. Worth noting, moreover, in this connection are the quite striking similarities between the contemporary ecological emphases on humanity's continuity with nature and place 'within' it, and those of the Great Chain of Being. Of course, there can be no direct analogue between a secular critique of instrumental rationality and of a 'technical fix' approach to nature, and a Neoplatonist theology which grounds its demand for human humility in the distance which separates man from the lowliest of divine beings. Ecology, moreover, is generally opposed to the hierarchical ranking of species that is the organizing principle of the Great Chain. But if we extrapolate the cosmological principles from their theological trappings, and focus simply on the idea of plenitude, diversity and organic interconnection informing the idea of the Chain, then there would at least seem some parallel here with current arguments concerning the interdependency of the eco-system, the importance of maintaining bio-diversity, and the unpredictable consequences of any, however seemingly insignificant, subtraction from it. Moreover, there is no doubt that, in a general way, ecology would have us revise our attitudes to 'nature' and the place of humanity within it, along lines that would reintroduce some of the conception of the Chain; rather than view 'nature' as an external and inorganic context, we should regard the eco-system as a plurality of beings each possessed of its particular function and purpose in maintaining the whole.

Human 'Nature'

The limitations of thinking of 'nature' as that which is independent of us, and external to us, are also brought into view when we consider the way in which we use the term in reference to ourselves. For we, too, it is said, are possessed of a 'nature', and may behave in more or less 'natural' ways. Now, it might be argued, that all that we should read into this vocabulary is the idea that human beings possess properties which are of their 'essence', with no presumption being made about their 'naturality' in any other sense. In other words, in speaking of 'human nature' we are not necessarily implying that human beings participate in the 'nature' we ascribe to animality or pointing to the continuity of their being with that of the 'natural' world. On the contrary, it might be said, we are precisely designating those features which are exclusive to them, and mark them off from 'nature' conceived on the model of 'animality'. Certainly, it is true that the idea of 'human nature' is very often used to emphasize our difference from 'natural' species, as when it is said, for example, that human beings are 'by nature' rational and moral beings in a way that no other species are, that it is against their 'nature' to behave 'like animals', or that in taking 'nature' as a model they are precisely reneging on what is true to their own.

It is in line with this view of 'human nature' that John Stuart Mill in his essay on 'Nature' denounces the immorality of following the course of nature and rejects any consecration of instinctual action. Since natural phenomena, he argues, are 'replete with everything which when committed by human beings is most worthy of abhorrence, any one who endeavoured in his actions to imitate the natural course of things would be universally seen and acknowledged to be the wickedest of men.'[15] Coming at the issue from a very different political perspective, Baudelaire employs a similar vocabulary in denouncing Romantic conceptions of 'nature' as a model of human beauty and goodness. 'Nature,' he writes, 'cannot but counsel that which is criminal . . . [In] all the actions and desires of the purely natural man, you will find nothing that is not ghastly.'[16] Yet there would be little point in moving these arguments were it thought that human beings are 'by nature' incapable of following the 'counsel' of nature, and their point, in fact, is not so much to assert the actual impossibility as to emphasize the immorality or cultural degeneracy of doing so. What is being disputed here is not so much the human possession of instinct or 'animal' desire, but the ethics of human conduct, and specifically the extent to which 'nature' offers itself as an appropriate guide to this; in other words, whether it is conceived essentially as a source of virtue or of vice, and thus as a mode of being we should seek to emulate or disown. Clearly, as Mill himself in effect points out,[17] there is little point in recommending that human beings either follow or reject the model of 'nature' if nature is here being construed as a set of powers or properties that they have no choice but to comply with. Admonitions of this kind implicitly reject a deterministic conception of 'human nature' even as they advocate a certain view of its 'order' and propriety. To suggest, for example, that 'human nature' is betrayed by following the course of 'animal' nature is paradoxically to acknowledge that human beings are capable of defying their 'nature' in ways denied to other animals. It is to suggest, in effect, that 'human nature' is such as to be realized only in compliance with a certain order of 'conventions' of a kind that no other creature can be expected to recognize or would require its fellows to observe. As Empson wryly notes, the animal 'is at least unconventional in the sense that it it does not impose its conventions.'[18]

Yet there is no doubt, too, that the idea of a 'human nature' cannot be so readily divorced from the assumption of humanity's sameness with the animal world and rootedness within the order of nature. This is in part because the notion of our having a 'nature' carries with it something of that same necessity we attribute to animal and inorganic modes of being: to speak of 'human nature' is to imply that we are possessed of preordained features, and subject to their order of needs in the way that other creatures also are. These features may be supposed to be very different from those of animals, but in describing them as 'natural' to us we are imputing a similar determination and necessity to them.

But we should note, too, the way in which the idea has

been used to condemn the 'perversity' of human behaviour where it is thought to *diverge* from that of other animals – as in the case, most notably, of certain forms of sexual practice. The 'convention' through which homosexuality has been perennially condemned as a 'crime' against nature would have us conform to, rather than contravene, a supposed 'norm' of animal conduct; and a similar rationale is at work in the condemnations of much else that is thought 'perverse' in our own behaviour: here the point is to exclude those human modes of conduct that have been deemed (though often mistakenly in fact) *not to conform* to those of other animals.

But against all those cases in which the 'healthy' human norm is established by reference to the custom of nature, must, of course, be set all those numerous others in which we become creatures of 'nature' in failing to conform with the custom of humanity. The conception of what is proper to human nature is thus arrived at both in approval and in rejection of what is thought 'spontaneous' or 'instinctual', and it is this ambivalence of attitude that Edmund in *King Lear* turns powerfully to his own account in calling upon God to stand up for the bastards bred in the 'lusty stealth of Nature' rather than for the 'tribe of fops' who are got in the 'dull stale tired bed' of matrimony.[19] (Although we might note that what God is to stand up for are rights of inheritance to land which no 'lusty Nature' ever bestowed.)

The history of the ways in which the idea or model of nature has figured in human self-conceptions is extraordinarily complex, and there can be no question of offering more than the sketchiest account of its convolutions in this context.[20] But one of the main divisions which can be drawn is between those ethical, political and aesthetic arguments that are constructed upon a view of culture as offering an essential corrective to 'nature', or providing the milieu in which alone it acquires any definitively human form, and those that view nature as releasing us from the repressions or deformations of culture and as itself a source of wisdom and moral guidance. The former regard human 'nature' as appropriately and fully reflected only in those achievements of 'civilization' that distance us from the sinfulness or naïvety or crudity of 'nature'; the latter would have us see the very process of authentic human fulfilment as jeopardized or distorted by the corrupting effects of cultural 'progress'. In the one conception, the emphasis falls on those human powers in which we transcend 'nature', and on the moral goodness which is realised only in our freedom from its order; in the other on the 'nature' within us that is the well-spring of human virtue and thus of social regeneration.

Broadly speaking, we can say that the one provides the animating idea of the high Enlightenment, the other of the Romantic reaction to its economic and social consequences. In releasing humanity from a Deist conception of the order of Nature as hierarchically fixed or Providentially designed to secure the 'best of all possible worlds', the Enlightenment sought to realize the inherent dignity of the individual as a self-motivating rational and moral being: the progressive development of art, science and culture is thus viewed as the vehicle for the realization of a 'human nature' previously held in thrall to superstitious fears of 'nature' and theological bigotry. In the Romantic reaction, which is profoundly influenced by Rousseau's summons to attend to conscience as the 'voice of nature' within us, the integrity of nature is counterposed to the utilitarianism and instrumental rationality through which the Enlightenment ideals were practically realized and theoretically legitimated: the point is not to return to a past primitivity, but to discover in 'nature', both inner and outer, the source of redemption from the alienation and depredations of industrialism and the 'cash nexus' deformation of human relations. In the aesthetic theory of the Romantic movement the artistic or poetic imagination is charged with the task of expressing this latent and occluded force of nature as redemptive resource, and this idea remains central to the forms of expressivism into which it subsequently flows. In social theory, the Romantic critique receives its most powerful elaboration in the argument of the Frankfurt School critical theorists: 'instrumental rationality', in oppressing nature, cuts us off from it as a source, and thus betrays its original promise to release us from thraldom to a Deistic order by entrapping us in relations to nature that are deeply oppressive of ourselves as well.[21]

Let it be said immediately, however, that this is to offer only a very general framework of opposing viewpoints, both of which are subject to numerous mutations and inflections, and neither of which provide compartments into which we can readily slot the argument of particular writers. The argument of Descartes and Locke, for example, was crucial in laying the foundations of the Enlightenment idea of subjectivity, but remained committed to Deistic or Providential conceptions of the social whole. Kant is a major architect of the Enlightenment conception of the autonomous subject, but exerts a lasting influence on Romanticism in rejecting the utilitarian ethic and the 'civilization' that 'progresses' in accord with it; Marx combines a Promethean aspiration to transcend all natural limits on human self-realization with a quasi-Romantic critique of alienation; and there are many other examples one might give of such hybrid modes of thinking and lines of influence.

We must allow, too, that very divergent and often antithetical moral postures and political ideologies can be defended from either of these perspectives on the model offered by 'nature'. An Enlightenment conception of our 'nature' as 'improvable' has been of critical importance to the promotion of the ideals of equality, justice and freedom which have come to ground the Western conception of progress. The (alas, continuing) horrors of the twentieth century have severely dinted the faith in the ameliorative powers of 'civilization', but in a sense this itself speaks to a presumption that our 'human nature' is such as to allow and require us to act in ways that transcend 'nature': to act in accordance with justice and to observe a system of rights. Moreover, the importance attached by a *tabula rasa* conception of nature to providing the appropriate cultural and physical milieu for human growth and self-realization has issued in some of the most progressive programmes of social reform.

On the other hand, it must be recognized that the emphasis on the role of culture in the formation or improvement of human nature can lend itself both to enlightened forms of educational and social policy and to the crudest forms of 'social engineering' and technocratism. The Enlightenment acclamation of human freedom and autonomy, moreover, carries within it a potentially repressive legacy of the modes of thought from which it breaks in the form of a continued elevation of mind over body, the rational over the affective. Though pitted against the more puritanical suppressions of bodily appetite and 'animal' instinct sustained in Christian dogma, the rationalist element of Enlightenment thinking may also be charged with fostering modes of 'corrective' education and regulation that have denied self-expression and served as the continued prop of class, race and gender divisions.

In view of this, it is not surprising that the Romantic conception of 'nature' as an essentially innocent and benevolent power has played such a key role in the discourses of sexual and social emancipation from the time of Blake and Shelley through to the 'flower power' politics of the sixties and much of the ecological argument of our own time. Liberating the 'nature' within or without us has been a constant theme of emancipatory discourse (and one might argue, some reference to a 'repressed' nature is a condition of the coherence of any such talk). But we should not forget the irrationalities and repressions to which this 'nature libertarianism' can also lend itself. Romantic conceptions of 'nature' as wholesome salvation from cultural decadence and racial degeneration were crucial to the construction of Nazi ideology, and an aesthetic of 'nature' as source of purity and authentic self-identification has been a component of all forms of racism, tribalism and nationalism. Equally, of course, the appeal to the health, morality and immutability of what 'nature' proposes has been systematically used to condemn the 'deviants' and 'perverts' who fail to conform to the sexual or social norms of their culture.

Finally we might note the ways in which some of these inflections of the pro-nature ethic have prompted a series of counter-Romantic denunciations of the quest for humanist redemption through 'nature', ranging from T. E. Hulme's rejection of any Rousseauan confidence in human amelioration and preference for all that is 'life-alien', to Baudelaire's protestations against 'ensouled vegetables';[22] from Oscar Wilde's professions of hatred for nature, to Foucault's conventionalist leanings towards an erotic-aesthetic of 'cruelty' and 'dandyist' ethic of style.[23] In these voices we encounter some of the more 'violent' attacks on the 'violence' of 'nature' and a systematic refusal to endorse its truth, authenticity or regenerative powers. But we should note that they also give expression to a form of resistance common to all those who have challenged the appeal to 'nature' to legitimate and preserve a status quo, whether of class relations, patriarchy, sexual oppression or ethnic and racial discrimination. What is put in question through such challenges is precisely the extent to which what is claimed to be 'natural' is indeed a determination of 'nature', and hence a necessity to which we must accommodate, as opposed to a set of conventional arrangements, which are in principle transformable. In the case of many of these expressions of dissent, however, it is not so much *any* invocation of nature that is rejected, but that construction of it which has pre-empted or distorted the potential forms in which it might be realized.

Within the general opposition to the naturalization of the social, therefore, we may distinguish between two rather differing types of claims: between those that reject the specific accounts that have been given of what is 'natural' in the name of the equal or more authentic 'naturality' of what they seek to institute; and those that insist on the non-natural, or normative, or culturally-constructed quality of all social arrangements, practices and institutions. Whereas the former position retains the idea of there being some sort of 'natural' order in human society, which if instituted will guarantee the well-being of its members and allow them to realise their essential 'nature' as persons, the latter emphasizes the discursive and revisable quality of what is claimed to be 'natural' to human beings and their societies at any point in history. For the latter position, then, 'nature' in human affairs is a concept through which social conventions and cultural norms are continuously legitimated and contested; it does not refer us to an essential or true mode of being from which we may think of ourselves as being culturally alienated at any point in time, or as having realized in some historical past, or as able potentially to realize in the future. The concept of 'nature' according to this 'culturalist' argument is certainly always employed *as if* it referred us to what is 'essential', 'true' or 'authentic' to us, but it is a usage that at the same time necessarily denies the historicity of what has been believed at any time to be the dictate of nature. Since 'progressive culture' has constantly re-thought the limits it has imposed on what is 'natural' or 'proper' to human beings and their society, the use of 'nature' as if it referred to an independent and permanent order of reality embodies a kind of error, or failure to register the history of the legitimating function it has played in human culture. From this 'culturalist' perspective, then, 'nature' is a kind of self-denying concept through which what is culturally ordained is presented as pre-discursive external determination upon that culture. From a 'realist' perspective, by contrast, nature refers to limits imposed by the structure of the world and by human biology upon what it is possible for human beings to be and do, at least if they are to survive and flourish. It is an order of determinations that we infringe only at the cost of a certain 'loss' of self or 'alienation' from what is true to ourselves, and in this sense provides the essential gage by which we may judge the 'liberating' or 'repressive' quality of human institutions and cultural forms, including those through which we relate most directly to the environment and other creatures.

The essential difference or tension is, then, as suggested, between a generally 'nature-endorsing' and a generally 'nature-sceptical' response. For the former, which may take either conservative or progressive forms, 'nature' is appealed to in validation of that which we would either seek to preserve or seek to instigate in place of existing actuality; for the latter, which is usually advocated as progressive, but may be charged with conservatism in the free hand it gives to cultural determination, the appeal is always to be viewed as a dubious move designed to limit and circumscribe the possibilities of human culture.

Notes

1 In his essay on 'Nature' John Stuart Mill speaks of nature in this sense as 'what takes place without the voluntary and intentional agency of man'. See Mill, *Three Essays on Religion* (Longman, London, 1874), pp. 3–65.

2 John Passmore, *Man's Reponsibility for Nature*, 2nd edn (Duckworth, London, 1980), p. 207.

3   Robert E. Goodin, *Green Political Theory* (Polity Press, Oxford, 1992), p. 41; cf. pp. 30–40.

4   Karl Marx, *The German Ideology* (Progess Publishers, Moscow, 1968), p. 59. (The observation is illuminatingly discussed by Neil Smith in *Uneven Development: Nature, Capital and the Production of Space* (Blackwell, Oxford, 1984), p. 54f. The idea of 'nature' as 'cultural construction' is more fully discussed in chapter 5.

5   Thus Goodin's general claim is that pristine nature is always to be preferred to that which has been tampered with, however congenial the effect. More specifically he argues that, if faced with the choice between a small-scale English village 'more in harmony with nature' and 'postmodern' Los Angeles, we must always opt for the former. All the same, 'grubbing out' nature to build even the most harmonious hamlet is a less acceptable option than leaving nature in its original state. See *Green Political Theory*, pp. 51–2.

6   The classic work on the subject is that of A. O. Lovejoy, *The Great Chain of Being* (Harvard University Press, Cambridge, Mass. and London, 1964) where it is argued that it is only in the late eighteenth century that the idea attains its widest diffusion. See esp. p. 183.

7   Ibid., pp. 59–60.

8   Alexander Pope, *An Essay on Man*, Epistle 1, 237–46 (Methuen, London, 1950), pp. 44–5.

9   Lovejoy, *Great Chain*, p. 67f.

10 *Libri Sententiarum*, II, 1, 8, cited in Lovejoy, *Great Chain*, pp. 186–7.

11 Keith Thomas, *Man and the Natural World* (Allen Lane, London, 1983), p. 25. In his preceding survey (pp. 17–24), Thomas cites, as instances of such anthropocentric ingenuity, the suggestion that horse-flies had been created 'that men should exercise their wits and industry to guard themselves against them'; that apes had been designed 'for man's mirth'; and the argument of the Elizabethan, George Owen, concerning the multiple purposes of the lobster: that it provided food to eat, exercise in cracking its legs and claws, and an object of contemplation in its wonderful suit of armour.

12 Lovejoy, *Great Chain*, p. 188f.

13 Ibid., p. 195.

14 Ibid., p. 196.

15 J. S. Mill, 'Nature' in *Three Essays on Religion*, p. 65.

16 Quoted in Charles Taylor, *Sources of the Self* (Cambridge University Press, Cambridge, 1989), p. 434.
17 J. S. Mill, *Nature*, pp. 13–19.
18 Willam Empson, *Some Versions of Pastoral* (Harmondsworth, Penguin, 1966), p. 212.
19 Shakespeare, *King Lear*, I, ii. Cf. John F. Danby, *Shakespeare's Doctrine of Nature* (Faber and Faber, London, 1949), esp. parts I, II.
20 One of the most illuminating and discriminating accounts of the role played by the idea of nature in shaping conceptions of human subjectivity is to be found in Taylor, *Sources of the Self*, especially parts IV and V. My discussion here draws extensively on this work.
21 The seminal text here is Theodor Adorno and Max Horkheimer, *Dialectic of Enlightenment* (Verso, London, 1979). For a full bibliography on the Frankfurt School, see David Held, *Introduction to Critical Theory* (University of California Press, Berkeley, 1980).
22 On both, see Taylor, *Sources of the Self*, pp. 426–9, 434–42, 459–63.
23 For an illuminating tracing of these veins of Foucaultian resistance to 'nature', see James Miller, *The Passion of Michel Foucault* (Harper Collins, London, 1993).

2

NATURE, HUMAN AND INHUMAN

Two closely connected distinctions have been central to Western thinking about nature: that between what is naturally given and what is contrived (the artificial) and that between what is dictated by nature and what is humanly instigated (the cultural or conventional). As R. G. Collingwood points out, in posing the question of the nature of nature the Ionian philosophers of the seventh and sixth centuries BC had already presupposed a difference between natural or 'self-occurring' things and the products of skill or artifice,[1] while by the fifth century a nature–culture demarcation is at least implicitly at work in the distinction between *nomos* (that which is a convention of culture, or socially derived norm or law) and *physis* (that which is naturally determined).

Both distinctions presume that there are certain ways in which humanity can – and indeed must – be counterposed to the rest of nature. The distinction between the natural and the artificial, for example, implies that there is a type of productive activity or creativity that is exclusive to human beings. Humanity, that is, has seen itself as differing from the rest of nature in virtue of the fact that it both reproduces and produces, or, if preferred, in virtue of the fact that it creates both natural and artificial 'products'. For while other living beings both produce in the sense of reproducing themselves, and create objects (nests, webs, hives, etc.), the latter have been denied the status of artifice precisely because they are viewed as purely instinctual and undeliberated, as the necessarily determined 'products' of their nature. This, it should be noted, is not quite the same as denying them the status of art, since, as Kant points out, we are 'pleased to call what bees produce (their regularly constructed cells) a work of art' and 'we recognize an art in everything formed in such a way that its actuality must have been a representation of the thing in its cause (as even in the case of the bees), although the effect could not have been *thought* by the cause'.[2] But, he argues, since no rational deliberation has gone into their making, we refer to such works of nature as 'art' only on the strength of their analogy with our own productions: 'where anything is called absolutely a work of art, to distinguish it from a natural product, then some work of man is always understood'.[3] It is this same insight that is registered in Marx's remark concerning the role played by the prior imagination of his construction in differentiating the work of the architect from that of the bee.[4]

Through the notion of the conventional we likewise draw a distinction, which is denied to obtain in the case of other creatures, between those of our practices and modes of behaviour that are naturally ordained and those that are self-instituted and hence in principle revisable. Other animals are here defined as beings who do not instigate conventions and for that reason are viewed as belonging entirely within the order of nature.

An opposition, then, between the natural and the human has been axiomatic to Western thought, and remains a presupposition of all its philosophical, scientific, moral and aesthetic discourse, even if the history of these discourses is in large part a history of the differing constructions we are asked to place upon it. Whether we are asked to view nature as an external realm, or ourselves as belonging within its order; as vitalist or mechanistic; as the mere object or instrument of human purposes, or as dialectically shaping us as much as we shape it; all such thinking is tacitly reliant on the appreciation of our difference from nature or 'the rest of nature', and would have no purchase on our understanding without it.

To point this out, it might be said, is not to say very much. Clearly, we cannot be asked to construe a conceptual distinction in this way rather than that, to adjust, undermine or collapse it altogether, unless we already in some sense observe it. Yet it may not be so idle to comment on this *a priori* dimension of the humanity–nature distinction, given its implications both for those who would emphasize the 'culturality' of nature, and for those who emphasize human affinities with nature. For a concept of the natural as that which is distinguished from the human or the cultural is implicitly at work in any attempt to deny its independent reality, or to have us view nature as itself an 'effect' or 'construct' of culture. Arguments that would assimilate nature to culture by inviting us to think of the former always as the effect of human discourse presuppose the humanity–nature dichotomy as the condition of their articulation. Nor can there be any claim to the effect that this dichotomy is itself conventional that does not tacitly rely for its force on precisely that objectively grounded distinction between what is humanly instituted and what is naturally ordained which is being rhetorically denied. When anti-realists insist upon the relative and arbitrary character of the nature–culture antithesis they are implicitly assuming what they purport to deny: that both terms have reference to distinguishable orders of reality.

But the same point must apply conversely to those who would emphasize human communality with nature, since they too necessarily presuppose the difference they might appear rhetorically to deny. Those who insist on human affinities with other animals, or would have us view humanity as belonging within the order of nature, must admit that they are speaking of an affinity or continuity between two already conceptually differentiated modes of being. Similarly, those who deplore the 'anthropocentricity' of human attitudes to nature must accept that the very coherence of their complaint relies on an acknowledgement of human exceptionality.

Indeed, all ecological injunctions – whether to sacrifice our own interests to those of nature, or to preserve nature in the interests of our future well being, to keep our hands off it, or to harness it in sustainable ways, to appreciate the threat we pose to nature or to recognize our kinship with it – are clearly rooted in the idea of human distinctiveness. For insofar as the appeal is to humanity to alter its ways, it presupposes our possession of capacities by which we are singled out from other living creatures and inorganic matter. Animals have in the past been morally blamed, and even brought to trial, for the havoc they have brought about to human lives and crops. But I have yet to encounter any ecological argument of our times that subscribes to this Mediaeval morality, which calls upon the Dutch elm beetle to be more responsible to the elm, or sees fit to blame the geological fault for the earthquake it precipitates. Green arguments are addressed to humanity's destruction of a nature from which it is distinguished, and impute responsibilities to human beings of a kind that it is presumed to be meaningless to ascribe to the rest of nature, organic or inorganic. Thus far, they credit us with powers to monitor and transform our impact on the environment that are denied to other forms of being. For, although other creatures certainly change their ways of living, sometimes with dramatic and calamitous impact on their immediate habitat and other species, this is deemed to be adaptive behaviour very different in kind from that which humanity is called upon consciously and pre-emptively to undertake.

This argument applies not only to ecologically motivated assertions of our affinity with the rest of nature, but to any and every theory that would have us view human attributes and culture as explicable in terms of features shared with the rest of animal life. For were humanity not – at least implicitly – being accorded powers of self-conceptualization denied to other species or inorganic matter, both the production and the claims to attention of such theories would be incomprehensible. No one stressing what is common between humans and other species devotes much attention to persuading those other species of the truth of their claims. Nor can anyone calling upon us to appreciate our affinities with other animals really deny that they are calling upon us to perform an act of cognition of which other beings are incapable – and which therefore renders them different from us. I take it, therefore, that, however carelessly formulated some claims about our communality with nature may be, they are not intended to be construed in ways that deny us our species-specific capacity to articulate and understand them.

What is then at issue in the humanity–nature division is not the positing of the distinction in itself, but the way in which it is to be drawn, and importantly whether it is conceptualized as one of kind or degree. Are we thinking of an absolute difference of realms or modes of being, or of a totality or continuum within which no hard and fast delineation can be drawn between the human and the natural? These questions have preoccupied both philosophy and the human sciences, though their levels of address have been rather different. In modern philosophy, the humanity–nature antithesis has on the whole been interpreted very broadly and abstractly as a Subject–Object division: as a division between the Humanity that is the thinking subject and the Nature that presents itself to thought, but is incapable of thought itself. Within the human sciences, by contrast, the humanity–nature relationship has for the most part been interpreted as the site of questions concerning the relations of difference or continuity between human beings and other animal species. While philosophy has been primarily concerned with what can be known of Nature construed as 'external' reality, and with whether humanity, as the knowing subject of this reality, is necessarily transcendent to and ontologically distinct from it, the human sciences have been concerned with the extent to which the empirical knowledge we have of biology, the evolution of species and animal ethology can provide a basis for understanding what is specific to human beings and their forms of life. Humanity–nature relations are under this aspect conceived essentially in terms of the opposition between the order of culture and the order of nature, where the former is defined in terms of language and symbolism, and socially instituted norms and conventions of behaviour, and the latter in terms of what is given and transmitted genetically. Here the central debates concern the definition of culture and the extent to which it is exclusive to human societies; the respective roles played by nature and culture in the constitution of human individuals; and the degree to which specifically human attributes and practices are deemed amenable to naturalistic explanation. In short, is there a rigid and theoretically unbridgeable divide between the 'cultural' and the 'natural', or is the distinction between humanity and animality (notably other primates) a matter of degree rather than a difference of kind?

The Human Subject and the Natural Object

There can be no question here of offering any systematic survey either of philosophical discourses on Nature, or of the controversies between naturalist and anti-naturalist approaches within the human sciences, and I shall do no more here than offer some illustration of the form they have taken. A first point to make here, perhaps, is that for Nature to be conceived as Object, as it is in philosophy from the time of Descartes onwards, it must already be opposed to the mental – as that which differs from the Subject in not possessing mind, spirit or soul. The Subject-Object conception of the Humanity-Nature relationship is the register in modern philosophy of the 'scientific revolution' which in the course of the sixteenth and seventeenth centuries replaced an animistic with a mechanistic view of nature. This cosmological shift, in which a conception of nature as 'ensouled' organism is supplanted by a conception of it as inorganic, fundamentally mathematical and hence objectively quantifiable, has its correlate in the philosophical dualism of Descartes, which opposed God (the Architect and Prime Mover of the 'machine') to Nature (the 'clockwork' set in motion), and mind or soul (as the essence of humanity) to the body or inanimate matter of the rest of existence. The abiding influence of Cartesian mind–body dualism on subsequent philosophical approaches to the humanity–nature relationship is readily understandable if we consider the limitations or philosophical difficulties of the two positions from which it is distinguished: a pantheistic conception of the natural world on the one hand, together with the superstitious or magical modes of understanding and relating to it which that encouraged; on the other, a materialism for which the mental was to be viewed as simply a rather special form of matter and comprehensible in physicalistic terms. But having noted that, one must immediately point to the deficiencies of Cartesian dualism itself, and most notably in respect of its failure to offer any convincing account of the interaction of mind and body. To accept the Cartesian picture is simply to accept that there exist two utterly different kinds of substance, that God saw fit to create them both, and that they miraculously but inexplicably operate continuously upon each other. Since, for Descartes, the essential being of humanity lies in thinking, and mind can in principle, if not in practice, exist independently of body, Descartes in effect places humanity outside the order of nature, and can only account for its existence in terms of its separate creation by the deity.

Yet if the Cartesian two-substance theory of mind and matter offers no satisfactory solution, the problem of how to respect their essential difference, without denying the unity essential to the existence of either, has continued to vex philosophy ever since, and the mind-body problem remains thereafter the axis around which Subject–Object, Humanity–Nature relations have been conceptualized. How do we accommodate the fact that as embodied entities we are clearly part of the order of nature, subject to its determinations and knowable in terms of natural science, while at the same time paying due heed to the fact that, qua Subjects, we are possessed of attributes – cognitive, moral and aesthetic capacities – seemingly unamenable to explanations of a physicalist kind?

The Kantian answer to these questions is notoriously double-edged: human subjects are both free of nature and determined by it, both 'noumenal' creatures whose rational and moral capacities place them beyond the ken of scientific understanding and release them from the grasp of a causal order, but also 'phenomenal' beings whose empirical existence makes them subject along with everything else to natural necessity and knowable to the 'human sciences'. Kant, then, resolves the question of our relations to nature by splitting the human subject, and relegating the problematic 'spiritual' dimension of self-hood to a realm beyond scientific cognition; as transcendent beings we cannot be understood in the terms with which we understand the world of Nature, but as objects of empirical knowledge we do indeed belong within that order. At the same time, since we cannot know of this order other than as it appears to us in our own experience and as moulded by the categories we bring to it, Kant in a sense allows for a wholly other and objective world of 'Nature'. In positing a noumenal 'reality' independent of human experience and cognition he can be seen to preserve the idea of a 'Nature' that is indifferent to human purposes and the unknowable condition of human (and all other) existence, rather than the mere servant and adjunct of human knowledge. The world as we know it appears to have been designed with a view to allowing human cognition of it, and thus far Kant's philosophy subscribes to the Enlightenment conception of Nature as specially adapted to human interests and uses. In the same process, it projects a view of humanity as the imbricated and yet transcendent agent through whom a harmony implicit in the ordering of the universe can find its realization. Yet in positing a noumenal world beyond the powers of human cognition, Kant at the same time registers a resistance to this teleology and hints at a resistance in Nature itself to its subsumption within human knowledge.

For Hegel, by contrast, this Kantian compromise between Nature and Humanity is altogether too timorous – an unwarranted and philosophically vacuous concession to the limitations of human knowledge. Hegelian idealism returns Nature to the fold of human knowing by revealing its very objectivity and difference as the dynamic vehicle of the realization of the Idea. Nature may appear as an utterly separate, other and indifferent realm of being, but it does so only to a consciousness that is not yet aware of its own conceptual role in positing Nature *as other* to itself. As consciousness proceeds to an awareness of its own alienation in presenting Nature as 'alien' to it, it transcends this alienation, subsuming the objectivity of Nature into its own subjective knowing. For Hegel, therefore, the very otherness of Nature becomes the vehicle through which Mind or Spirit realizes the transcendence of the cognizing subject to that which is cognized. The Subject, as it were, subsumes the Object of Nature through an appreciation of the dependency of the ideas it has of the latter on its own powers of conceptualization.

For Marx, this subsumption of Nature represents the height of idealist abnegation, and there can be no comprehension that does not proceed from recognition of the dependency of all forms of human knowing on the material world, both in the sense that knowledge is the acquisition of embodied subjects who must eat before they can think, and in the sense that it is acquired only in and through the practical encounter with a physical environment. For Marx, indeed, there can be no posing of the question of humanity–nature relations that abstracts from this practical engagement and its consequences in transforming both the natural environment itself and the 'nature' of the human subjects who are continuously interacting with it. In Marx's conception, Nature figures as a kind of inorganic body of human subjectivity, and in transforming the 'object' we necessarily transform the subject – to the point, Marx suggests in his early work, of constituting even our very senses of sight, taste and touch. In humanizing nature we also naturalize ourselves in the sense that by creating the objective world of our existence we also will determine the nature of even our most immediately sensory responses to it.

Unlike other animals, however, whose 'nature', it might be said, is also formed (and transformed) in response to an environmental context, human beings are quite capable of interacting with nature in ways that are profoundly untrue to themselves, and alienating of their 'species being' – as happens, according to Marx, under relations of private ownership and capitalist exploitation. Humanity is thus presented both as belonging with the order of Nature, and sharing in a structure of dependencies on the environment that is common to other animals; but also as differentiated from that order in its very capacity to create the conditions of its own alienation (and, so Marx would argue, of its eventual emancipation). Humanity viewed as a collective Subject is thus both a 'spontaneous' or 'natural' product of its interaction with Nature, but also an active agent who – unlike the spider or the bee – is responsible for the forms of that interaction and in principle capable of transforming them. Humanity is both the creature of nature and its creator, and it is this dialectic – or tension – between active and passive dimensions that has made Marxism such a fertile, if problematic, resource for both naturalist and culturalist approaches within the human sciences.

Part of the problem, it might be said, of construing the humanity–nature relationship as a Subject-Object antithesis is that it already presupposes a division between 'subjects' and 'objects' that is strictly speaking illegitimate. For is this not to bring to the world a prior knowledge of its forms of 'being' : to suppose that we already know what it is to 'be' a 'subject', what it is to 'be' an 'object'? Such, at any rate, is Heidegger's challenge to the Western metaphysical tradition. For Heidegger, all scientific thinking and all philosophy, at least from the time of the pre-Socratics, has failed to concern itself with this fundamental question of 'being'. It has failed, that is, to stand back from its metaphysical assumptions of mind and body, subject and object, to engage in a kind of presuppositionless awe over the sheer fact of existence. Instead of pausing to wonder why there are existents rather than nothing, or why the myriad of things by which we are surrounded take the form which they do, rather than some other, science and philosophy take this fundamental 'beingness' of the world as if it were inevitable and unproblematic. For Heidegger, however,

'Nature' in this sense is precisely not a necessary order, but an extraordinary contingency that might either not have existed at all or happened in some entirely other kind of way. Moreover, there is no way in which it can be thought of as an 'external' world, since *Dasein*, or the Being-of-humanity, is always a Being-in-the-world and inseparably bound up with it. To consider the world of Nature as 'object' is already to have stood back from a primary and pre-cognitive familiarity and imbrication with it; it is already to have adopted a theoretical mode of 'knowing', which necessarily overlooks or distorts the more primordial level at which Nature is already simply 'there' for us and we ourselves 'thrown' into its midst. The entities of the world therefore present themselves as 'objects' only to a theoretical and technological mode of thinking that is permanently dislocated from a more unthinking pre-understanding of the world.

Heidegger therefore comes close to suggesting that we are alienated from the world in the very act of cognitively reflecting upon it; that our 'authentic' relations with Nature are those in which we have only an immediate, unthinking, sensory or aesthetic responsiveness to it. Hence his tendency to celebrate the immanent non-reflective relations to Nature of an idealized 'peasantry'. Yet it would be mistaken to present Heidegger as engaged in a simplistic nostalgia for a pre-technical world, since 'technology' is not a dispensable feature of human relations to Nature, but part of the intrinsic structure of *Dasein* from whose destiny there is no escape or turning back. It is built into *Dasein*'s own nature that it should overlook and forget its originary being in the world, and there is in this sense no collective political project by which this loss might be recuperated. *Dasein* in its 'mass' or average or collective existence is thus presented by Heidegger as doing no more than following a predetermined and quasi-natural course in the very 'fallenness' or inauthenticity of its relations to

Nature. Only the rare individual, the poet or artist, so Heidegger suggests, is in a position to realize, by means of an aesthetic transcendence of technological wisdom, the promise of authentic relations to Being.

This is no more than an outline of some of the more influential discourses on the humanity–nature relationship that have been developed in modern philosophy. Yet enough has been said to indicate the extent to which thinking in this area is troubled by the paradox of humanity's simultaneous immanence and transcendence. Nature is that which Humanity finds itself within, and to which in some sense it belongs, but also that from which it also seems excluded in the very moment in which it reflects upon either its otherness or its belongingness. To insist on our naturality, it seems, is to pay too little heed to those exceptional powers and capacities through which we have exercised an ecologically destructive dominion over Nature, but without which there can also be no question of overcoming this alienation. To insist, on the other hand, on our 'super-naturality' or essential separation from Nature is to sever us too radically from the material context of existence, to conceptualize human nature in idealist terms (by viewing its essence as 'mentalistic' or 'spiritual'), and to open the way to a purely conceptual or subjectivist – and hence ecologically irrrelevant – resolution of the problem of alienation.

Humanity and Animality

This dilemma is reflected in the tension between what may very broadly be described as dualist and monist approaches to the questions of humanity's relations with the rest of animality. For the dualist, our attributes, realized capacities and potentialities as human beings are so radically different from those possessed by other species that there is no proper analogue between humans and other animals. For the monist, by contrast, all the ways in which we differ from other species are matters of degree, which can be all the better illuminated by seeing them as gradations within an essential sameness of being.

It is important, however, to recognize that this is an extremely broad brush distinction that cannot really do justice to the complex and divergent arguments associated with either perspective. In the first place, there is a distinction to be drawn between 'separate creationist' dualism and those who would accept an evolutionary account of the emergence of *homo sapiens* as a distinct biological species, but are dualist in the sense that they view certain distinguishing features – notably the use of language – as exclusive to humanity and as offering a clearcut criterion for dividing between the 'cultural' and the 'natural'. Disputes about the origins of the human species have in this sense to be distinguished from disputes about the defining properties of the 'human' and the 'cultural', and about the extent to which the latter are explicable in terms of natural features. Monists and dualists are not necessarily in dispute about evolution (though there has been a recent revival of Creationism in the USA,[5] it is now generally accepted that *homo sapiens* is not a distinct creation, the divine work of the sixth day of Genesis); nor do they dispute the species-specific attributes of *homo sapiens*. What is at issue, rather, is the extent to which these properties or powers are entirely exclusive to human beings, and whether they provide the grounds for a rigid demarcation between the 'being' of human beings and that of other creatures.

If, for example, we pursue a monist or naturalist line on this issue, then there are no hard and fast discriminations to be drawn between our capacities and those of the higher primates, who, it is said, do have some limited linguistic capacity, and also give evidence of learnt, as opposed to genetically inherited, forms of behaviour. The, admittedly rather meagre, success in teaching 'language' to chimpanzees is frequently cited in support of these claims, and indicates, it is argued, the fundamental mistake of attempting rigidly to distinguish between the cultural and the natural:

> 'Language' facility, existence of learned and shared behaviour among non-human primates do not mean that there are not large differences between humans and other primate species. What they do indicate, however, is that these differences are the product of evolutionary transformation and not of a – theoretically – unbridgeable gap between ourselves and other species. Human capacities and abilities are the product of evolution, they are not the gifts of God.[6]

The dualist, however, may well agree that humanity is not the 'gift of God' while nonetheless arguing that it is not the gift of 'nature' either – but precisely of culture. One is born *homo sapiens* (distinctively biological animal), but one becomes human, which is to say that one does things (uses language in a non-inverted commas sense of the term; is subject to rules of behaviour) that are, definitionally, symbolic – which is to say, inexplicable by reference to natural properties. As Marshall Sahlins puts it:

> The 'symbolic faculty' defines culture. Human beings are not socially defined by their organic faculties but in terms of symbolic attributes, and a symbol is precisely a meaningful value . . . which cannot be determined by the physical properties to which it refers.[7]

Claude Lévi-Strauss, likewise, while speaking of the rule which establishes culture (the incest taboo) as a 'transition' from nature to culture, nonetheless insists on the irreducibility of the cultural defined as a matter of rule-following rather than obedience to natural laws:

> The prohibition of incest is in origin neither purely cultural

nor purely natural, nor is it a composite mixture of elements from both nature and culture. It is the fundamental step because of which, but above all in which, the transition from nature to culture is accomplished. Before it culture is still non-existent; with it, nature's sovereignty over man is ended. It brings about in itself the advent of a new order.[8]

Hence, in a general sense:

The absence of rules seems to provide the surest criterion for distinguishing a natural from a cultural process. Wherever there are rules we know for certain that the cultural stage has been reached.[9]

From a culturalist perspective, then, what matters is not the possession or absence of biological properties, but the presence or absence of certain practices. It is therefore not a question of seeing how far chimpanzees can be taught 'language' or persuaded to perform in quasi-human ways. Any falling short of the symbolic capacities of normal human beings will be enough to deny them 'cultural' status; as, indeed, will be the fact that, left to themselves, they will manifest not even the minimal 'linguistic' skills they acquire as a consequence of intensive human training. Indeed, from a culturalist point of view, such attempts to 'prove' the potential of other animals to approximate in their behaviours to human comportment are largely irrelevant, as is the choice of only the higher primates for the exercise. For it is of the essence of their definition of the cultural that it consists in a set of capacities and practices that are *normally* displayed by all members of the *homo sapiens* species. Moreover, it follows from the logic of this definition, that were *any* animal community, however remote from us in evolutionary terms, to show evidence of these practices (to behave, for example, after the manner of the donkey whom Aristotle reports having been seen to throw itself over a cliff face on perceiving that it had

had intercourse with its mother),[10] then, presumably, they would have to qualify as cultural creatures. It might be very improbable for biological reasons that any animals other than those closest to us in evolutionary terms would manifest any evidence of human-like behaviour, but the culturalist would go by the achievement, not by the nature of the beast.

What matters, then, to those insisting on the absolute duality of the human (or cultural) and the natural is the gap between what chimpanzees can be taught, usually with much effort, to do in the way of sign-using, and the human facility in language and dependence upon its acquisition for normal life; the difference between human and animal production (between, say, the beehive, bird's nest or ant heap, and the opera house, power station or cathedral); or between animal and human sociality and culture (between the pecking order and the rules of kinship, the migration of birds and the tourist industry). For the dualist, that is, any attempt to explain what human beings alone are able, or potentially able, to do, by reference to what other species do, or might become able to do, is mistakenly reductive. For the monist, by contrast, to insist on an absolute division of realms is to impose an arbitrary and anthropocentric demarcation belied by everything that zoology and human biology, evolutionary theory and animal ethology has taught us about animal life in general, including that of *homo sapiens*.

The claim that animals are essentially different from people is traceable back to Aristotle, is a prominent feature of Stoic thinking, and is scarcely much challenged before the nineteenth century. One of its most radical versions is to be found in Descartes' claim that animals, being deprived of a soul, are in effect no more sentient than plants, and therefore lack the capacity of feeling pleasure and pain in any subjective sense. For Descartes, since the capacity for language was essential to thought, and thought essential to the experience of selfhood, animals were in effect like machines, which might send out behavioural signals of joy or distress, but lacked any corresponding sensibility of the kind possessed by human beings.[11]

It is not essential to a dualist view, however, to accept this Cartesian picture of the indispensability of language and thought to the capacity to feel. One might agree that animals experience pleasure and pain in a subjective sense, while still arguing that they differ absolutely from people in lacking cognitive, moral and aesthetic capacities and sensibilities. Kant argued, for example, that humans differed from other animals in being 'ends in themselves', by which he meant creatures who, in virtue of their possession of reason, came with certain entitlements 'in their own right' (by which they also acquired duties), and for whom alone it made sense to speak of 'just' and 'unjust' dealings. Animals, then, differ essentially from us in not being morally culpable for their actions; but, by the same token, neither do they possess rights of the kind which must be respected in people (though this is not, of course, to imply that we should not take account of the sensibilities they do have in our treatment of them).

It is also true that one could accept Descartes' dualist position on language as a cardinal divider between humanity and animality, while disagreeing with almost everything else he said. Structuralist and post-structuralist theories reject the Cartesian treatment of consciousness as the primary source of understanding, while yet subscribing to the view that it is language use that marks us off from animality. From this perspective, language is indeed the defining property of humanity, but since language is itself a social system not an individual property (a truth which Descartes failed sufficiently to recognize), entry into its symbolic order is essential to becoming a human subject and its system of meaning is socially pre-given to the individual. For this 'culturalist dualist' position, what is definitional of being 'human' is the possession not of certain biological properties defining of *homo sapiens*, but of certain capacities and behaviours that are theorized as acquirable only in a human cultural and social environment. One becomes a human (or 'cultural') being only insofar as as one is subjected to a social and conventional set of norms and meanings and organizes ones's identity in terms of it. Culturalist dualism is marked, therefore, by a resistance to accounts of the human in terms of properties locatable at the level of the individual.

Yet the Cartesian distinction between 'language-users' and the 'rest of nature' has also been defended by Naom Chomsky from a position which emphasizes the individual biological basis of language and thus challenges the idea that *human* nature must be conceived as an entirely cultural construction. Chomsky criticizes Descartes' assumption that all the phenomena of the natural world, save consciousness and human creativity, could be explained in terms of 'push-pull' mechanics,[12] while nonetheless agreeing about the uniqueness of human language: 'all normal human beings acquire language, whereas acquisition of even its barest rudiments is quite beyond the capacities of an otherwise intelligent ape – a fact that was emphasized, quite correctly, in Cartesian philosophy.'[13]

In contrast to culturalist dualism, however, Chomsky emphasizes the indispensability of the particular structure of the human brain to the capacity for language; and he has suggested that, were it not in virtue of neural mechanisms exclusive to *homo sapiens*, it would be remarkable that other species had failed to become language users.[14] Chomsky therefore questions the assumption that what distinguishes us essentially from other species must be attributed to social and historical conditions and cannot be traced to natural features. It is this preparedness to accept that 'human nature' might be a discovery of science that distinguishes his position, so he has suggested, from that of Foucault and culturalist approaches in general. The key difference, he argues, lies in their much greater scepticism about 'developing a concept of "human nature" that is independent of social and historical conditions, as a well-defined biological concept.'[15] In other words, while Chomsky seeks to differentiate humans from other animals in terms of a common biological essence, the culturalist takes the view that what is critical to the difference between humanity and the rest of nature is not some individual and a-historic property of the mind, but the forms of human sociality themselves. Both regard culture as the defining attribute of the human species, but, while one sees this as conditional upon attributes internal to individuals, the other views it as external to them. Yet in the end, the difference here, Chomsky suggests, should be viewed as one of emphasis rather than an absolute division, and, while he himself has stressed the universal features of the human mind, this is not to dispute the relevance of the culturalist attention to social and historical conditions. Some compromise of this order certainly seems the most convincing, since, while it is no doubt true that we do not become fully human other than in a specific and always historical human social context, it is difficult to explain the emergence of such contexts without reference to biologically predisposing properties.[16]

It may be objected, however, that a position such as Chomsky's is not properly speaking to be viewed as dualist at all, since by making biology rather than culture the basis of the distinctive character of human language, he undermines rather than sustains the rigid divide between man and animal. Such a view is certainly implied by Paul Hirst and Penny Woolley, when they appeal to Chomsky's argument in support of their claim that 'in evolutionary terms a "talking ape" is as possible as is a "naked" ape: there is no *essential* difference between Homo Sapiens and

any other animal.'[17] All the same Chomsky's approach
must be differentiated from a monist (or naturalist) position that objects in principle to the drawing of any absolute
boundary between humanity and animality. According
to this view, humanity can be divided from other species neither by sign, symbol or taboo, nor is it alone
in possessing culture, even if its culture, or cultures, are
markedly different from those of other animals. There is,
therefore, no 'essence' of the human or the cultural whose
explanation is to be sought in properties of biology or
sociality that are entirely exclusive to *homo sapiens*. The
differences, in short, between ourselves and other animals
are all to be theorized as differences of degree, gradations
within an essential sameness of being.

As with dualism, however, a monist perspective encompasses quite widely divergent forms of argument, and we
must distinguish here between more and less reductive
approaches. We may define as reductive, or biologically
determinist, any attempt to explain individual behavioural
dispositions and abilities, or past and present social
arrangements, as the inevitable consequence of biology.
In some of the crudest versions of the determinist
argument, differences of 'character' or ability have been
directly associated with such features as body shape
and weight (morphology), brain size (phrenology), skin
colour (theories of so-called 'racial' difference), and sexual
anatomy and function (biological explanations of gender
difference). Much contemporary theory of criminality,
deviance, mental functioning and mental illness is likewise
underwritten by a determinist approach, as are the 'pop
ethology' accounts of human territoriality, aggression and
sexuality offered in the works of such writers as Konrad
Lorenz, Robert Ardrey and Desmond Morris.[18]

Within the reductive bracket we may also include the
currently very influential attempts within sociobiology to
explain all human and other animal forms of 'social'

behaviour in terms of the individual genotype or 'selfish gene'.[19] These attempts are reductive in the sense that all forms of apparently learned and culturally transmitted behaviours are accommodated within, or made to conform to, a narrow range of evolutionary hypotheses based on the theory of natural selection. The essential thesis of sociobiology, in short, is that the individual organism is to be viewed as the vehicle for the reproduction of the gene and that all overt forms of altruistic or cooperative behaviour are explicable in terms of an underlying 'competition' for genetic inheritance. Individual actions, however apparently self-sacrificial, can always be interpreted as indirect strategies designed to secure genetic survival, and what we think of as 'morality' is simply a circuitous device for preserving genetic material. Even those behaviours which appear directly to confound the thesis, such as the rules of exogamy, are explicable, so it is claimed, in terms of the advantages they secure for the individual genotype.[20] Such theories have been widely denounced for the incoherence of their assumption of an 'intuitive calculus of blood ties' and for their failure to address the obvious fact that the human groups that exchange in marriage are by no means determined exclusively by ties of blood, but by many other circumstances (adoption, migration, clientship, etc.). Exogamy, in other words, is not a practice confined to those who happen to be naturally related, and kinship rules cannot therefore be viewed as biologically determined.[21] More generally, sociobiological explanations have been charged with reading biology in the light of existing relations of class, gender and racial exploitation, and thus with deploying genetic theory in the interests of socially inculcated ideologies and the preservation of the capitalist order. The theory has been criticized for its naturalization of tribalism, racism, entrepreneurial activity, xenophobia, male domination and social stratification; feminists have roundly condemned the tracing of differences in sexual behaviour to the determination exercised by the 'selfish' gene (in 'causing' females to 'invest' in nurturing, males in 'philandery' and both in strategies of 'mutual exploitation');[22] and the argument of sociobiology has been extensively accused of bias and circularity. Thus, it has been said, that what is determined as 'deviant' is deemed by sociobiology to be the object of a corrective programme at the level of the gene thought to determine the trait; while what is deemed more universal and acceptable (male assertiveness, for example) is legitimated as the norm and invites no such programme of genetic intervention.[23] The sociobiologists, in short, would have it both ways: they would both deny that their argument has any political motivation or relevance, and seek to explicate the political and social consequences that supposedly follow from their objective science.[24]

A deterministic naturalism, however, might be critical of the specific explanations offered by sociobiology, while nonetheless maintaining that human beings are no better placed than any other of nature's species in respect of their powers to change their 'nature', whose effects on the environment may be of a different order from those of other creatures but no less 'pre-programmed'. Such a view would have us regard human culture as itself no less a part of nature than the culture of other species, the generation of nuclear power or rock-music coming just as 'naturally' to us as the creation of the spider-web to the spider or nectar-gathering to the bee. The critical indifference of this form of philosophical determinism to the impact of different types of human activity – which are all viewed as equally inevitable consequences of our occupation of the planet – makes it problematic, as we have noted, from the point of view of any form of ecological recommendation. Certainly, the attribution to humanity of moral responsibilities for nature are incoherent for a naturalism of this type, though an ecological version of such determinism might take the form of arguing that, if humanity does come to adjust its attitudes to nature, this will have followed from its nature in much the same way as other species are constantly adapting their behaviours to changes in their environmental conditions.

Non-reductive naturalism, by contrast, purports to respect all the ways in which humanity differs from animality, including those ethical capacities that make meaningful the attribution of responsibilities for the natural world. It thus has many quarrels with reductive approaches and would reject their political fatalism and legitimation of the status quo. But it also rejects any form of culturalism that refuses to accept that the possible range of human behaviours is ultimately biologically determined, and insists that all human capacities and 'cultural' attributes are grounded in the biological species being of *homo sapiens*. It is thus opposed to the idea that there is any fundamental ontological division to be drawn between the human and the animal. There are many particular arguments that may be construed as defending a non-reductivist naturalism. Much in the writing of Marx and Engels tends in this direction, even if, particularly in the case of Marx, there are a number of more dualist themes that gainsay it.[25] Freud, likewise, though very resistant in much of his argument to any reductive explanations of human culture and psychic experience (hence the justification for the Lacanian insistence on a linguistic interpretation of psychoanalysis), nonetheless offers accounts of the cultural as taking the form it does in virtue of somatic instincts and needs, which are shared with the animal world at large. Evolutionary perspectives that emphasize the gradual emergence of what is distinctively human out of a previously more animal state of being, and the analogues between human and animal 'culture' would also claim to be anti-biologistic, while nonetheless refusing to recognize any absolute division of the cultural and the natural. We may also note here the 'critical realist' defence of naturalism elaborated in the work of Roy Bhaskar, and Ted Benton's defence of a non-reductive naturalism (some of the ecological implications of which are discussed in chapter 5).[26]

Civilized Conceptions

One of the difficulties, one may argue, in any formulation of the humanity–nature distinction in Western discourse concerns its reliance on a metaphysical vocabulary that has developed in tandem with the development of Western culture or 'civilization' itself. To the extent that the very concept of the 'human' has been arrived at in the light of the practices and relations to nature of 'developed' or 'civilized' society – practices and relations which, by definition, are not 'primitive', 'wild', 'savage' or 'exotic' – its very meaning may be said to be dependent on a history of exclusion of some of those members or groups of the *homo sapiens* species for all of whom it purports to speak. What is deployed, as if it were a universal concept, carries within it the traces of a semantic history that has always defined what is more properly or truly 'human' on the model of Western culture, and has selected in favour of that in its very disposition to think of other societies as 'primitive', 'closer to nature' or less alienated from it. Very often, moreover, what is being said of the human side of the equation in discussions of humanity–nature relations or forms of interaction is meaningful only if we assume that we are talking of the relations of Western humanity to nature, rather than of humanity in general.

One needs, however, to be careful in making such claims, for not all Western discourses on what it is to be 'human' are equally ethnocentric, and many of them seek explicitly to avoid an interpretative bias in favour of 'civilized' humanity. To make claims concerning the structure of the 'human' brain, or about the 'human' symbolic or linguistic capacity, its bipedalism, use of tools or rule-governed behaviour, is to make claims that precisely do not discriminate between the different members of the *homo sapiens* species or types of human societies. Such representations of what is common to humanity or to human culture are indeed the product of Western science and dependant for their dissemination on its academic institutions, but they pertain to all human beings or societies regardless of race, creed, colour, or type of cultural development. Those who have sought to provide explanations in terms of an invariant human essence have also linked this quest to the avoidance of ethnocentric bias. Chomsky views his insistence on language as the invariant and exclusive property of humanity as offering a 'modest conceptual barrier' against racism and other ethnocentric tendencies, precisely because it avoids the empiricism for which other attributes, such as colour, might be deemed relevant to the definition of the 'human'. A structuralist conception of human societies as differentiated only in the variety of their symbolic systems is, for Lévi-Strauss, of critical importance to avoiding the ethnocentric limitations of previous anthropology. Since from the structuralist perspective there is no meaning prior to signification, there is no meaning to which we could reduce the variety of symbolic systems, nor can we order them hierarchically in terms of a linear 'progressive' evolution. In refusing to explain social phenomena by reference to feeling or experience (and tracing instead the content of all forms of human experience to a common unconscious structure or system of shared categories), structuralist anthropology precisely aims to avoid the usual concern with understanding 'native' experience, and thus to escape the dangers of interpretations of other cultures that are predetermined by the expectations of the investigator. In explaining totemism, myths and kinship systems as forms of an invariant structure of human cognition, it aspires to an 'objectivism' for which all cultural systems of thinking, including that of Western anthropology, must be viewed as having equivalent status.[27]

All the same, even where the theory is arrived at in awareness of the possible distortions of viewing other cultures through the lens of our own attitudes and interpretations, a problem remains concerning the status of its own discourse. If, as Lévi-Strauss has suggested, his theory of myth is itself on a par with myth, why should we take it seriously as explanation, and how are we to reconcile its claimed 'mythical' status with its claim to scientific objectivity? Why should we not, it has been asked, view the very quest for such objectivity as part of the mythology of the West? Perhaps the very attempt within Western thought to develop a genuinely 'objective', non-ethnocentric discourse on 'humanity' is in this sense necessarily self-defeating – caught up in a quest for a universalist truth which is itself a piece of cultural 'imperialism'?

As a preliminary to his discussion of the work of Lévi-Strauss, Jacques Derrida makes the general point that the discursive character of ethnology means that:

> whether he wants to or not – and this does not depend on a decision on his part – the ethnologist accepts into his discourse the premises of ethnocentrism at the very moment when he denounces them. This necessity is irreducible; it is not a historical contingency. We ought to consider all its implications very carefully. But if no one can escape this necessity, and if no one is therefore responsible for giving into it, however little he may do

so, this does not mean that all the ways of giving in to it are of equal pertinence. The quality and fecundity of a discourse are perhaps measured by the critical rigor with which this relation to the history of metaphysics and to inherited concepts is thought. Here it is a question both of a critical relation to the language of the social sciences and a critical responsibility of the discourse itself. It is a question of explicitly and systematically posing the problem of the status of a discourse which borrows from a heritage the resources necessary for the deconstruction of that heritage itself. A problem of *economy* and *strategy*.[28]

If considered in this light, Lévi-Strauss, claims Derrida, is less than critically rigorous in remaining committed to the endeavour of science and the provision of a universal – 'humanist' – discourse: in seeking still to explain the indefinite 'play' of the sign in terms of some ground or origin that escapes the sign, and that is discovered in a 'science' which necessarily returns us to Western culture as the privileged culture of reference.[29]

But the difficulty here is whether one could begin to discriminate between more or less ethnocentric positions in the way that Derrida acknowledges we can, and should, – for, as he says, not all the ways of yielding to ethnocentricity are of equal pertinence – without some recourse to the 'scientific' objectivity we are here asked to forego. In other words, if structuralism is at risk of resorting to Western culture in the midst of its effort to transcend its reference point, post-structuralist critique tends to a position of such extreme cultural relativism that it risks conflating the very differences it would seek to sustain between theories that are more or less blind to the problems of ethnocentric bias. Western science and anthropology have indeed been guilty of bringing many culture-bound assumptions to their studies of 'humanity', but they have also, as Derrida notes, developed discourses that have sought to expose that guilt and avoid its errors; and it is difficult to see how we could finally distinguish between the two while denying that there is *anything* that can be said to be common to all human beings. Whether or not we are convinced by the arguments of Chomskyan linguistics or structuralist anthropology, it would seem perverse to argue in ways that might appear to assimilate their pursuit of scientific objectivity to the forms of ethnocentric bias they have sought to avoid.

More generally we may argue that there are no grounds at all for assuming that it is automatically more democratic or politically progressive always to respect cultural difference rather than to insist on sameness. Universalist discourses about 'humanity' are indeed at risk of introducing an ethnocentric bias into their view of what is common to us all; but discourses that would deny any shared structure of cognition, need and affectivity may also license a callous political neglect of the sufferings and deprivations of others. At a theoretical level, moreover, they necessarily undermine the very basis of their own critique, since to pursue an entirely relativist approach to human cultures is to define them all as equally ethnocentric, and Western culture can no more be called to account at this level than can any other. Indeed, if we deny the applicability of any form of 'humanist' discourse, it is difficult to see what it could even mean to move the charge of 'ethnocentricity', let alone assert its 'oppressive' character.

It is, then, important to be scrupulous in laying charges of ethnocentric bias against Western discourses on the humanity–nature distinction, and to recognize the extent to which those discourses have themselves been the vehicle of its exposure. In pointing to ways in which Western metaphysics has conceptualized humanity on the model of its own culture, I do not mean to imply that any attempt to speak in universal terms about the nature or condition of humanity is to be resisted. My point, rather, is that Western culture has arrived at its normative conception of the 'human' in the light of its own development, and that this concept remains residually in play in the very terms in which it condemns its cultural record. Western thought invokes a notion of 'civilized' values drawn from its own self-image even when it is most critical of the 'brutality' or 'barbarism' of its treatment of other cultures. I am not here simply drawing attention to the actual historical record of Western colonialism and to the ways in which the identification of 'humanity' with 'civilized' humanity has been used to justify the historical oppression, and even extermination, of 'savage' or 'primitive' communities. The extent to which Western society has historically constituted itself through the denial of the 'other' and violent oppression of whole constituencies of the human species is indisputable and today increasingly well-documented. So, too, is the process through which it began to question these exclusions, and to open itself to the possibility that these 'others' had been illegitimately excluded. The point I am making here is not that Western society did in fact treat other groups and cultures as if they were less than human, but that its thought has been reliant on an implicit assimilation of the 'being' of humanity at large to the being of 'civilized' man; and that there is a legacy of this in the very discourses with which it criticizes the suppressions and abuses, whether of its own species, or of animals or of inorganic nature, that have been perpetrated in the name of 'civilization'. When Western society condemns its own 'savagery' or 'inhumanity', it does so from a perspective that has already conceptualized what it is to be properly human in the light of its own modes of comportment. When we speak of 'humanity's' alienation from, or dominion over, or destruction of, nature, we are talking in ways that implicitly assume the greater propinquity to nature of primitive or non-industrialized societies. Even if we accept, as Martin Bernal has argued we should, that Western civilization has involved extensive suppression of its non-Western Afro-Egyptian origins, this point remains valid, since the dispute about origins is essentially a dispute about which acts of colonization are to be credited with laying the foundations of Western culture, rather than a dispute about its 'civilized' quality.[30] Bernal's challenge to the conventional picture of the 'white' roots of Western culture is itself conducted within a conceptual framework that privileges the achievements of 'civilized' humanity and views them as an advance over primitivity.

In fact, to ask what it would have been for 'primitive' cultures to have provided the standard by which developed societies historically judged the degree of their own 'humanity' is rather like asking what it would have been for man to have been constituted the subordinate 'other' to woman. Such questions are literally utopic, outside the time and space of history. Entertainable though they may be in the sense that we can understand the rhetorical force of their posing, in another sense they take us beyond the bounds of conceptualization. For we have no resources other than those supplied us in the actual course of history for thinking these hypothetical scenarios; yet those resources themselves inform us that such putative alternatives cannot be thought within the framework of historical actuality. For them to have been possible in history would be for history as we have known it to have been impossible. Had the 'savage' or the 'primitive' been regarded as the norm of humanity, the 'civilized' or the 'developed' as the anomaly, then the record of humanity–nature relations would also, we may surmise, have been very different. When Western thought reflects on the record of its relations to nature, it necessarily thinks in a vocabulary that has presupposed that 'civilized' man is representative of the 'humanity' that is nature's antithesis.

Notes

1   R. G. Collingwood, *The Idea of Nature* (Oxford University Press, Oxford, 1965), pp. 29–30. For an extended account of conceptions of nature in classical antiquity, see C. J. Glacken's monumental work, *Traces on the Rhodian Shore, Nature and Culture in Western Thought from Ancient Times to the End of the Eighteenth Century* (University of California Press, Berkeley and London, 1967); see also Louis Dupré, *Passage to Modernity: An Essay in the Hermeneutics of Nature and Culture* (Yale University Press, New Haven and London, 1993), chs 1, 2. I owe the concise and apt expression of the 'self-occurring' to my son, Jude Ryle.
2   Immanuel Kant, *Critique of Judgement*, Book II, 43, 304, ed. James Meredith (Clarendon Press, Oxford, 1952), p. 163.
3   Ibid.
4   'A spider conducts operations that resemble those of a weaver, and a bee puts to shame many an architect in the construction of her cells. But what distinguishes the worst architect from the best of bees is this, that the architect raises his structure in imagination before he erects it in reality.' Karl Marx, *Capital*, vol. I (Lawrence and Wishart, London, 1954), ch. VII, i, p. 174.
5   See Dominique Lecourt, *L'Amerique entre la Bible et Darwin* (PUF, Paris, 1992).
6   Stephen Horigan, *Nature and Culture in Western Discourses* (Routledge, London, 1988), pp. 108–9.
7   Marshall Sahlins, *The Use and Abuse of Biology: an Anthropological Critique of Sociobiology* (University of Michigan Press, Ann Arbor, 1976), p. 61.
8   Claude Lévi-Strauss, *The Elementary Structures of Kinship* (Eyre and Spottiswoode, London, 1969), pp. 24–5. Elsewhere, Lévi-Strauss speaks of the incest taboo as the 'scandal' which is both 'natural' in being a universal and spontaneous feature of human society, and 'cultural' in being normative, *The Raw and the Cooked* (Harper and Row, New York, 1969), pp. 5–6. As Jacques Derrida points out, however, there is no scandal 'except within a system of concepts which accredits

the difference between nature and culture' – a difference which the incest taboo may be said to both escape and to ground. See *Writing and Difference* (Routledge, Kegan Paul, London, 1978), pp. 283–4.

9 Lévi-Strauss, *The Raw and the Cooked*, p. 8.

10 I confess I have been unable to trace this reference. Perhaps I have dreamt it.

11 See Stephen Clark entry on 'Animals', J. O. Urmson and Jonathan Rée (eds), *The Concise Encyclopedia of Western Philosophy and Philosophers* (Unwin Hyman, London, 1989), pp. 14–16.

12 Naom Chomsky, *Language and Responsibility* (Harvester, Sussex, 1979), pp. 96–7.

13 Naom Chomsky, *Language and Mind* (Harcourt, Brace, Jovanovich, New York, 1972), pp. 66–7; cf. 'Review of *Verbal Behaviour* by B. F. Skinner', *Language*, 35, 1959.

14 Naom Chomsky, 'Review of Skinner', passim and p. 30, note.

15 Chomsky, *Language and Responsibility*, p. 77.

16 Cf. Paul Hirst and Penny Woolley, *Social Relations and Human Attributes* (Tavistock, London, 1982), p. 87f.

17 Ibid., p. 82.

18 Konrad Lorenz, *On Aggression* (Methuen, London, 1966); Robert Ardrey, *The Territorial Imperative* (Collins, London, 1966); Desmond Morris, *The Naked Ape* (Cape, London, 1967), and *The Human Zoo* (Cape, London, 1969). 'Pop ethology' is a term coined by Stephen Gould – see Kamin and Lewontin, *Not in Our Genes* (Penguin, Harmondsworth, 1984), p. 239.

19 The founding works are those of E. O. Wilson, *Sociobiology* (Harvard University Press, Cambridge, Mass., 1975); *On Human Nature* (Harvard University Press, Cambridge, Mass., 1978). See also Richard Dawkins, *The Selfish Gene* (Oxford University Press, New York, 1976).

20 For a clear and succinct discussion of Wilson's account of exogamy, and of the criticism it has evoked, see Hirst and Woolley, *Social Relations*, pp. 66–91 (who here draw largely on Marshall Sahlins's 'classic' critique of sociobiology in *The Use and Abuse of Biology*). See also, A. L. Caplan (ed.), *The Sociobiology Debate* (Harper, New York, 1978); S. Rose (ed.), *Against Biological Determinism* (London, 1982); L. Kamin and R. C. Lewontin, *Not in Our Genes*. For a critique of determinist approaches to the study of human intelligence, see S. J. Gould, *The Mismeasure of Man* (Norton, New York, 1981). For some

astute comments on the ways in which current revivals of biological determinism feed into the New Right's sanctification of possessive individualism, see Andrew Ross, *The Chicago Gangster Theory of Life* (Verso, London, 1994), ch. 5, esp. pp. 250–9.

21 Hirst and Woolley, *Social Relations*, p. 75.

22 As evidenced, for example, in R. L. Trivers, 'Parental Investment and Sexual Selection' in B. Campbell (ed.), *Sexual Selection and the Descent of Man 1871–1971* (Aldine, Chicago, 1972); Richard Dawkins, *The Selfish Gene*. For an exposition and critique of sociobiology's determinist approach to human sexual behaviour, see Janet Sayers, *Biological Politics* (Tavistock, London, 1982), chs 4, 5; cf. Linda Birke, *Women, Feminism and Biology* (Harvester, Brighton, 1986); Donna Haraway, *Simians, Cyborgs and Women: the Reinvention of Nature* (Free Association Books, London, 1989).

23 Kamin and Lewontin, *Not in Our Genes*, p. 173.

24 Ibid., p. 28.

25 See Ted Benton, 'Humanism = Speciesism? Marx on humans and animals', *Radical Philosophy* 50, pp. 4–18 and other works cited in chapter 3, note 39.

26 See chapter 5, note 7.

27 For two excellent guides to what is distinctive to Lévi-Strauss's anthropological argument, see E. R. Leach, *Lévi-Strauss* (London, 1970, rev. edn, New York, 1974) and Dan Sperber, 'Claude Lévi-Strauss' in John Sturrock (ed.), *Structuralism and Since* (Oxford University Press, Oxford, 1979), pp. 18–51.

28 Derrida, *Writing and Difference*, p. 282.

29 Ibid., pp. 288, 292.

30 Martin Bernal, *Black Athena: the Afroasiatic roots of classical civilisation* (Free Association Books, London, 1987).

3

NATURE, FRIEND
AND FOE

I have suggested that there can be no adequate engagement
with the question of what nature is that fails to address the
ways it is spoken of and represented in cultural discourse
and imagery. But to attend to this symbolic dimension is
immediately to be struck by the diversity and complexity
of our descriptions and images of nature. Nature is both
machine and organism, passive matter and vitalist agency.
It is represented as both savage and noble, polluted and
wholesome, lewd and innocent, carnal and pure, chaotic
and ordered. Conceived as a feminine principle, nature
is equally lover, mother and virago: a source of sensual delight, a nurturing bosom, a site of treacherous
and vindictive forces bent on retribution for her human
violation. Sublime and pastoral, indifferent to human purposes and willing servant of them, nature awes as she
consoles, strikes terror as she pacifies, presents herself as
both the best of friends and the worst of foes.

That nature is endowed with these contradictory characteristics is indicative of the extent to which this supposed
antithesis to the human is being thought through a process
of anthropomorphism, in which we project on to that
which we are not those very qualities and attitudes
that we deem exclusive to humanity. To explore these
configurations and human projections upon nature is to

attend to the humanity–nature distinction as a site of equivocation wherein we can read a narrative of human self-doubts, not only about our use of nature conceived as a clearly delineated 'other', but also about where to draw the line between ourselves and this 'other' to ourselves in the first place.

To engage with this history of the definitions of the 'natural' and the 'human' is not to suggest that these terms acquire such meaning as they have only in and through a series of semantic oppositions. The very fact that we can point to definitional dependencies at this level, and discriminate between our differing representations of nature, presupposes the reference of the term to a distinguishable order of reality; and it would not in the end be possible to account for the ways in which our language registers a difference between the 'natural' and the 'human', were this to be denied. Nor is my engagement in this chapter with the symbolism and representation of nature intended to imply support for any conventionalist position that would have us view it as nothing but 'discursively constructed'. I have already suggested that such a position is incoherent and self-stultifying, and can provide no sound basis from which to challenge specific ideologies of nature, and I shall have more to say on this in subsequent chapters. But while conventionalist approaches are altogether too dismissive of realist objections to their insistence on the 'discursive construction' of 'nature', realists are often a little reluctant to give full due to the symbolic and conceptual dimensions to which the conventionalists would have us attend. There is a gestural acknowledgement of the always conceptually mediated quality of our relations to nature, and of the ideological functions served by its various representations; but it is rare to find an extensive engagement conducted from within a realist framework with 'nature' as signifier rather than as signified. This chapter is offered as some modest corrective to this tendency. The aim here is not to offer a comprehensive or systematic account of Western conceptions of nature, but simply to illustrate their divergent and equivocal character; and to consider those ways in which it may fairly be said that we 'never speak about nature, without at the same time speaking about ourselves'.[1]

I have argued, in the preceding chapter, that all discourses about the humanity–nature relationship, even those most critical of humanity's role in the destruction of nature, or those most keen to recall us to our affinities with it, are ultimately reliant for their coherence on a prior distinction between 'ourselves' and the world of nature. I have also suggested that it has been a prevailing tendency of Western thought to identify what it is to be 'human' with 'developed' or 'civilized' humanity. But since humanity so conceived has constantly re-thought the nature of the human, we are speaking here of a discrimination that is itself possessed of a history. Even if Western civilization has tended to associate its course with that of humanity at large, it has also, as part of its very development, continuously questioned the barriers it has erected around the 'human community', and seen its 'progress' as consisting in a gradual enlightenment in regard to its own exclusions. To take account of this, however, is necessarily, I suggest, to acknowledge the instability of the humanity–nature distinction itself, since as the 'human' has been re-thought, so too has the 'nature' to which it has been opposed. What is then presented as if it registered an absolute and static division of realms is in reality a rather mutable construct, within which the 'nature' that always figures as the antithesis to the 'human' also always bears the imprint of our equivocations and changing perceptions about ourselves.

In this sense, 'nature' may be viewed as a register of changing conceptions as to who qualifies, and why, for full membership of the human community; and thus also to some extent as a register of Western civilization's anxieties and divisions of opinion about its own qualities, activities and achievements. Among those, for example, whom Western culture has at various points in its development deemed 'inhuman' or less than properly human, we may cite the following categories: barbarians (those who do not speak one's own language), slaves, negroes, women, Indians, savages, 'wild' or 'wonder' men, witches, sorcerers, dwarfs and idiots. Such groups, that is, have been associated with functions or attributes that place them nearer to nature and render them not quite fully human (they are lacking in reason; or bestial in their behaviour; or immersed in the body and reproductive activity; or untamable, and so on). What is 'proper' to humanity, that is, has been thought in relation to a number of excluded dimensions, of which the 'primitive', the 'animal', the 'corporeal' and the 'feminine' are the most notable, and those I propose to address here. But this, I shall suggest, is a history of exclusions that reveals a profound uncertainty about the policing exercise itself: a desire to re-find humanity in the very dimensions of being from which it has sought to discriminate itself, and to re-locate its position *vis-à-vis* nature accordingly. Humanity, that is, may have defined itself in opposition to these relegated 'others', but it has also never really managed to confine them very securely within their supposedly natural domain.

Nature as Primitivity or 'Cultural Other'

Let us first consider some of the variants that have marked approaches to the cultural 'other'. One notable ambivalence here has been between the treatment of this 'other' as a kind of 'marvel' of nature and his dismissal as 'savage' or dumb beast – creature without speech, and incapable of it. The cultural 'other' has, after all, been a source of both awe and disdain, mythologized as both semi-divine and less than human. From the classical period through to the late Middle Ages, the 'East', and especially India, was viewed as a site of wonders, peopled by races of super-human capacities or monstrous forms (giants, pigmies, satyrs, cyclops, martikhora, sciapodes, cynocephali, men with no heads, or heads in their chests, people with ears so protracted they slept in them at night, with multiple toes or inverted feet):[2] creatures, whose very difference commanded a certain respect even as it provided the grounds for fear and pejorative discrimination. Of course, this is not to imply that the 'East' was thought to be exclusively, or even predominantly, peopled by such curiosities. These were indeed thought of as exceptions to the more ordinary exemplars of humanity to be encountered in those parts, and many of the stories of fabulous creatures brought back to the West were derived from Indian epic myths themselves. It is interesting to note that, when St Augustine faced the dilemma as to whether these monstrous races were derived from the stock of Adam and the sons of Noah, he pronounced astutely that *if* they were human then they did derive from Adam just as did monstrous births in individual races; and added, for good measure, that God may have created fabulous races so that monstrous births among ourselves should not be regarded as failures of his wisdom.[3] The point is not so much that the peoples of the 'East' were thought in general to take these 'marvellous' forms, but that in virtue of its distance and unfamiliarity, the 'East' was conceived as a site of ambiguity.

Speaking very generally (and the point stands in need of considerable qualification in the light of Greek and Roman attitudes to the 'barbarian'),[4] one may say that it is only with the opening up of the New World and the development of colonialism in the sixteenth century that amazement gives way to more confident assumptions of superiority, rooted in the idea of the cultural 'other' as a creature without soul or capacity for language. In other words, it is only as imperialism brings about a fuller and more direct contact with the mythologized 'other' that a clearer distinction gets drawn between those who are indeed men (not marvels, monstrosities or freaks of nature), but sub-human by comparison with civilized humanity. The 'other', as Stephen Greenblatt has suggested, is a Caliban bereft of speech, or the savage of Spencer's *Faerie Queen* (Book VI), who has:

> But a soft murmure, and confused sound
> Of senseless words which Nature did him teach.[5]

This view of the 'barbarian', Indian or savage as a beast without speech then feeds into an antithetical, and, if anything even more insulting,[6] assumption that there was no significant language barrier between Europeans and savages. To prove his credentials as human, the primitive had to acquire our language, assume our religion, submit to our rule and behave in accordance with our rationality. Typical expressions of this form of oppressive patronage were Pope Paul II's claim, in his 1537 Declaration, that while the Amer-Indians could be considered human, their acceptance into the human race was conditional upon their conversion to Christianity;[7] or the Spanish Requerimiento of 1513, which was a document to be read to all peoples encountered in the New World demanding subservience to Spanish rule in the name of equal descendancy from Adam and Eve.[8]

This attitude to the negro, savage or primitive 'other' was to culminate in the Enlightenment idea of the 'Family of man': no longer were such groups to be viewed, in Sir Walter Raleigh's words, as 'half-men, fit only for the place below man himself in the hierarchy',[9] but as carrying within them the potential for becoming fully human insofar as they adopted the values and mores of civilized man. No longer was the savage to be relegated to the side of nature in virtue of his animality, but only in virtue of his failure to conform to those standards of behaviour that were proper to humanity.

This is not to suppose that colonial oppression was in any sense curbed by such a transformation of attitude. On the contrary, to regard the savage as potentially human was in many ways the better to licence his abuse as one who, though capable of civilized comportment, was maliciously resistant to conversion. To view the 'other' as endowed with the makings of civilized humanity was, in effect, to construe any manifestation of diversity from its values and behaviour as a wilful, and hence punishable, rejection of the intentions of Providence. When interpreted in this fashion, then, the idea of the equality or sameness of all human beings became a legitimation for the oppression of all those potential members of the 'Family of Man', who, by their persistence in heathen rites, bestial practices and rebellious resistance to the civilizing mission, revealed their refusal to comply with the basic rules of kinship. On this logic, any and every vile treatment of the native could be justified, as it was, not only for the colonists of the New World, but through into the high period of British imperialism in the nineteenth century, when whole populations were systematically destroyed in the name of 'civilization'.[10]

But, of course, the discourse of civility was a two-edged weapon that could very easily be turned against the savagery of the colonizer, as it was by the patriot leader, President Aguinaldo, when he denounced the American seizure of the Phillipine islands as 'the dominion of force accompanied by the repugnant barbarity of primitive tribes';[11] and Western critics of colonial arrogance and repression had earlier made use of a similar rhetorical inversion. In the argument of Bartolomé de Las Casas, the whole idea of the 'barbarian other' was turned against the oppressor:

A man is apt to be called barbarous, in comparison with another, because he is strange in his manner of speech and mispronounces the language of the other ... But from this point of view, there is no man or race which is not barbarous with respect to some other man or race ... Thus, just as we esteemed these peoples of the Indies barbarous, so they considered us, because of not understanding us.[12]

In this connection, moreover, we may note that however ready Western thought has been to relegate the 'savage' to the side of nature, this natural man has just as persistently returned as critic of the incivility of civilized man, and thus as idealized image of humanity. One is speaking here of a perdurable equivocation within 'civilized' thinking, which has no sooner constructed its own 'humanity' by way of a contrast with wild bestiality and primitive savagery than it discovers within the excluded domain of the 'natural' its own intrinsic nobility. This ambivalence, which historians of ideas have often mapped in terms of the contrary impulses of positivism and romanticism – the one to promote the cause of science and industry, the other the 'return to nature' – is perhaps registered most forcefully only at that point where Western civilization becomes most closely identified with industrialism, and hence prompts an immanent critique of this identity. Yet it is a tension traceable back much earlier, and it has always found expression in a schizoid projection of the barbarian 'other' as both brutal and noble, wild and gentle, fiercely impervious to the civilizing influence of art and science, or righteously repelling its pernicious effects.

What is involved here is a rather complex form of splitting whereby 'primitivity', although opposed in general as a state of nature to civilized society, is itself divided between 'harder' and 'softer' forms, both of which are equally invoked as human ideals. Thus the 'primitive' as the 'natural' state of life can be applauded either for its simple rudeness or for its gentle innocence. It can figure either a proud and ruthless autonomy: a moral defiance of social convention in its most courageous and principled individuality; or a pacific collectivism, a life of blissful communion, freed from the torments and strifes of moral maturity and factitious self-assertion. Nature has in this sense been valued both as an image of sublime transcendence of the 'civil', and as an image of the harmony that would prevail in the absence of a civilized zeal to transcend a more animal state of being.

In classical thought, the milk-drinking Albioi, the Lotus eaters and other such mythological or semi-mythological communities are celebrated for their mildness, the Scythians and Germanic peoples for their ferocity – with the Scythians representing, it has been said, the 'noble savage' for the Ancient World much as the Amer-Indians were to become the 'hard' primitives of the sixteenth and seventeenth centuries.[13] In the Middle Ages, the 'wild man' was deemed both brutal and benevolent, monstrous savage and innocent child – and we can trace a similar instability in later approaches to the phenomenon of 'feral' children.[14]

By the time of the French Revolution, the savage had entered European thought as a symbol of revolutionary freedom and even as an ideal of human perfectibility – with Rousseau being credited, if somewhat misleadingly, as one of the major architects of this idea. Rousseau, in fact, was no simple advocate of the 'noble savage', but this ideology was sufficiently associated with his political argument to prompt the rebuke from his contemporary, Mary Wollstonecraft, that had he

. . . mounted one step higher in his investigation, or could his eye have pierced through the foggy atmosphere, which he almost disdained to breathe, his active mind would have darted forward to contemplate the perfection of man in the establishment of true civilization, instead of taking his ferocious flight back into the night of sensual ignorance.[15]

Yet alongside this ennobling of a wild or 'harder' primitivity, we find a comparable dignification of a more luxuriantly sensual, less hardy mode of naturality, as represented, for example, in the Tahitians, who were praised by Diderot for their 'softness',[16] and who notoriously figured in the nineteenth century as an exotic culture that paradoxically approached almost to decadence in its disregard for civilized norms.[17] Conversely, we might note, the idle and Sybaritic primitivity of the Southerner was associated with climatic conditions and a natural plenitude inimical to the industriousness essential to civilization. Annette Kolodny has drawn attention to the play of this dialectic among the colonizers of America, who depicted the South both as a paradise of plenty and sensuous ease, and as a place to be avoided at all costs as an invitation to 'sponging', corruption and indolence; or, as one of them put it, because 'the over-flowing of riches [is known] to be an enemie of labour, sobriety, justice, love and magnanimity: and the nurse of pride, wantonnesse, and contention'.[18] Laziness, in fact, itself often enough viewed as induced by an overly generous abundance of natural provisions, has standardly been associated with backwardness even as freedom from the curse of labour has been a central aspiration of human progress, and figured very prominently in utopian argument.[19] The struggle against nature has thus been conceived as both a necessary vehicle of civilization–humanization and as emblematic of an unnatural repression of our more truly human selves; correlatively, primitivity as idleness has been construed both as slothful regression and as playful advance beyond the realm of necessity.

Animals and Us

The association of the primitive with either animal simplicity or brutish ferocity clearly draws on a prior discrimination between man and beast. I now turn to this more directly in order to illustrate the ways in which it has served both as a conceptual tool through which humanity thinks its difference from the rest of animality and as an assertion of its communality with it. For it is clear that human attitudes to animals serve both to express and to conceal a dualistic conception of ourselves as creatures who are both 'cultural' (i.e. 'non-natural') and yet subject to 'natural' functions and possessed of 'purely animal' properties.

As we have seen in chapter 2, this dualism has its theoretical reflection in the debate between 'culturalist' and 'naturalist' approaches to the human-animal divide, with the one side claiming that human beings differ absolutely from animals in virtue of their symbolic capacities, the other insisting that the differences between humanity and the higher primates are matters of degree. But whatever view we take on this issue, there is little doubt that, in the common way of seeing things, animals are opposed to human beings as creatures who belong to the order of nature. Western thought has therefore, in an important sense, regarded the animal as the antithesis to the human, and done so very largely on account of its lack of speech. It is 'dumbness' that is regarded as the primary characteristic of the beast, and that places it most firmly in the camp of nature, even if other features (hairiness, non-erect posture, absence of tool-using, incapacity to laugh) have been invoked to confirm this classification. This is not to

suppose that, long prior to evolutionary theory, there were
not some doubts about the absoluteness of the distinction.
In his *Systema Naturae* of 1736, Linnaeus classified the
'animal' as *mutus*, *hirsutus* and *tetrapus* [dumb, hairy, and
quadruped]. But, like Rousseau and Monboddo, he was
also inclined to suppose that the orang-utan was a kind
of human, and in fact classified it as *homo nocturnus*.[20]
But if these 'border line cases' could occasion doubts in
the mind of the classifier, lay thinking on the whole has
not experienced much hesitation about where the divide
falls, nor doubted that, despite the immense diversity of
the creatures who are lumped together as 'animals', they
are all creatures of nature in a way that humans are not.

But even as we distinguish ourselves in this way, our
relations with animals are profoundly marked by our
disposition to view them as a mirror of humanity, to
project our features on to them, or to regard their features
as symbolic or representative of our own. Animals mediate
our relations to the world and each other in an immense
variety of ways. They are both treated 'like animals';
that is, without compunction about their suffering or
loss of dignity, and as objects of extreme reverence and
fierce taboo. They symbolize everything that is most
hallowed and most reviled. They provide metaphors for
the entire gamut of human emotions, and have been one
of 'primitive' and 'civilized' humanity's primary means of
classification and representation (as in their totemic use
explored by Lévi-Strauss and others; or the classification
and heraldic use of animals as emblematic of human social
hierarchies).[21] They are also, of course, semiotically ever
present in our own culture in their use to name a whole
range of commodities from cigarettes to motor-cars to
insurance schemes. They are, in general, as Lévi-Strauss
has suggested, 'good to think with'; but also we might say,
'good to dissimulate with', too, in that when used as means
of naming and thinking, they often seem to offer themselves

as a kind of manifest text or displaced commentary on a more latent and less consciously acknowledged perception of the world. It is as if through the semiotic use of animals we are spared the embarrassment of a more direct confrontation with our own follies and aggressions. We name cars after wild animals, put 'tigers' in their tanks, for example, rather than admit directly to human ferocity, and through animals we surreptitiously acknowledge an envy or admiration of qualities we are officially supposed to deplore (the fox's cunning, the lion's pride, the cock's vanity, and so forth). Animals, of course, are also constantly used as a means of moral or satirical commentary on ourselves (as in Aristophanes' *Birds, Frogs, Wasps*; Aesop's *Fables*; Chaucer's *The Fowls' Parliament* or *The Nun's Priest's Tale*; Mandeville's *Fable of the Bees*; Orwell's *Animal Farm*, and numerous other instances); but also, by way of what Mary Midgley has termed the 'Beast Within', as a means of self-exculpation:

> If . . . there is no lawless beast outside man, it seems very strange to conclude that there is one inside him. It would be more natural to say that the beast within us gives us partial order; the task of conceptual thought will only be to complete it. But the opposite, *a priori* reasoning has prevailed. If the Beast Within was capable of every iniquity, people reasoned, then beasts without probably were too. This notion made man anxious to exaggerate his difference from all other species, and to ground all activities he valued in capacities unshared by animals, whether the evidence warranted it or no. In a way this evasion does the species credit, because it reflects our horror at the things we do. Man fears his own guilt and insists on fixing it on something evidently alien and external. Beasts Within solve the problem of evil.[22]

Our proneness to anthropomorphize animals has, of course, been generally recognized, particularly in its two most obvious, if contrary, aspects: our eagerness to endow animals with human personality, and our use of them to dissociate from our own animality. Both aspects reveal a dialectic. Under the first, we show our affection for animals through allowing them to share a human 'life' and our fondness for ourselves in projecting onto them the feelings we deem exclusive to us. Under the second aspect, we express our distance from animals by viewing them as the alien embodiment of all that is less truly human (our lower, carnal, more bestial selves), and our distaste for the human insofar as this is irrevocably tied to animality, hence in need of distantiation.

The animals chosen for these projections are very often those with whom we live in close propinquity, whether voluntarily or involuntarily (pets, domestic animals, pests). Pets, for example, are very often treated as if they too were 'persons' in their own way, possessed of names, passions, foibles, even a way of 'talking' to us. Their nature is also our nature, viewed with a certain indulgence, an empathetic tolerance for everything that is delightful, comic, lovable and absurd in ourselves. At the same time, many of the qualities that we deplore in the human being (pomposity, pride, deceit, stealth, greed, fickleness) are smiled upon, and even admired, in our pets, whose 'natural innocence' turns vice into virtue; and who allow us, through identification with them, a measure of forgiveness for the sins we displace onto them.

Indeed, it is as if we use our pets in part to mitigate the inevitable elements of alienation that attach to a genuinely inter-subjective engagement. They allow us, as it were, to escape the strains and responsibilities of dealing with the other's autonomy. By transferring onto our pets a personality that we know in a sense to be a product of our own fantasy, we allow ourselves a privilege we cannot in our human personal relations: to feel confident that we are fully loved by a subject even as we gratify the urge for a total – and necessarily objectifying – possession of the other. More facetiously, we might say that the pet animal relieves us of the tensions theorized by Hegel in his Master-Slave dialectic (and later applied by Sartre to the situation of the lover): through the fantasy of its autonomy, speech and cognition, we can be recognized by a 'subject' who poses no threat to our subjectivity. Or, to express the point in more Lacanian terms, the animal here, in virtue of its being at once both a 'person', and bereft of speech, absolves our subjectivity from dependency on the other's interpretation of our message. For to the pet we can impute whatever understanding of ourselves we intend to convey.

In the case of our affection for animals, then, one may speculate that a positive anthropomorphism, or humanization of nature, allows us a measure of relief from the rigours of being human. It permits a certain suspension from the moral universe that governs relations between persons, and from the struggles for autonomy that attach to that. Conversely, it has been suggested that the strains of human life are sometimes betrayed in the artistic depiction of animals as freer from bondage than their masters precisely because, being soul-less, they are destined neither for heaven nor hell.[23] In this general connection, we may also note the powerfully suggestive points that Donna Haraway has made about the motives of primatology and the domestication of the higher primates:

> Underlying the language and home-reared ape studies is the simple, enduring Western question: what would it be like not to be barred from nature? Is touch possible? Since traditionally language has been imagined to be the source of the barrier, perhaps if language could be shared, contact with apes, almost as extraterrestrials, could be made, and 'man' would not be alone . . . Teaching apes human language and learning from them how to

communicate with their own kind were both efforts to
open the border inherited from the separation of nature
and culture. Surrogates, rehabilitants, language students,
and adopted children: apes modelled a solution to a deep
cultural anxiety sharpened by the real possibility in the late
twentieth century of Western people's destruction of the
earth.[24]

But if we have turned to animals in an attempt to
transcend the 'loneliness' or 'alienation' of our cultural
status, we have also persistently used them to preserve
the culture-nature barrier. In the case of pests and vermin,
for example, whose parasitism is experienced as entirely
negative, anthropomorphism is employed to denounce the
vileness of human habits and dependencies. The rat, or
flea, or wasp, figure the human only in those aspects in
which it is considered most abject and revolting: where it
is scrounging, mean, cowardly, vicious and sycophantic. If
we endow such creatures with the attributes of personality,
it is to reject our own beastliness rather than discover
ourselves in 'nature', and thus to reinforce rather than
loosen the grip of the moral order. The animal is here
used to police rather than confuse the human-nature
divide; by associating all our 'lowlier' characteristics and
bodily functions with animality, we assert the importance
of sustaining those higher or more spiritual attributes that
grant us human sovereignty over the beast. Nature here
represents not a desirable state of innocence or freedom
from a too exacting cultural law, but that which it is
treachery to yield to. To act the animal (to be dirty,
lewd, selfish, etc.) is precisely to be 'brutal': to betray
what is proper to humanity. Nor is it any accident that
we often invoke creatures who are indeed very physically
lowly to express contempt for characteristics in our own –
erect – selves, which it is really quite meaningless to impute
to these species (as when we speak of the worm as 'cringing'
or the snake as 'deceptive').

Human attitudes to animals are revealed as particularly ambivalent where the beast in question is both relatively familial and eaten by us. Many commentators have remarked on the complexity of the iconography we bring to domestic animals, with the pig being selected here as of particular interest. It has been pointed out that many of the negative characteristics of domestic animals – the pig's proverbial greed or filthiness, for example – have been induced in them by the manner in which they are reared, and are indissociable from their positive utility to us:

> The pig is the only animal bred by man entirely for the sake of its meat. It is fed inordinately on garbage in order to make it fat. It becomes dirty because it is kept in a sty. It is made lazy only because it is confined. Yet the pig – not the breeder – is designated piggish.[25]

That the pig could be confined to the backyard and fed on waste meant, moreover, that it was not only an extremely economic source of meat, but also of human hygiene. The pig's 'dustbin' habits provided its owner with a primitive form of sewage and refuse disposal, and a voraciousness and filthiness imputed to pig 'nature' was enforced in the interests of human appetites and cleanliness.

At the same time, it has been suggested that it was the very propinquity of the pig, both in the sense that it, more than other domestic animals, occupied the household space, and in the sense of its anthropoid features (its hairlessness, the resemblance of its young to human embryos), which made it so apt for a complex projection through which humanity disowned its 'piggish' features while yet expressing a certain endearment for them.[26] Fraser Harrison has claimed, in fact, that ambivalence towards the pig only becomes more prevalently hostile as a result of its metamorphosis at the hands of breeders and transference to the slums of the early nineteenth century industrial towns and cities:

Its hitherto valued capacity to grow fat on the cheapest
rations now transformed it into a kind of latter-day
plague. It becomes an object of hatred and revulsion not only because it contributed to the mass of
dirt, and flourished on it, but because it stood as
a sign of the gross immiseration of its fellow slum
dwellers.[27]

Only then does the aggression towards the pig allow its
use as an uncomplicated term of abuse of the 'pigs' who
police the law and order of society (and later of the 'male
chauvinists' who defend its patriarchal rule).

Prior to this transformation, the pig, as member of the
family who was yet to end up on its table, was an object of
more confused emotions: a creature whose revolting habits
both gained it a certain indulgence as wayward child and
justified its eventual slaughter. Indeed, it has been said that
the vilification of the pig can be attributed to the need to
assuage the guilt of killing and eating such a commensual
associate.[28] If this is so, it perhaps also helps to explain
the tendency – very prevalent still among Continental
pork butchers – to depict the pig as eager and cheerful
participant in its own consumption. The pig who savours
the smells of its own bacon and revels in the prospect of
the meal it supplies expiates the crime of its own killing
by joining us at the feast. (And some similar motive may
be traceable in poetic imagery which has the pheasant,
partridge and other delicacies 'willing', as Jonson put it,
'to be kill'd'.)[29]

Yet it is questionable whether such ethical projections
go to the heart of our ambivalence towards the pig,
which John Berger has argued is better viewed as a
vestige of a primitive dualism in human attitudes to
animals, who were both 'subjected *and* worshipped,
bred *and* sacrificed'.[30] To pursue such a line of inquiry
is, in turn, to place consideration of the pig (and by
association of our own 'piggishness') in the context of

the ambivalence of religion itself towards the 'pollution' from which the 'sacred' and 'holy' must be preserved. For the sacred is both the uncontaminated and that whose worship requires transgression of its taboos and defilement of its purity. Holy days are, after all, feast days, when the normally forbidden excess is permitted and even prescribed – as in the extreme example cited by Georges Bataille of the islanders of the Pacific, the death of whose king prompts a frenzy of sacrilegious acts.[31] The taboo, in fact, Bataille suggests, is only 'there to be violated', and the sacred world must be viewed as embodying contradictory meanings. Whence he concludes: 'we are not perhaps justified in asserting that religion is based on breaking rules, rather than on the rules themselves, but feast days depend on a readiness to make great inroads upon savings, and feast days are the crown of religious activity'.[32]

In her justly celebrated study of the disposition to sacralize the unclean, Mary Douglas has sought to explain this in terms of the tension between the order and systematicity imposed by the holy (which requires and enjoins the 'purity' of absolute separation and differentiation) and the practical impossibility of keeping life free from a profaning mélange and confusion.[33] Pollution taboos, she argues, such as the dietary rules in *Leviticus*, are neither to be understood in terms of hygiene, nor yet dismissed as irrational, but should be seen as demarcating the edible in terms of the unity and distinctness of the species category to which it was assigned. Impure animals (whom it is defiling to eat) are those that do not fit clearly into any single category, but have a 'mixed up' nature.[34] But since purity is the enemy of change and growth (chastity, for example, or the non-mixing of the sexes, is incompatible with life), the 'impure', which is first repelled for its lack of proper differentiation, returns as an apt symbol of creative formlessness. But it is from its first phase that it derives its power. Those vulnerable margins and those attacking forces which threaten to destroy good order represent the powers inhering in the cosmos. Ritual which can harness these for good is harnessing power indeed.[35]

Hence, she suggests, abominations are made powers for good as weeds and lawn-cuttings are turned into compost; and if the holy king or priest vicariously lives the abstinence and celibacy that ordinary mortals cannot, he also is imbued through transgressive forms of worship with the power that accrues to the danger of defilement. (Thus, an act of ritual incest is part of the sacralization of the king, the normal precedence of right hand over polluting left is reversed in religious ceremony, and through a cult use of blood, ordure and excreta, dirtiness becomes adjacent to godliness.[36] The fundamental taboo on eating human flesh is likewise transgressed in religious acts of cannibalism, whether involving actual human sacrifice, or the symbolic partaking of flesh and blood).[37]

When placed in the perspective of such religious attitudes and practices, it should hardly surprise us to find even the reputedly most filthy of animals endowed with the aura of the sacred, especially where its 'sacrifice' has been so essential to promoting the festive excess.

The Repulsion and Reintegration of the Body

This brings us to a cognate series of ambivalences that attach to the mind–body dualism of the humanity–nature distinction. As we have seen, a good part of our attitudes to animals is at the service of a policing exercise that preserves the 'human' from the 'natural' by identifying it with the mental and spiritualistic. That which is distinctively human is defined by exclusion of the carnal (more 'bestial') dimension, this being conceived as a 'lower' aspect or region. Such an exercise serves a number of social functions, notably to preserve class and gender hierarchies. Where the distinctively human is identified with the aesthetic sensibilities and intellectuality whose acquisition is the privilege of an educated elite, the 'lower orders' of society necessarily figure as something less than human: as an uncouth, simple peasantry or proletariat, whose closeness to the earth and its animals also places it nearer to nature. The genderization of mind–body dualism, whereby the 'human' as productivity/creativity is associated with the male, 'nature' as reproduction with the female, has likewise served as a support for patriarchy, and some of the dimensions and contradictory aspects of this symbolism will be examined in the final sections of this chapter.

Here I shall focus on some more general parallels between the way in which the excluded body returns to subvert the humanity–nature distinction, and the reversals in thinking that have rendered this division so ambiguous in respect of the 'savage' and the 'animal'. In a broad sense, we are here talking of a materialist challenge to the puritanism and elitism of the idealist refusal of the body. Though this has been registered in materialist approaches in philosophy from very early on, it is not until the nineteenth century that it is given powerful and sustained expression – notably in the argument of Nietzsche, Marx and Freud. Thus Nietzsche exposes the repudiation of the body as a morbid moralization through which humanity learns to be ashamed of its own instincts, and invites us to read the history of philosophy as 'an interpretation of the body, and a misunderstanding of the body'. Philosophy, he suggests, can be read as narrative about the body that takes the form of a denial of its philosophical validity, since it says 'away with the body, this wretched *idée fixe* of the senses, infected with all the faults of logic that exist, refuted, even impossible, although it be impudent enough to pose as if it were real'.[38] Marx, for his part, concurs in the rejection of a priestly 'ascetic' while analysing its ideological service on behalf of the ruling class, and its function in sustaining an exploitative division between 'mental' and 'manual' labour.[39] Freud likewise, in his theory of the repression of the Id, his presentation of culture as sublimation of sexuality, and his attention to the punitive and authoritarian dimensions of super-ego, points to the price humanity pays for its 'denial' of the body, even as he analyses its necessity. For if Freud regards repression as essential to the constitution of a distinctively human identity and culture, he also emphasizes the precariousness of this achievement and the extent to which conscious life is subject to the disruption of those impulses that it has been compelled to forego. In his suggestions, moreover, that there is something directly unwholesome about the guilts and tribulations that are the cost of rejecting 'animality', he comes close to implying that humanity is too exacting in the 'cultural' demands it makes of itself.[40]

But if it is only in the work of those whom Terry Eagleton has described as the three great 'aestheticians' of the body[41] that the ideological dimensions of mind–body dualism have been rendered theoretically explicit, a more cultural-symbolic use of carnality to undermine idealist cosmology, and the political hierarchy it helped to affirm, was in evidence much earlier. One might cite here the carnivalesque reversals of mind–body values and symbolism that have been explored so interestingly by Mikhail Bakhtin in his study of Rabelais and the Renaissance.[42] In these, what Bakhtin terms the 'grotesque body' and 'lower bodily stratum' are employed to debunk and invert the prevailing order. The below becomes the above, the derided body a site of celebration, the 'backside' of humanity the source of revolutionary power, the 'pig' the 'god':

> This downward movement . . . is inherent in all forms of popular-festive merriment and grotesque realism. Down, inside out, vice versa, upside down, such is the direction of these movements. All of them thrust down, turn over, push headfirst, transfer top to bottom, and bottom to top, both in the literal sense of space, and in the metaphorical meaning of the image . . . debasement is the fundamental principle of grotesque realism; all that is sacred and exalted is rethought on the level of the material bodily stratum or else combined and mixed with its images.[43]

This downward movement is found in ritual fights, beatings and blows, which trample the adversary to ground, but only to become the source of a creative flowering; in curses and expletives which draw their force from the energies of the body; in carnival uncrownings whereby the king's attributes become those of the buffoon; in images and acts whose carnal excess is turned in rebellious mockery against the pomposity of Church and State. Head, spirituality, refined sensibility: those features said to place us 'above' nature are here ridiculed as symbols of everything that is cramping and moribund. So far from figuring nature in its immanence and repetition, the body becomes the source of a creative and transcendent renewal. It is life against death, eros pitted against the reactionary and destructive qualities of a spirituality that would seek to immortalize its hold by presenting its values as eternally fixed. The excluded body thus returns from its repressions in order to reverse the dualism which cast it to the beyond of nature. As creative energy, it figures humanity in its refusal of fixity and its resistance to a supposedly 'natural' hierarchy. What clerics and kings here represent is a spiritual order whose self-exaltation and pretensions to permanence associate it symbolically with nature in its most degenerative and inertial aspects.

Of course, the inversions of the carnival were the temporary and in a sense permitted transgressions of the holiday. Moreover, to invert a mind–body dualism and the humanity–nature divide it maps is not in itself to break with its fundamental values. In many respects, we can see the conventions of the mind–body opposition sustained in the celebration of bodily energy and excess as an expression of creativity and cultural renewal.

The animal and corporeal are not so much freed from their traditional coding as subordinate to spirit, as themselves elevated as spiritual powers through which humanity may triumph over the dead forces of nature and their mundane representatives. All the same, the reversal instantiates the instabilities and ambiguities that we have seen to mark all attempts to demarcate between a higher 'humanity' and a 'lower' nature with respect to the 'cultural other' and to bestiality. Bakhtin's seminal work has been richly instructive here, as have the many studies that have drawn on it. The discussion of the hybridization and transgressions of the human–animal divide in Peter Stallybrass and Allon White's discussion of Jonson's *Bartholomew Fair* is particularly enlightening and very relevant to much of my argument here.[44]

Let us note, in conclusion, the attention that Bakhtin has drawn to what might be termed the 'paradox of Prometheanism' – to the ways, that is, in which a cosmological re-thinking that begins with a 'return to nature' becomes the basis for a celebration of human powers to master it. For Bakhtin argues that we must view Rabelais's use of 'grotesque realism' as deployed in the interests of something more than political satire.[45] Rabelais's exercise is not that of the intellectual opportunist, who plunders the tropes and imagery of folklore in order to offer an ironically coded commentary on the events and figures of his day. He was seeking rather to place carnivalesque inversion at the service of a revolutionary cosmology that would topple the Mediaeval conception of the universe, and thus release man from those cosmic fears which religion had always used to oppress him. Bakhtin writes:

> The starry sky, the gigantic material masses of the mountains, the sea, the cosmic upheavals, elementary catastrophes – these constitute the terror that pervades ancient mythologies, philosophies, the systems of images, and language itself with its semantics. An obscure memory of cosmic perturbations in the distant past and the dim terror of future catastrophes form the basis of human thought, speech, and images. This cosmic terror is not mystic in the strict sense of the word; rather it is the fear of that which is materially huge and cannot be overcome by force. It is used by all religious systems to oppress man and his consciousness. Even the most ancient images of folklore express the struggle against fear, against the memories of the past, and the apprehension of future calamities, but folk images relating to this struggle helped develop true human fearlessness. The struggle against cosmic terror in all its forms and manifestations did not rely on abstract hope or on eternal spirit, but on the material principle in man himself; he discovered them and became vividly conscious of them in his own body. He became aware of the cosmos within himself.[46]

The device used by Rabelais to assist this struggle against 'cosmic terror' was to decentralize the universe of traditional Christianity (the vertical hierarchy of the Great Chain of Being) by means of a relative re-centring of it on the underworld/underground conceived as a 'lower bodily stratum', which was also the source of all true wealth and abundance. Associating Rabelais with a tradition of earlier writing that had depicted Hades or hell as places of gaiety, Bakhtin argues that the essential aim was to 'laugh down' fear by re-presenting all that was normally viewed as most gloomy and terrible as an object of mirth and source of vitality. Grotesque realism is here pushed beyond the confines of the fertility cult to become emblematic of mankind's real future. 'The downward movement that penetrates all Rabelaisian images is ultimately directed towards this gay future';[47] the body, at home in the cosmos, is the 'gay matter which confronts cosmic power and laughs it down';[48] it is the historic, progressive body of mankind, 'the living sense that each man belongs to the immortal people who create history'.[49]

Where mediaeval scholasticism had repelled the body in order to sustain the 'humanity' of man, in other words, his propinquity to God relative to the beasts, Rabelais and other thinkers of the Renaissance (notably Pico della Mirandola, Giambattisto Porta, Giordano Bruno, Tommaso Campanella and Marsile Ficino)[50] employed it as a principle of a new Promethean humanism. The cosmos is here reconstructed, not on a vertical, but on a horizontal axis, which allows, in Pico's argument, man to be superior to all beings, including those of the celestial realm, because he alone has a nature that is not fixed but always in process of becoming. Man falls outside the linear hierarchy conceptualized in the Great Chain of Being because hierarchies can determine only what represents a stable and immutable nature. To view man, in proto-existentialist fashion, as unfinished and incomplete, is to allow him to become capable of anything. In Rabelais this vision is a new awareness of the cosmos as 'man's own home, holding no terror for him',[51] and its Prometheanism emerges very clearly in the eulogy to Pantagruelion, symbol of human technical capacity:

> . . . those heavenly creatures we call gods, both terrestrial and maritime, took fright when they perceived how, thanks to the blessed herb pantagruelion, the Artic peoples, under the very eyes of the Antarctic, crossed the Atlantic Ocean, passed the twin tropics, pushed through the torrid zone, spanned the zodiac, frolicked beneath the equinox, and held both poles within sight of the

horizon. Faced with such a situation, the gods, terrified, said:

'Pantagruel has, by this mere herb, caused us more worry and labour than ever the Aloides or Giants, Otus or Ephialtes, when they sought to scale Olympus. He will soon marry and beget children by his wife. This is a fate we cannot forestall, for it has been woven by the hands and shuttles of the three fatal sisters, daughters of Necessity. Who knows but that Pantagruel's children will discover some herb equally effectual? Who knows but humans may, by its means, visit the source of hell, the springs of the rain, the forge where lightning is produced? Who knows but they will invade the regions of the moon, intrude within the territories of the celestial signs? Some, then, will settle at the sign of the Golden Eagle, others at the Ram, others at the Crown, others at the Harp, others at the Silver Lion. They will sit down at our divine board, take our goddesses to wife, and thereby become themselves divine'.[52]

The humanity–nature antithesis has here gone through a kind of symbolic volte-face. Where the body and animality had previously been pushed to the side of 'nature' in order to preserve the spirituality of the 'human', these forces have now come to represent everything most triumphantly human. Their 'materialist principle' is the intelligence that exposes adulation of the spirit as the product of superstition, religious bigotry and cosmic fear, their energy symbolizes the human technological capacity for mastery over that 'nature' to which the 'gods', as false idols of our own thinking, had previously held us in thrall. Paradoxical as it may seem in some ways, the reversion to human nature in all its carnality and affinity with animality provides the support for an Enlightenment type of confidence in technical mastery and human dominion over nature. The celebration of the 'lower bodily stratum' leads on to that of instrumental rationality, the belly laugh at the spirit serves as the basis for a new credo in humanity's privileged powers of transcendence.

We might note, furthermore, that in this clash between a 'materialist' and a theological conception of the cosmos, the one seeking to subvert a presupposed order in human affairs, the other to preserve it, we have a prefiguring of the tension which has persisted into our own time between those who would invoke a mystical or 'theological' version of nature as a caution against Prometheanism, and those who would expose the reactionary function of all forms of nature 'idolatry' in perpetuating social divisions and hierarchies. The manifestation of this tension in contemporary arguments about nature will be examined more closely in subsequent chapters. Suffice it to say here, that while the de-divinization of the cosmos may have served as the support for ecologically very damaging practices, this is no reason to overlook its progressive function in challenging the supposed fixity and hierarchy of human relations, and both these aspects of Prometheanism need to be kept in mind in the appraisal of our political discourses about nature.

Naturalized Woman and Feminized Nature

One such supposedly natural fixity is that of relations between the sexes, and I shall here consider in conclusion some of the ways in which the naturalization of woman, and correlative feminization of nature, have served as symbolic support of sexual hierarchy.

(1) Woman as 'Nature'

As suggested earlier, the association of femininity with naturality represents a more specific instance of the mind–body dualism brought to conceptions of nature, since it goes together with the assumption that the female, in virtue of her role in reproduction, is a more corporeal being than the male. If we ask, that is, what accounts for this coding of nature as feminine – which is deeply entrenched in Western thought, but has also been said by anthropologists to be cross-cultural and well-nigh universal,[53] – then the answer, it would seem, lies in the double association of women with reproductive activities and of these in turn with nature. As feminists from de Beauvoir onwards have argued, it is woman's biology, or more precisely the dominance of it in her life as a consequence of her role in procreation, that has been responsible for her allocation to the side of nature, and hence for her being subject to the devaluation and de-historization of the natural relative to the cultural and its 'productivity'. The female, de Beauvoir tells us, is 'more enslaved to the species than the male, her animality is more manifest'.[54] Others have pointed out that in virtue of their role in the gratification of physiological needs, reproductive activities are viewed as directly linked with the human body, and hence as natural. As Olivia Harris puts it, 'since the human body is ideologically presented as a natural given, outside history, it is easy to slide into treating domestic labour as a natural activity, also outside the scope of historical analysis'.[55] In the argument of Sherry Ortner, woman's

'natural' association with the domestic context (motivated by her natural lactation functions) tends to compound her potential for being viewed as closer to nature because of the animal-like nature of children, and because of the infra-social connotation of the domestic group as against the rest of society. Yet at the same time, her socializing and cooking functions within the domestic context show her to be a powerful agent of the cultural process constantly transforming raw material resources into cultural products. Belonging to culture, yet appearing to have stronger amd more direct connotations with nature, she is seen as situated between the two.[56]

In the view of Ortner, then, and other anthropologists, what is at issue here is not so much a simple conflation of woman with nature, as an alignment of the two that derives from the female role in child-birth and her consequent activities as initial mediator between the natural and the cultural.[57] As those responsible for the nursing and early socialization of children, women are 'go betweens' who stay closer to nature because of their limited and merely preparatory functions as 'producers' of the cultural.

Patriarchal relations, moreover, have protracted and reinforced this set of associations by the limitations they have placed on female participation in and access to culture. Ortner remarks that 'in virtually every society there is a point at which the socialization of boys is transferred to the hands of men', and that even cooking, which ought by rights to align women with the cultural, is not regarded as truly cultural until it is conceived as an 'art' form – whereupon it typically becomes the province of the male chef. The *haute cuisine* transfer to the male thus replicates the pattern in socialization: 'women perform lower level conversions from nature to culture, but, when culture distinguishes between a higher level of the same functions, the higher level is restricted to men'.[58] This same pattern, we might note, tends to be repeated even in societies that have ceased to impose any formal or legal ban on the engagement of women in 'high level' socialization – as is evidenced, for example in the preponderance of males over females the higher up one goes through the echelons of the educational system. The ratio of men to women in professorial posts is more or less the inverse of that of teachers in the primary school class.

We might also note, in this connection, the extent to which the presumption that 'art' is a distinctively male preserve has influenced the reception of female cultural production. As Griselda Pollock and Rozsika Parker have pointed out, certain subject matters and art forms (the painting of flowers, for example) were typically viewed as appropriate to women in virtue of their similarity to their own nature, so that 'fused into the prevailing notion of femininity, the painting becomes solely an extension of womanliness, and the artist becomes a woman only fulfilling her nature'.[59] At the same time, for needlework, quilt work and other forms of craft traditionally produced by women to be perceived as 'art', their origins as craft had to be overlooked. They cite (adding their own italics) the deliberate amnesia of the critic, Ralph Pomeroy:

> I am going to forget, *in order really to see them*, that a group of Navajo blankets are only that. In order to consider them as I feel they ought to be considered – as Art with a capital 'A' – I am going to look at them as paintings – created with dye instead of pigment, in unstretched fabric instead of canvas – *by several nameless masters of abstract art.*[60]

What is interesting about this remark, we may add, is not only its blindness to the chauvinism of its patronage of female 'art', but its failure to appreciate that the abstract pattern of a Navajo blanket could be viewed as 'art' only *after* (male) 'high art' had come to encompass and value abstraction. In this sense, female cultural production was actually in advance of 'masculine' aesthetic conceptions.

More generally, it must be said that the antithetical equivalence: woman = reproduction = nature versus man = production = culture offers a doubly distorting picture: firstly, in that it invites us to suppose that 'production'

proceeds without reliance on nature, when in fact any
form of human creativity involves a utilization and transformation of natural resources; and secondly because it
presents 'reproduction' as if it were unaffected by cultural mediation and innured against the impact of socio-
economic conditions. Production, however, can no more
be regarded as independent of biological and physical
process than reproduction can be viewed as reducible
to an unmediated matter of biology outside the cultural-
symbolic order. This does not mean that there are no
distinctions to be drawn between the production of human
beings and the production of armaments, or between the
different kinds of work and activity involved when human
beings transform natural materials. Feminists, for example, have pointed to the ways in which any economic
theory (that of Marx, for example) that conceives of 'production' as essentially a matter of producing objects or
commodities will tend to overlook the productivity of
domestic labour and skew perceptions of its contribution accordingly.[61] The adequacy of the 'object' model
of production for thinking about agricultural production
has also been justly questioned.[62] Equally there is no
denying that insofar as human reproduction is a biological
process, the sexes are differently involved in it, and have
tended to assume distinctive social roles as a result of
that. The point is only that a simple mapping of the
culture-nature opposition onto these various differences
obscures rather than assists the discriminations necessary
to thinking clearly about them.

(2) Nature as 'Woman'

If women have been devalued and denied cultural participation through their naturalization, the downgrading
of nature has equally been perpetuated through its representation as 'female'. Looked at from this optic, too,

the symbolization testifies to considerable confusion of thought, and its very complexity indicates some profound ambiguities about 'man's' place within and relations to the natural world.

Nature has been represented as a woman in two rather differing senses: 'she' is identified with the body of laws, principles and processes that is the object of scientific scrutiny and experimentation. But 'she' is also nature conceived as spatial territory, as the land or earth which is tamed and tilled in agriculture (and with this we may associate a tendency to feminize nature viewed simply as landscape – trees, woodland, hills, rivers, streams, etc. are frequently personified as female or figure in similes comparing them to parts of the female body). In both these conceptions, nature is allegorized as either a powerful maternal force, the womb of all human production, or as the site of sexual enticement and ultimate seduction. Nature is both the generative source, but also the potential spouse of science, to be wooed, won, and if necessary forced to submit to intercourse. The Aristotelian philosophy, claimed Bacon, in arguing for an experimental science based on sensory observation, has 'left Nature herself untouched and inviolate'; those working under its influence had done no more than 'catch and grasp' at her, when the point was 'to seize and detain her';[63] and the image of nature as the object of the eventually 'fully carnal' knowing of science is frequently encountered in Enlightenment thinking and famously captured in Louis Ernest Barrias's statue of *La Nature se devoilant devant la science*, a copy of which stood in the Paris Medical Faculty in the nineteenth century.[64]

Nature as physical territory is also presented as a source of erotic delight, and sometimes of overwhelming provocation to her masculine voyeur-violator. Describing the confluence of the Potomac and Shenandoah rivers, Thomas Jefferson writes:

For the mountain being cloven asunder, she presents to your eye, through the cleft, a small catch of smooth blue horizon, at an infinite distance in the plain country, inviting you, as it were, from the riot and tumult roaring around, to pass through the breach and participate of the calm below.[65]

Wordsworth's poem, *Nutting*, offers one of the most powerfully voluptuous descriptions of the 'virgin scene' of nature, and one of the most disturbed accounts of the ravishment it provokes:

> Then up I rose,
> And dragged to earth both branch and bough, with
>   crash
> And merciless ravage; and the shady nook
> Of hazels, and the green and mossy bower,
> Deformed and sullied, patiently gave up
> Their quiet being; and, unless I now
> Confound my present feelings with the past,
> Even then, when from the bower I turned away
> Exulting, rich beyond the wealth of kings,
> I felt a sense of pain when I beheld
> The silent trees and the intruding sky.[66]

With less compunction John Montague urges the reader of his poem, *Message*, to

> ease your
> hand into the
> rot smelling crotch
>
> of a hollow
> tree, and find
> two pebbles of quartz
>
> protected by a spider's web
> her sunless breasts.[67]

But it is in the perception of the colonizer, for whom nature is both a nurturant force – a replenished bosom or womb of renewal – and a 'virgin' terrain ripe for penetration, that the metaphor of the land as female is most insistent; and also most equivocal – for it is one thing to cajole – or force – a virgin to surrender to her lover (rapist), another for the son to direct his sexual attentions towards his mother. Incestuous desires, or acts,(which constitute, indeed, a crime against nature) are of an altogether different order from those of a suitor overwhelmed by a natural interest in possessing the rightful object of his desire.

As a site of both reproduction and seduction, nature is here a complex, composite 'female', a metaphoric register in her feminization of the same divisions and anxieties that have characterized male attitudes to women themselves, who are, of course, both mothers and sexual partners, and who have been cherished and abused in both these roles. Moreover, nature can also turn against her seducer with all the flightiness and unpredictability of woman. She may prove a shrew untamable, a thankless spouse to her toiling 'husband', a vengeful Fury unleashing her wrath against all those who dare to mess with her. As woman, then, nature is all things that women are, her sexuality everything it has been said to be: tender and nurturing, alluring and gratifying, irresistibly but dangerously compelling, formidably cold and voraciously hot. Her hills and downlands are the soft curves of bosom and thigh, her streams and rivers delightful clefts and sources of fertility. Yet her jungles and forests may prove impenetrable, her arctic zones repellently frigid, her bogs and morasses all too engulfing. And though she does 'unveil' herself to her explorer, her charms are not always what they first appear to be, and if tampered with too far or too clumsily she is well known to turn very ugly indeed.

Many have remarked on the analogies between the domination of nature and the oppression of women. Fewer have noted the equivocation in the mother–virgin–lover imagery, which is surely expressive of the conflicting feelings that 'real' nature has induced in 'men'. If Nature is, after all, both mother and maid, this surely reflects a genuine tension between the impulse to dominate and the impulse to be nurtured. The urge to feminize nature contains within it, that is, something of the contrariness of attitude that is inspired by the interaction with it; or, as Annette Kolodny has put it in her study of the 'pastoral impulse' in American art and letters, it combines both a 'phallic' and a 'foetal' aspect, the conflict between them testifying to deep-seated ambiguities about the use of nature. For the American colonizer, suggests Kolodny, who was 'beginning again', nature was a site of rebirth, but only on condition of its settlement and taming – a 'violating' intervention by the phallic pioneer upon the nurturing womb, which was bound to prove a source of guilt. The mother's body as the first ambience experienced by the infant becomes a kind of 'archetypal primary landscape' to which subsequent perceptual configurations of space are related. As such, moreover, it is expressive of a nostalgia for a mother–child unity, this unity itself being a figure of a desired harmony and 'at oneness' of man and nature.[68]

To pursue this idea further is to suggest that there is a parallel mapping of the regrettable but inevitable mother–child separation onto the relation to nature as inevitable object of 'phallic' intervention. The Oedipal drama, whereby the child acquires masculine subjectivity in 'giving up' incestuous desires for the mother in exchange for eventual possession of another female, is here inscribed in the 'body' of nature itself as both protective mother to be shielded from ravishment, and (as Thomas Morton described New England) the 'faire virgin, longing to be sped/ And meete her lover in a Nuptiall bed'.[69] If viewed in this light, nature's retributions on those who would force her to yield her secrets or submit to 'husbandry' can readily appear to be maternal punishments; or the desire to be overwhelmed by nature indicate a remorse felt for her violation.

Feminized nature is not therefore emblematic simply of mastered nature, but also of regrets and guilts over the mastering itself; of nostalgias felt for what is lost or defiled in the very act of possession; and of the emasculating fears inspired by her awesome resistance to seduction.

Some, doubtless, will want to dispute the force of the psychoanalytic account of feminine representations of nature, or at least wish to restrict its pertinence to the colonial experience (though Wordsworth's 'merciless ravage' suggests a wider relevance). It is not, however, essential to the symbolic tensions explored here that it is a *virginal* woman-territory that is also a nurturant Mother, but only that Nature is perceived as both sexual partner and maternal womb. In any case, given the extent to which the 'virginal' metaphor remains residually in play in the disposition – very prevalent in ecological thinking – to represent nature as a domain of purity that has been defiled by human intervention, there is a kind of legacy of the colonial imagery in contemporary representations. As Alexander Wilson has noted, moreover, the idea of 'nature' as the untouched zone beyond the encroachment of human culture remains powerfully compelling and an ideological mainstay of leisure and tourist industry advertising.[70] 'Getting back to nature' or 'really in touch' with it is getting back to, or in touch with, what has not yet been broached. Whether or not these attitudes to nature are clarified by viewing them through an Oedipal optic, there is no doubt that the investment of geographical territory with femininity offers an interesting record of human ambivalence towards the land and its exploitation.

(3) Fatherland and Motherland

There are also interesting inconsistencies, though of a

somewhat different order, generated by the application of sexual imagery to the territory of the nation. The nation state is bisexualized – both fatherland and motherland – even if the tendency is for the *patria* to figure the nation in its temporality, the maternal image to figure it in its spatiality in a reproduction of the classic gendering of the time–space divide.[71] The fatherland, that is, registers the nation in its history and tradition, in its existence as a sedimented stock of customs and values, as a temporally inherited and transmissible 'culture'. The idea of the motherland, by contrast, invokes nationality in its supposedly eternal territorial fixity as land or earth, as 'natural' precondition and spatial background to its historical and cultural existence, and is often more prominent in the nationalist iconography of rural societies. The nationalist mythology of Ireland (which I shall draw on as a case study in this discussion) is heavily reliant on the depiction of the nation as female: as the woman epitomized in the pre-Christian 'sovereignty goddesses', in their Mediaeval personifications (Dierdre, Queen Medbh of Connacht), and in a continuous allegorization of the indigenous land as female victim of the 'masculine' colonizer from the seventeenth century onwards (she is the 'aisling', Eriu, Fodla, Banba, Roisin Dubh, Sean Bhean Bhocht, Caitlin Ni Houlihan, etc.).[72]

If the self-image of one nation is more feminine, while that of another is more masculine, this in part reflects the way in which gender imagery itself 'maps' the rural-industrial, primitive-civilized, space-time conceptual oppositions within which national identity is conceived. (The more a nation identifies itself with its 'masculine' feats of military conquest and industrial enterprise, the less inclined it is to mythologize itself as feminine). But it also in part reflects the application of that imagery to international relations, where the imperialist nation conceives of itself, and is conceived by those it suppresses, in the 'phallic' mode, the colonized identifying itself as a female brutally assaulted by the male oppressor.

To the extent, however, that all nationalist rhetoric 'feminizes' the nation in its encouragement of the idea of this as 'home' or 'family', then patriotic loyalty to it, as Ross Poole has noted, embodies a kind of gender paradox. For the request to the sons of the nation to concern themselves with its 'domestic' interests, and, if necessary, to die in their service, is an injunction to adopt what is traditionally thought of as a feminine set of loyalties and moral postures.[73] Nationalist symbolism, in other words, runs athwart the conventional gendering of the public–private divide, which has always been seen to correspond to the state–family, male–female, division of spheres and moral responsibilities.

Hegel's justification of this division, for example, which is perhaps the most sophisticated in philosophy, is premised on the assumption that men and women are naturally differentiated in their ethical concerns and capacities.[74] Thus the proper ethical domain of the woman is that of family, and her loyalties are those of Antigone: loyalties to kith and kin, to the ties of blood, which it is her specific duty to defend against the universalist and secular law of Creon. Female concerns, then, are essentially particularist. The male, by contrast, is able to transcend the familial domain, in virtue of his ethical concern and identification with the collective interests of the State; and he alone, in his moral maturity, appreciates the necessity of sacrificing the bond of blood in the furtherance of these higher, 'universal' aims.

To the extent, then, that nationalism draws on familial and tribal imagery for its patriotic appeal, it is invoking a feminine ethical mode, since this is an appeal to the tie of kinship and to altruistic self-sacrifice on behalf of the 'family'. Hegel's purportedly 'masculine' universal values, the patriarchal 'public' interests, are here legitimated on the very basis of what are conceptualized as 'inferior' female duties and moral modes.

At the same time, the deployment of the idea of the nation as tribe or family, whose members are linked by the blood-tie, is manifestly an attempt to create a piece of 'nature': to obscure the artificial, or 'fictional' (Ernest Gellner) or 'imaginary' (Benedict Anderson) or 'fantastical' (Slovoj Žižek) quality of the national entity.[75] By means of nationalist bonding – the ideology of the tribe – the attempt is made to secure and legitimate a conventional order of civil power by projecting it back into a primordial state of nature. What is in reality a cultural construction, and a quite recent one at that,[76] is massaged into existence by means of a myth of its immemorially archaic origins and 'natural' evolution. Nationalism therefore works by means of a certain self-delusion whereby an idealized image of the archaic land masks the more complex and fractured realities of its actual history. Thus – to invoke again the example of Ireland – in the Land League propaganda of Michael Davitt, or the writing of the Literary Revival, a romanticized version of the nation as a people whose frugal life-style and spiritual values set them as a race apart from their commercial and materialist oppressors served to 'redeem' or even to screen out the actual oppressions of their existence.[77] Indeed, not only did the Celticism espoused by Synge, Yeats and other writers of the Revival obscure the rather less than picturesque aspects of rural life, and the aspirations of many Irish to something more than a beatified state of 'primitivity' and 'frugality', it also perpetuated the English myth of Ireland as a backward nation of 'pigs and paddies' – and thus served, as G. J. Watson has observed, as a reminder of the extent to which English culture had constructed Ireland's own image of its national identity.[78] James Joyce's resistance to 'ruralism' and his option for cosmopolitanism against the ghetto of Celticism were motivated by a desire to expose the bigotries masked by Irish nationalism and its mythical status as a pure, indigenous cultural legacy.

Many of these bigotries, moreover, were peculiarly oppressive of women. Nationalism very frequently makes use of the iconography of the land as female to reinforce, by way of the woman-nature association, its legitimacy as 'natural', and then appeals to this 'natural' status to justify the oppression of women. Idealized affinities between woman and the land and earth-bound values thus function as the support for a politics that employs iconic female figures and pastoral idylls to veil the deeply reactionary quality of its policies towards women and the gender division of labour.

We may add that even those who are sensitive to, and critical of, the mythologizing functions and regressive effects of nationalism may make use of the gender imagery in ways that reproduce rather than problematize the stereotypical associations of woman with the natural, the spatial and the immanent. Joyce's *Ulysses* is working within an essentialist and mythologizing conception of the feminine (as earth-bound, cosmic, cyclical, the representative of humanity in its reproductive immanence) even as it exposes the reactionary dimensions of these modes of thinking in respect of nationalism.[79] Patricia Coughlan also questions the essentializing implications of the gender symbolism in the poetry of Seamus Heaney and John Montague, and the temporal conflations of which it is the vehicle:

> One must question in general the elision of history which is involved in this smooth passage from memory to myth – an elision which precludes the possibility of understanding history as the product of human actions and not merely as fate, cyclical natural process. It is also necessary in particular to interrogate the notions of essential femininity and immemorially assigned female positions as the vehicles of this myth-memory passage, and to notice that

it requires an implicit assumption of the inescapability of a gendered allocation of subject-positions, by means of which rationality, speech and naming are the prerogatives of the autobiographically validated male poet, and the various female figures dwell in oracular silence, always objects, whether of terror, veneration, desire, admiration or vituperation, never the coherent subjects of their own actions.[80]

In subsequent chapters, I shall pursue some further dimensions of the forms of naturalization discussed here, placing them in the context of contemporary ecological calls for nature conservation and preservation. I shall thus be seeking to advance the discussion beyond the level of symbolism and representation at which it has largely remained in this chapter, in order to engage with some central tensions between ecological theory and politics and culturalist approaches that emphasize the mythical and normative functions of 'nature' in Western culture. In the first instance, I turn to the particularly acute and interesting form in which these tensions present themselves in respect of feminist and gay theories of gender and sexuality. The issue of sexuality is thus offered as a specific illustration of the contestation over 'nature', which I shall be addressing in broader terms at a later stage.

Notes

1   F. Capra, *The Tao of Physics* (Shambhala, Berkeley, 1975), p. 77.
2   The main sources for these stories of the 'Marvels of the East' were Ktesias of Knidos (fourth century BC); Megasthenes' report on India (*c.* 300 BC); Pliny's *Historia naturalis* (AD 77) and Solinus' *Collectanea rerum memorabilium* (3rd century AD). For an account and survey of the pictorial tradition, see Rudolf Wittkower, 'Marvels of the East' in *Allegory and the Migration of Symbols* (Thames and Hudson, London, 1977), pp. 46–77;

cf. Stephen Horigan, *Nature and Culture in Western Discourses* (Routledge, London, 1988), pp. 55–7; Mikhail Bakhtin, *Rabelais and His World*, trans. Hélène Iswolsky (MIT Press, Cambridge, Mass., 1968), pp. 344–7.

3 Wittkower, *Allegory*, pp. 47–8.

4 Since, according to Strabo (Book xiv), the Greeks thought of 'barbarians' as mispronouncing the Greek language, and despised them accordingly.

5 Stephen Greenblatt, *Learning to Curse: Essays in Early Modern Culture* (Routledge, London, 1990), p. 2

6 Greenblatt, *Learning to Curse*, p. 26f.

7 Cf. Margaret Hodgen, *Early Anthropology in the Sixteenth and Seventeenth Centuries* (University of Pennsylvania Press, Pennsylvania, 1964), cited in Horigan, *Nature and Culture*, p. 60.

8 Greenblatt, *Learning to Curse*, pp. 28–30.

9 Hodgen, *Early Anthropology*, cited in Horigan, *Nature and Culture*, p. 61.

10 Over the period 1840–50, for example, the entire native community of Tasmania was eradicated. On these and other 'civilizing' effects of British imperialism, see Victor Kiernan, *The Lords of Human Kind: European Attitudes towards the Outside World in the Imperial Age* (Penguin, Harmondsworth, 1972).

11 Ibid., p. 327.

12 See Greenblatt, *Learning to Curse*, p. 19.

13 Cf. Horigan, *Nature and Culture*, p. 54.

14 Cf. Richard Bernheimer, *Wild Men in the Middle Ages* (Harvard University Press, Cambridge, Mass., 1952); see also Horigan, *Nature and Culture*, p. 62f.

15 Mary Wollstonecraft, *Vindication of the Rights of Women* (Penguin, Harmondsworth, 1983), p. 99.

16 Diderot, *Supplément au Voyage de Bourgainville* in *Selections*, ed. A. Adams (Garnier-Flammarion, Paris, 1972), pp. 141–86.

17 See Kiernan, *The Lords of Human Kind*, pp. 246–56.

18 Annette Kolodny, *The Lay of the Land* (University of North Carolina Press, Chapel Hill, 1975), p. 19.

19 Thus Marxism and socialist theory closely associate human emancipation with the release of free time, and this is a 'utopian' thematic developed in the argument of the Frankfurt School theorists, notably in the second part of Herbert Marcuse's *Eros and Civilisation* (Beacon Press, Boston, 1966). More recently, André Gorz has promoted a vision of post-capitalist society

114   *Nature, Friend and Foe*

rooted in the idea of the liberation from work, see in particular, *Paths to Paradise: On the Liberation from Work*, trans. Malcome Imrie (Pluto Press, London, 1985).

20 See Keith Thomas, *Man and the Natural World* (Allen Lane, London, 1983), pp. 129–31; cf. Horigan, *Nature and Culture*, p. 74 (who also notes in this connection that Monboddo's claim, that the intelligence of apes was evidenced in their use of sticks, had drawn forth the objection at the time that Monboddo was simply drawing on pictures of apes, to which the iconography of the stick had been introduced because of the religious offence in the idea of the ape being able to walk erect unassisted).

21 See Dan Sperber in John Sturrock (ed.), *Structuralism and Since* (Oxford University Press, Oxford, 1979), pp. 27–33; Keith Thomas, *Man and the Natural World*, ch. 2, pp. 51–81, 100–20.

22 Mary Midgley, *Beast and Man* (Harvester Press, Hassocks, 1979), p. 40.

23 John Berger writes in his essay on animals in *Second Nature*, ed. R. Mabey, S. Clifford and A. King (Cape, London, 1984), p. 99, that 'the strain of subordinating life to the laws of the closed symmetrical systems was often betrayed by a response to animals', and cites as an example the much freer expression given to animals than to humans in twelfth-century church carvings.

24 Donna Haraway, *Primate Visions* (Routledge, London, 1989), p. 132.

25 John Berger, 'Animal World' in *Second Nature*, p. 100. Cf. Fraser Harrison, 'Vile Piggishness' in *Strangeland* (Sidgwick and Jackson, London, 1982), pp. 46–7.

26 Fraser Harrison, *Strangeland*, p. 60.

27 Ibid., p. 61.

28 Edmund Leach, 'Anthropological Aspects of Language: Animal Categories and Verbal Abuse', in Eric H. Lenneberg (ed.), *New Directions in the Study of Language* (MIT Press, Cambridge, Mass., 1964), p. 51. Cf. Fraser Harrison, *Strangeland*, pp. 61–2, though Harrison's suggestion that a similar inversion is discoverable in our attribution of 'fowlness' ('foulness') to those of our feathered friends whose flesh we most delight in ingesting (p. 62) is based on an etymological confusion.

29 On the whole, however, such imagery – which is discussed at greater length in chapter 6 – is better explained in terms of the pastoral fantasy of an 'abundant nature'.

30 John Berger, 'Why Look at Animals' in *About Looking* (Writers and Readers Publishing, London, 1980), p. 5.
31 Georges Bataille, *Eroticism* (Marion Boyars, London, 1987), p. 66. Bataille is here drawing upon Roger Caillois's accounts in *L'Homme et le Sacré*, 2nd edn (Gallimard, Paris, 1950), p. 151.
32 Georges Bataille, *Eroticism*, p. 68.
33 Mary Douglas, *Purity and Danger* (Routledge, Kegan Paul, London, 1978).
34 Ibid., pp. 55–7. Hence, Douglas argues, Jewish abstinence from pork eating has nothing to do with the dangers of disease, but is solely to do with the pig's 'failure as a wild boar to get into the antelope class' (p. 55).
35 Ibid., p. 161.
36 Ibid., pp. 159–60.
37 Cf. Georges Bataille, *Eroticism*, pp. 71–2; see also Catherine Clément, *Le Gout du Miel* (Grasset, Paris, 1987), pp. 15–19.
38 Friedrich Nietzsche, *The Gay Science*, trans. Walter Kauffmann (New York, 1974), pp. 34–5, and p. 18.
39 See in particular, the attack on the mind–body inversions of German idealism in *The Holy Family* and *The German Ideology* in Karl Marx, Friedrich Engels, *Collected Works* (Lawrence and Wishart, London, 1970–), vols 3, 5. But while Marx emphasizes the materialism of his premises over those of German idealism, he is also highly critical of the ahistoric materialism of Feuerbach, and is not one to collapse the 'cultural' into the 'natural' order. He has been criticized for his neglect of the biological (or over-socialized account of it), notably by Sebastiano Timpanaro in *On Materialism* (Verso, London, 1975), and has more recently been charged with sustaining an 'anthropocentric' human-animal dualism, at least in his early work, by Ted Benton (see 'Humanism = Speciesism? Marx on humans and animals', *Radical Philosophy* 50 (Autumn 1988), pp. 4–18) and cf. his *Natural Relations* (Verso, London, 1993). For a sense of the debates on Marx's views on biology, human nature, and the humanity–nature relationship, see *Issues in Marxist Philosophy*, vol. II, *Materialism*, ed. J. Mepham and D. H. Ruben (Harvester Wheatsheaf, Hemel Hempstead, 1979); Norman Geras, *Marx on Human Nature: Refutation of a Legend* (Verso, London, 1983); Peter Dickens, *Society and Nature: Towards a Green Social Theory* (Harvester Wheatsheaf, Hemel Hempstead, 1985), esp. ch. 3.

40 See the writings in Sigmund Freud, *Civilisation, Society and Religion* (Pelican Freud Library, vol. 12, Harmondsworth, 1985); The literature is vast here. For some excellent discussion see Leo Bersani, *The Freudian Body* (Columbia University Press, New York, 1986); Paul Ricoeur, *Freud and Philosophy: An Essay in Interpretation* (Yale University Press, New Haven, 1970); Paul Rieff, *Freud: The Mind of the Moralist* (London, 1959); Terry Eagleton, *The Ideology of the Aesthetic* (Blackwell, Oxford, 1990), ch. 10; Jonathan Dollimore, *Sexual Dissidence: Augustine to Wilde, Freud to Foucault* (Oxford University Press, Oxford, 1991), pp. 169–204.

41 Eagleton, *Ideology of the Aesthetic*, p. 197.

42 Bakhtin, *Rabelais*, p. 197.

43 Ibid., pp. 370–1.

44 Peter Stallybrass and Allon White, 'The Fair, the Pig, Authorship' in *The Politics and Poetics of Transgression* (Methuen, London, 1986). Stallybrass and White emphasize that what is at issue in animal-human transgression is not just inversion, but also hybridization, i.e. 'the in mixing of binary opposites, particularly of high and low, such that there is a heterodox merging of elements usually perceived as incompatible, and this latter version of the grotesque unsettles any fixed binaryism' . Inversion, they argue, is mere topsy-turvy, whereas hybridization – as in the circus use of the pig – is more complex (see pp. 44–59). Cf. *The Reversible World*, ed. Barbara Babcock (Cornell University Press, Ithaca, 1978).

45 Bakhtin, *Rabelais*, ch. 5.

46 Ibid., pp. 335–6.

47 Ibid., p. 378.

48 Ibid., p. 341.

49 Ibid., p. 367.

50 Ibid., pp. 363–6.

51 Ibid., p. 365.

52 Book 3, ch. 51, cited in Bakhtin, *Rabelais*, p. 366.

53 Its universality is stressed by Sherry B. Ortner in 'Is Female to Male as Nature is to Culture ?' in *Woman, Culture, Society*, ed. Michelle Zimbalist Rosaldo and Louise Lamphere (Stanford University Press, Stanford, Calif., 1974), pp. 67–87; cf. Michelle Zimbalist Rosaldo, 'A Theoretical Overview', ibid., pp. 18–19; but see also, E. Ardener, 'Belief and the problem of women' in *Perceiving Women*, ed. S. Ardener (Malaby, London, 1975); and *Nature, Culture and Gender*, ed. C. MacCormack and M.

Strathern (Cambridge University Press, Cambridge, 1980), esp. the essay by G. Gillison, 'Images of Nature in Gimi Thought', pp. 143–73.

54 Simone de Beauvoir, *The Second Sex*, trans. H. B. Parshley (Penguin, Harmondsworth, 1953), p.239; cf. pp. 24–7, 58–60.

55 Olivia Harris, 'Households as Natural Units' in *Subjectivity and Social Relations*, ed. Veronica Beechey and James Donald (Open University Press, 1985), p. 129.

56 Sherry Ortner, 'Is Female to Male?', p. 80.

57 It is this ambiguous status, she claims, that may help to account for the fact that in specific cultural ideologies and symbolizations, woman can occasionally be aligned with culture, and 'in any event is often assigned polarized and contradictory meanings within a single symbolic system'. Ibid., pp. 85–6.

58 Ibid., p. 80.

59 Griselda Pollock, Rozsika Parker, *Old Mistresses* (Routledge, Kegan Paul, London, 1981), p. 58.

60 Ibid., p. 68.

61 See the excellent recent discussions by Linda Nicholson and Nancy Fraser in Seyla Benhabib and Drusilla Cornell (eds), *Feminism as Critique* (Polity, Oxford, 1987), which also offer some survey of earlier debates around this issue.

62 See Ted Benton, 'The Malthusian Challenge: Ecology, Natural Limits and Human Emancipation' in *Socialism and the Limits of Liberalism*, ed. Peter Osborne (Verso, London, 1990), ch. 10, pp. 261–7.

63 Francis Bacon, *Thoughts and Conclusions* in B. Farrington, *The Philosophy of Francis Bacon: An Essay on its development from 1603 to 1609 with new translations of fundamental texts* (Liverpool University Press, Liverpool, 1964), sec. 13, p. 83; and *Novum Organum* I, aphorism CXXI, in *The Physical and Metaphysical Works of Lord Bacon*, ed. J. Devey (George Bell, London, 1901), p. 441. Cf. Genevieve Lloyd, *The Man of Reason* (Methuen, London, 1984), pp.10–17.

64 Cf. Elaine Showalter, *Sexual Anarchy* (Virago, London, 1992), pp. 144–5.

65 Cit. Kolodny, *Lay of the Land*, p. 28.

66 William Wordsworth, Samuel Coleridge, *The Lyrical Ballads*, ed. Derek Roper (Collins, London, 1968), pp. 206–7.

67 John Montague, *Collected Poems*.

68 Kolodny, *Lay of the Land*, pp. 127–8, 148–60.

69 Ibid., p. 12.

70 Alexander Wilson, *The Culture of Nature: North American Landscape from Disney to the Exxon Valdez* (Blackwell, Oxford, 1992).

71 For a challenging discussion of its persistence within geographical study itself, see Doreen Massey, 'Politics and Space/Time', *New Left Review* 196 (November–December, 1992).

72 See T. O. Johnson and D. Cairns (eds), *Gender in Irish Writing* (Open University Press, Milton Keynes, 1991), and esp. the article by D. Cairns and S. Richards, in this edited collection, pp. 121–38.

73 Ross Poole, *Morality and Modernity* (Routledge, London, 1991), pp. 100–5.

74 G. W. F. Hegel, *Phenomenology of the Spirit*, trans. A. V. Miller, (Oxford University Press, Oxford) sections 444–76, pp. 266–90; cf. Genevieve Lloyd, *Man of Reason*, pp. 80–5.

75 Ernest Gellner, *Nations and Nationalism* (Cambridge University Press, Cambridge, 1983); Benedict Anderson, *Imagined Communities* (Verso, London, 1983, revised edition 1991); Slovoj Žižek, 'Eastern Europe's Republics of Gilead', *New Left Review* 183 (September–October 1990), pp. 50–62, reprinted in Chantal Mouffe (ed.), *Dimensions of Radical Democracy* (Verso, London, 1991); cf. Jonathan Rée, 'Internationality', *Radical Philosophy* 60 (Spring 1992), pp. 3–11.

76 Most of the contemporary studies of the issue, including the works cited above, agree, despite their other differences, that nationalism is a comparatively recent phenomenon, hardly met with before the period of the French Revolution.

77 See the very illuminating discussions by G. J. Watson, *Irish Identity and the Literary Revival* (Croom Helm, London, 1979).

78 Ibid., p. 24f.

79 Or so I myself have argued elsewhere, see 'Stephen Heroine' in *Troubled Pleasures* (Verso, London, 1991, pp. 246–68).

80 Patricia Coughlan, '"Bog Queens": the Representation of Women in the Poetry of John Montague and Seamus Heaney', in *Gender in Irish Writing*, ed. T. O. Johnson and D. Cairns.

4

NATURE AND SEXUAL POLITICS

The terms, and political implications, of the tension I wish to address in this chapter have been well summed up by Jonathan Dollimore in his recent book on *Sexual Dissidence*, a work offering many insights on the ideological service that the concept of nature has been called upon to perform in the field of gender politics. In response to calls by socialists and those of a left-liberal persuasion for the injection of a new naturalism into Left thinking, he writes:

> If, in the process of 'recovering' nature, Marxism or any other political movement ignores the violence and ideological complexity of nature as a cultural concept, it will only recover a nature imbued with those ideologies which have helped provoke recent crises. In short, there is a danger that much reactionary thought will return on the backs of nature and of those who rightly recognise ecological politics as of the utmost urgency. Of course, there are obvious and fundamental distinctions which can help prevent that – between human nature and the nature that is destroyed by human culture; between the ecological and the ideological conceptions of nature. But . . . they are distinctions which the concept traditionally slides across and between.[1]

This seems a helpful formulation of the problem, because,

while it targets very precisely the potential site of abra-
sion between the 'nature-sceptical' critiques of a progressive gender politics, and the valorization of nature at the
heart of ecological politics, it does so in terms which
make clear that it would be no more appropriate for
those whose primary interest is in sexuality to pit their
'nature' deconstructions against the ecological cause, than
for ecologists to ignore the slidings of a signifier so central
to their own concerns.

Dollimore's main concern is with the violence that has
been done to homosexuals through the representation of
their sexual practices as a crime against nature; and his
own and other writings provide powerful illustration of
the ways in which same-sex relations have been stigma-
tized and repressed on the grounds of their 'perversity'.[2]
Indeed, homosexuality has been so persistently demonized
as 'unnatural' that one can sympathize with the very
extensive suspicion of the concept of nature within the gay
community today and the reluctance of many gays to make
use of the 'nature-endorsing' language of their opponents
in promoting their own cause. Rather than have recourse
to what Foucault has termed the 'reverse discourse' of
self-authentication, wherein homosexuals began, in the
nineteenth century, to contest their repression in the
name of their own nature or naturalness, many would
today follow Foucault in rejecting the very attempt to
ground the discourse of the 'natural' and 'perverse' in
some 'authentic' reality that it purportedly misrepresents.
There is no 'nature' external to the cultural discourse that
constructs its 'truth'.[3] To seek to legitimate homosexuality
in the self-same vocabulary by which it was medically
disqualified is, they would argue, to give credence to the
category of 'nature' responsible for its oppression, and
to mistake the role it has played in the construction of
the homosexual subject. Rather than persist in the idea
of a natural or essential sexuality that has been socially

repressed, we should recognize the key role played by the discourse of 'nature' in constituting and endorsing certain sexual identities at the expense of others.

But it is not only gay theory and politics which has been resistant to the policing of sexuality through the concept of nature. So too has the feminist movement from its very origins, and, despite the very considerable spectrum of arguments that are found within it, they are united in rejecting the naturalisation of sexual hierarchy. The inaugural move of feminism, in fact, was the challenge it delivered to the presumed 'naturality' of male supremacy – a challenge registered in that conceptual distinction between sex and gender, which, although now under attack as itself too ready to naturalise sex, became institutionalized within modern feminist theory, providing it with the cornerstone of its critique of patriarchy. Feminism, as it were, gets off the ground through a deconstructive move whose effect is to expose the discursive 'eternizing' function of 'nature' in endowing with the seal of necessity what in reality is a matter of convention – and in this sense shares in the 'nature-scepticism' of much gay theory.

Yet in the case of feminism the tensions noted by Dollimore have a particular complexity because of the widely perceived congruence between the ecological and feminist agendas. Despite the pervasive resistance of feminism to any naturalization of gender relations, there has been an equally widespread sense that there is an overall affinity and convergence of feminist and ecological political aims. Patriarchal oppression has frequently been linked with those forms of rationality and technocratic values that ecologists cite as responsible for the domination and destruction of nature. Feminist critiques of mainstream, 'male' science and philosophy chime with ecological demands for a revision of 'anthropocentric' attitudes to humanity's place in the eco-system; the feminist emphasis on relational ethics is echoed in green arguments which have highlighted the integration and mutual dependency of the eco-system.

Indeed, the ecological call for a re-thinking of our approach to the natural world has seemed not only to be consistent with, but in a sense to encompass, the feminist demand for an end to sexual hierarchy, and for a revaluation of all those activities and dispositions traditionally linked with femininity. This prescriptive overlap, moreover, has a very obvious underlying rationale in the symbolic alignment of woman with nature. For just as ecological valorization of nature expresses dissent from Enlightenment conceptions of the natural and animal world as a lower order to be exploited in the interests of humanity, so feminism dissents from the idea of woman as a lesser type of human being whose subordination is explicable and justified by reference to male superiority. The respective critiques moved by ecology and feminism therefore reflect the ideological parallels in the conception of nature as bestial 'other' to human culture, and the conception of woman as inferior 'other' to man.

It is therefore not surprising that this communality of themes has found amalgamated expression in ecofeminist denunciations of the violation of 'mother' earth, whose feminine, nurturant powers, so long abused and suppressed by the hubris of male science and technology, are viewed as the energizing source of a renaissance at once both sexual and ecological. The emergence of a proper respect for nature is thus conceived as more or less coincident with a cultural prioritization of 'womanly' feeling and the establishment of a distinctively female orientated ethic.[4]

However, it is precisely with reference to such images of ecofeminist harmonization that many who count themselves as both feminist and green sympathizers have felt inclined to start talking about tensions, and bring some ideological critique to bear. The main objection here has been that they reproduce the woman–nature equivalence that has served as legitimation for the domestication of women and their relegation to maternal and nurturing functions.[5] As we have seen, too, the ideal feminization of the land has frequently served as the prop for a reactionary politics that would restrict the political and civil liberties of actual women.

There have been many feminist critiques of the ways in which the coding of femininity with naturality has served to justify the differential treatment of women, and to endow oppressive forms of polity with a mythologized aura of primordial authenticity, and I do not propose to add further to them here. Suffice it say that they are guided by a de-naturalizing impulse that puts them at odds with the altogether more nature-valorizing quality of ecological argument. This ideological tension, moreover, is reflected in divergencies of a more directly political character – for example, between feminism's generally favourable response to the interference in biology made possible by medical technology, at least in regard to contraception and abortion, and the ecological injunction to respect the rhythms and modalities of 'nature'. I am speaking here of a contrast in bias rather than of any necessary contradiction of approach. The forms of control represented by contraception and abortion are not at odds with the conceptions of good ecological management that inform what are sometimes referred to as the 'shallower' or more 'anthropocentric' currents of the Green Movement, since these latter – quite rightly in my opinion – have argued for the importance of harnessing technology in the preservation of nature, and deem the imperative to leave nature to its own devices to be both theoretically incoherent and practically disastrous. But they certainly represent an intervention in biological process that conflicts with those forms of submission to nature's ways recommended in some of the more extreme versions of the 'eco-' or 'cosmo-centric' argument.[6]

This is not to deny a certain contrariness at the very heart of this conflict. Thus, the extreme anti-human speciesism promoted by a minority of 'deep' ecologists – their insistence on the subordination of human interests to those of other species – makes for a certain nonchalance about the preservation of *human* life of a kind clearly at odds with the 'pro-life' arguments of the anti-abortion lobby. Conversely, feminists who have relatively little problem defending the intervention in biology represented by birth-control or abortion, because of the 'rights to choose' that they afford to women, are often, by the same token, highly critical of a technocratic approach to medicine wherever they detect in this the hand of an invasive and disciplinarian 'male' science. One may surmise that feminist responses to the kinds of control over reproduction that genetic theory and bio-technology look likely to proffer in the future will embody similarly complex attitudes.

I make these points to indicate the range of disagreements and possible complexities of outlook that we are likely to encounter at the practical, political level, and in respect of specific policy issues, where there are many more divisions and ambiguities of position within and across the feminist and ecological camps than can be registered in the more general tension on which I want to focus here. But by addressing the general tension, we may become a little clearer about those 'fundamental' (though perhaps not so 'obvious') distinctions about nature which Dollimore suggests need to be observed if we are to reconcile the critiques of feminism and sexual politics with those of ecology. These are distinctions, I shall argue, that reveal not only the potentially reactionary dimensions of ecological naturalism, but also the limitations, and indeed ultimate incoherence, of the anti-naturalism professed in contemporary approaches to sexuality. In other words, if the perspectives of the two camps are to be reconciled, the one may need the corrective of the other, or more precisely, both may need to reconsider their ways of talking about nature in the light of their respective critiques and political aims.

Confirming and Confounding Nature

Eco-politics, for its part, certainly needs to be alert to the implications for sexual politics of the emphasis it often places on the affinities between human beings and other animals. For this inevitably tends to abstract from critical differences in respect of the role played by language and symbolism in mediating human relations to biology. Animals, notably other primates, do indeed manifest sexual hierarchies, and appear to observe certain rules of intercourse, but it is only human beings, who, in virtue of language and conceptualization, can be said to experience themselves *as* sexual beings, with all the sources of pleasure and pain which that entails; and it is only human cultures that in any strong sense can be said to establish norms of sexual behaviour and sexual 'identity' in relation to whose codes and conventions all individuals must necessarily experience and organize their own sexuality, whether this be in conformity or resistance to them. To neglect these distinguishing features of human sexuality is to risk ignoring the varying, historical and constantly contested forms in which human beings experience their desires, their bodily existence and their functions in reproduction. To argue this is not to deny the biological basis of these cultural variants or the role played by a specifically human biology of sexuality in both circumscribing and enabling the forms they can take. Human beings, like all other living creatures, are determined by biology in the sense that they are embodied, mortal entitities with specific genetic endowments, and possessed of a particular sexual anatomy and physiology. But relative to other animals, and in part in virtue of their specific biological evolution, they are biologically under-determined in respect of the ways in which they will experience and respond to these conditions. The 'violence' that has been done through the cultural concept of nature must be associated with the refusal to respect these distinctions, and it is therefore important that ecological argument avoids talking about the 'communality' of humans and animals in ways that conflate the biological and cultural and symbolic dimensions.

It also needs to recognize the extent to which any romantic critique of industry and modernity is working within a binary structure of attitudes to nature, which is problematic from a gender point of view. This is a binary structure within which nature is both degraded and exalted: viewed both as the mere instrument of human self-fulfilment, and as the locus of an order and beauty imperilled by the feverish quest for transcendence. But since nature has also in an overall sense been coded 'female'. the structure incorporates contradictory attitudes to femininity itself, which is either that from which masculinity must assert its autonomy and separation, or that untroubled state of wholesomeness and innocence to which it would return. Femininity is in this sense both that which it is desirable to transcend and that state of immanent self-oblivion which is sacrificed in the act of transcendence – and both these representations are offensive to women.

To the extent, then, that ecology reveres nature and subscribes to the positively accented conceptions of it, it may be dissociating itself from the explicit insult to women embodied in utilitarian-instrumental approaches to the use of nature, but it is less obviously distancing itself from the more tacit disdain implied by 'her' sentimentalization as the innocent and desirable other to a distinctively human rapaciousness. For whether nature is viewed as sublime other that has been lost to human culture, or as mere instrument of its advance, 'her' space is still defined in opposition to that which is characteristically 'human'. For this reason, as various critics have suggested, an ecofeminist politics that calls on us to celebrate previously derided 'feminine' values, or that would look to that feminine 'difference', which culture has hitherto excluded, as the site of renewal, does not necessarily go very far in de-gendering the implicitly masculinist conception of humanity that has gone together with the feminization of nature.[7] Any eco-politics, in short, which simply reasserts the claims of 'nature' against its 'human' dominion, is at risk of reproducing the implicit identification of the species with its male members in its very denunciations of 'humanity'.

On the other hand, there is something equally questionable about the extreme forms of anti-naturalism that have been voiced by some theorists of gender and sexuality. I am referring here to that culturalist or constructivist orientation that has denied not only the naturality of gender, but that of sex and the body as well, thereby challenging the very distinction between sex and gender that I earlier suggested has provided the conceptual groundwork of modern feminist theory. Such arguments have been polemically defended in the writing of Monique Wittig and Christine Delphy, and are sustained and elaborated in a good deal of Foucaultian-influenced theory at the present time. For Wittig and Delphy, there are no extrinsic biological determinations on selfhood and sexuality, and, although people may come equipped with different genitalia and so-called secondary sexual characteristics, it is already to have endowed this equipment with a cultural genderism to have accorded it such a central significance in determining subjectivity. As Delphy has put it:

> Feminists have been shouting for at least twelve years, and still shout, whenever they hear it said that the subordination of women is caused by the inferiority of our natural capacities. But, at the same time, the vast majority continue to think that 'we musn't ignore biology'. But why not exactly?[8]

Wittig and Delphy have come under attack for the inconsistency of their use of such anti-essentialist arguments to defend a 'lesbian body' and erotic sensuality that they present as in some sense more authentic, dare one say 'natural', to female being.[9] But insofar as such attacks target the inconsistent application, rather than the tenets, of their anti-naturalism, they share its basic premises and would insist, rather, that it is the radical non-fixity of sexual identity, lesbian or otherwise, that has been exposed by these critiques of the sex-gender divide. Thus Judith Butler has drawn on Foucault's arguments to lend force to Wittig's rejection of 'sex' as a category produced in the interests of the heterosexual contract, and would have us view the sex-gender distinction as reinforcing of sexual identity and modes of relating that are constraining on the complex and shifting subject places we might otherwise choose to occupy. Sex, she argues, is the construct of gender discourses and practices that seek to ground themselves in a pre-discursive 'nature', and feminist critiques that would 'merely' expose the distortions and misrepresentations of the stereotyping gender discourses are themselves repeating the cardinal distortion of viewing sex as pre-cultural and prior to gender.[10] She and others working within a Foucaultian framework have also been highly critical of any conception of the body as 'natural'. Butler herself has taken issue with the residue of this idea in Foucault's invocation of bodily 'forces' and would insist that the body be theorized as an entirely culturally constructed set of signifying surfaces.[11] Others have simply read Foucault as denying the naturality of the body and pressed their case in the light of this idea. Thus Susan Bordo invokes his argument against any view of the body as a set of natural 'instincts' repressed or distorted by cultural forms:

> Rather, there *is* no 'natural' body. Cultural practises, far from exerting their power *against* spontaneous needs, 'basic' pleasures or instincts, or 'fundamental' structures of bodily experience, are already and always inscribed, as Foucault puts it, 'on our bodies and their materiality, their forces, energies, sensations and pleasures'. Our bodies, no less than anything else that is human, are constituted by culture.[12]

'For Foucault,' writes another of his followers, 'bodies are fabricated historically', and his work 'holds out the tantalizing promise of bodies whose truth is not ultimately the truth of sexuality or sex.' One must question, she argues, 'whether it is possible to use biological "sex" and not be trapped by some notion of "nature".'[13]

Arguments of this stamp do not object to invocations of nature and biology simply on the grounds of the ideological use to which they have been put in authenticating certain norms of sexual conduct. They refuse to allow that there is any natural dimension at all to human subjectivity, bodily existence or sexual disposition. They are therefore at odds with all those critiques that have focused on the ways in which culture has been gender biased or repressive of bodily need or sexual desire. Contesting though they do the *supposed* naturality of current sexual practices and institutions, their extreme conventionalism on nature, strictly speaking, denies them any basis either for justifying this critique of existing practice, or for defending the more emancipatory quality of the alternatives they would institute in its place. For if there are, indeed, no 'natural' needs, desires, instincts, etc., then it is difficult to see how these can be said to be subject to the 'repressions' or 'distortions' of existing norms, or to be more fully or truly realized within any other order of sexuality The prescriptive force of these critiques is thus systematically undermined by their insistence on the arbitrary and purely politically determined character of the divide between the supposed givens of nature and the impositions of culture. Their denunciations of the 'merely' normative character of specific forms of sexual institution is, in other words, directly incompatible with their ontological anti-realism Equally, of course, such anti-naturalism is at loggerheads with ecological realism and with any argument appealing to the nature we share in common with the rest of the animal world, or to our biological dependency upon the eco-system.

Rhetoric and Realism

The source and quality of these incompatibilities may be best illuminated by way of certain discriminations in the use of the term 'nature' that are seldom observed in the discourse of either sexual politics or ecology. Importantly, it seems to me, one must distinguish between the ways in which these arguments on sex and the body conflict with ecology in virtue of their resistance to a *monist* or *naturalist metaphysics*, and the ways they do so in virtue of their *anti-realism* about nature. In an overall way, I shall be arguing that it is anti-realism rather than metaphysical anti-naturalism that is the major obstacle to any rapprochement of the two perspectives, even though it is the presumption of much green thinking that the development of responsible policies on the environment requires the adoption of metaphysical naturalism. At the same time, I shall be arguing that insofar as a theory of sexuality and the body denies a realist conception of nature, it is not only incompatible with ecological thinking, but incoherent in itself.

By metaphysical anti-naturalism I refer to the view (discussed more fully in chapter 2) that human culture constitutes a quite distinct order from that of the rest of animality, and cannot be adequately accounted for in terms of the latter. According to this view, all attempts to explain human attributes and capacities by reference to what human beings share with other primates are inherently reductive, and fail to respect what is specific to humanity. Culturalist approaches to gender and sexuality that have emphasized the distinctiveness to human culture of language and symbolization, and resisted any by-passing of their role in the construction of desire and behaviour, presuppose a duality of realms in this sense and are thus underpinned, whether it is explicitly acknowledged or not, by an anti-naturalist metaphysics.

It is, as suggested, precisely this dualist approach to the culture-nature divide that is usually deemed inimical to green concerns and that is frequently cited as the source of those 'instrumental' and 'anthropocentric' attitudes which have brought about the destruction of nature, and which we must now revise. A great deal of ecological argument, in other words, presumes that the desired change in our approach to nature can only come about through a better appreciation of our communality with it. The adoption of a naturalist metaphysics, which recalls us to our affinities with other species and emphasizes our continuity with, rather than distinctness from, the rest of nature, has therefore commonly been viewed as an essential aspect of any improvement in environmental policies.

Now, the dualist position has indeed frequently served to legitimate the abuse of animals and destructive appropriations of natural resources. It is by no means obvious, however, that any devaluation or misuse of nature automatically follows from the insistence on our difference in kind from the rest of organic and inorganic nature – which might equally, in principle, provide the grounds for emphasizing our special responsibilities and pastoral role towards it. It does not logically follow from the fact that we think ourselves as different from – or even superior to – the rest of nature that we shall maltreat it; it follows only that, if we are looking for reasons to justify the maltreatment, this may be one that gets invoked. Conversely, anti-dualism may be invoked in support of more or less responsible eco-attitudes: either in defence of the idea that we should grant ourselves no privileged status *vis-à-vis* other animals and inorganic being, and hence no special rights over the use of nature, or else to argue that human beings are no more able than any other of nature's creatures to transcend their particular mode of doing things, however ecologically destructive this may have proven to be The issues involved here are pursued further in the following chapter, and I would here insist only that there would seem to be no necessary entailment between being green in one's politics and being monist in one's metaphysics. In this sense, I think there is no inherent contradiction between the anti-naturalism that underlies much contemporary theory of gender and sexuality (its insistence, that is, on the irreducibly symbolic dimension of culture and on the essential differences it introduces between human and animal orders), and respect for eco-logical priorities.

What is, however, critical to any compatibility here is a proper recognition of nature in the 'realist' sense, by which I mean nature as matter, as physicality: that 'nature' whose properties and causal processes are the object of the bio-logical and natural sciences. To speak of 'nature' in this conception is to speak of those material structures and processes that are independent of human activity (in the sense that they are not a humanly created product), and whose forces and causal powers are the necessary condition of every human practice, and determine the possible forms it can take.[14] Such a concept of nature as the permanent ground of environmental action is clearly indispensable to the coherence of ecological discourse about the 'changing face of nature' and the need to revise the forms of its exploitation. But it is also essential to the coherence of any discourse about the culturally 'constructed' body and its continually changing gender 'significations'.

If those denying the 'naturality' of sex and the body are inviting us to deny their physical reality, then they are committed to a form of idealism that is clearly incompatible with ecological argument. But they have purchased the 'freedom' of human sexual practice from any dependency on or determination by biology only at the cost of sacrificing all explanatory and prescriptive force. For to deny nature in the realist conception would be to render any form of culturalist theory or politics quite meaningless. The very emphasis on the variable and culturally relative quality of human sexuality requires as its counterpart a recognition of the more constant and universal features of embodied existence as a condition of its coherence. If the body is viewed as entirely the historical effect of cultural powers, then no plausible explanation can be given of why it is that all human bodies are subject to processes of growth, reproduction, illness and mortality; nor would it make sense to challenge the effects of the imposition of any specific cultural 'norm' or discipline upon their experience, to speak of a controlling intervention in those processes or use of the body in displaying or contesting specific gender identities. The very demand for a shift in the significance accorded to a difference of sexual anatomy and function presupposes what the constructivists purport to deny: that there is an extra-discursive and biologically differentiated body upon which culture goes to work and inscribes its specific and mutable gender text. There is in fact no possible understanding we can bring to the idea of the body as a site of gender inscription if we do not presuppose the body as natural organism subject to causal processes of a continuous and constant kind: to those processes that allow us through surgery or cosmetics or dieting or 'body-building' to alter bodily shape and appearance in accordance with (or in defiance of) social norms of beauty and gender identity; which, for example, cause amenorrhea as a consequence of fasting; or make possible the pleasures of sexuality, however and with whomsoever enjoyed. It is precisely this conception of the body as a natural organism that must inform the idea of its being 'produced' (confined, disciplined, distorted . . .) by discursive formations and social and sexual norms and powers. It is only if we recognize the body in its transhistoric natural properties that it makes sense to advocate a 'stylistics' of gender as a means of parodic contravention of existing norms.

I submit, then, that a good deal of anti-naturalist talk is politically incoherent if taken literally. Perhaps, then, it is to be construed in a more rhetorical sense: what is being denied is not the existence of a natural body in the realist sense, but the assumption that the phenomenally experienced body – the body of 'lived experience' is natural. Indeed, it seems difficult to interpret Foucault's own claims in any other way, since he precisely refers to an 'inscription' of cultural practices upon a natural body (a body described in terms of 'materiality', 'force', 'energy', 'sensation' and 'pleasure'). But if we are charitable and construe denials of the naturality of the body in this sense, then what exactly is being argued – what is the force of the vocabulary of 'construction' and 'production'? Why should we not refer to the body of lived experience as a 'natural' (albeit culturally conditioned) entity in order to distinguish it from those objects that are 'products' or 'constructions' out of realist nature (watches, nappies, computers, etc.), unless it is being assumed that bodies are no less artefactual than such articles, and that cultural forces construct them in the same manner in which watches etc. are put together? But if this is what the Foucaultians intend by their anti-naturalist rhetoric, then they are surely inviting us to make an extremely mistaken comparison, since what differentiates the body as it is lived from any artificially constructed object is precisely the fact that it is a vital organism that is experienced subjectively. Both bodies and watches might be said to be objects in the sense of occupying space and both, I have suggested, are natural entities in the realist sense of being composed of physical matter, but the body is natural in the further sense that it is not an artificial construct but a subject-object, a being that is the source and site of its own experience of itself as entity. To employ a vocabulary that invites us to overlook these differences and to view the embodied subject as the wholly objective product of cultural forces is paradoxically to deny that element of lived experience and creative 'self-making' essential to the political force of the constructivist critique.

It is also to elide important distinctions between two rather differing ways in which culture may be said to 'work' upon nature – between those that involve the cultural processing of what is naturally produced and reproduced, and must necessarily exist in some form prior to that cultural work upon it, and those that make use of natural materials to inaugurate a product which previously did not exist. The body is in this sense not a 'product' of culture but a creation of nature whose existence is the condition of any cultural 'work' upon it, whereas an entity such as a watch comes into being only in and through its 'construction'; and while watches are once and for all made as finished products, bodies are not, but remain continuously in the making, either as a consequence of what we deliberately contrive ourselves or as a result of involuntary processes (of ageing, disease, hormonal change, cell-renewal, etc.).

Moreover, if we do follow the suggestion of the constructivist rhetoric and view all embodied existence and sexual practice as equally artefactual, then some critically important distinctions between 'invented' and 'noninvented' nature will simply not be registered. There is, for example, a considerable difference in the modes whereby culture may be said to 'inscribe' or 'construct' the body. The 'inscriptions' of dress or cosmetics are rather different from the transformations effected through drill or exercise, dieting or drug use; nor are the latter of the same order as those achieved through surgical intervention. But there is also a considerable difference between any of these interventions or *re*-makings of the body and the making of entirely new organisms of the kind permitted by recombinant DNA technology (which has led to the inclusion of plant and animal varieties within the patenting laws precisely on the grounds that they are now considered as 'inventable').[15] Given the potential, and the dangers, of the genetic engineering capacity to 'invent' (and patent, and hence privately own and exploit) bits of nature, it seems important not to cloud the issues of bio-politics raised in this area by suggesting that culturally conditioned transformations of bodily and sexual being are on a par with the constructions of the laboratory.

What I am trying to highlight here is the conceptual poverty of the constructivist refusal to discriminate properly between those forms of being (bodies, geographical terrain) that are culturally transmuted and those kinds of things (telephones, aeroplanes) that are indeed culturally 'constructed' and have a natural existence only in the realist sense that they are constructed out of natural materials (though often highly processed ones). The distinction here is not between forms or entities that have or have not been culturally affected, but between those forms or entities that are natural in the sense that we have no choice but to experience them in some form prior to whatever form we impose upon them, and those that we literally bring into being. Bodies and landscape may be said to be culturally formed in the double sense that they are materially moulded and transformed by specific cultural practices and in the sense that they are experienced through the mediation of cultural discourse and representation. But they are not artefacts of culture, and it is no more appropriate to think of bodies and sexualities as the 'construct' of cultural practice and discourse than it is to think of the landscape as 'constructed' out of agricultural practices or as the discursively constituted effect of Romantic poetry.

On the other hand, if the culturalists are dismissing the naturality of the body, gender and sexuality only on the mistaken assumption that in regarding them as natural we are implying that they are entirely biologically determined and unaffected by cultural norms and interventions, then there would seem to be less incompatibility between ecology and sexual politics. This is because for the most part when the ecologists speak of nature meaning the environment and many of its resources (forestry, waterways, much plant and animal life) they are speaking about what is very obviously and recognizably a product of human cultivation and transformation upon nature in the realist sense. The reference, in short, is to a nature that is itself a work of agri*culture* rather than to some hypothetical humanity-free zone or essential being that is clearly disconnected from the impact of humanity. What is more, the nature in question here ought not to be spoken of as if it were the product of some universal 'human' subject, since it has acquired the form it has only in virtue of divisive and inegalitarian social and sexual relations of production, in other words, in virtue of historically specific cultural forces.

It is true that these points about the 'culturality' of nature are not always as well appreciated as they should be in eco-political discourse, where appeals to nature can draw on, and reinforce, reactionary use of the concept to 'eternize' class and gender divisions. On the other hand, the extreme contructivist position on gender and sexuality is also guilty of lending itself to regressive forms of thinking. Constructivists are clearly loath to allow any reference to nature or biology for fear of opening the floodgates to biological determinism and its political ideologies. But to take all the conditioning away from nature and hand it all to culture is to risk re-trapping ourselves in a new form of determinism. If we are disallowed any appeal to natural needs, instincts, pleasures and pains, we remove the objective grounds for challenging the authority of custom and convention, and must accept that it is only on the basis of personal preference (or prejudice) that we can contest the 'necessity' of a practice such as clitoridectomy or footbinding, challenge the oppression of sexual minorities, or justify the condemnation of any form of sexual abuse or torture. Though promoted in the name of freeing the subject from the policing of cultural norms, post-structuralist conventionalism ends up by ceding to culture that very right to arbitrate between what is or is not 'natural' that its progressive aspirations require it to deny. Nor can any theory that presents all sexual need and desire as the 'construct' of culture offer any convincing account of the source of the existential freedom requisite to its recommended policy of 'gender invention'. Indeed, if gender identity is entirely disconnected from sex and sexuality, it is not clear what constitutes a distinctively *gendered* practice, signification or behaviour in the first place, or how we could distinguish between those performances that are manifestations of gender identity and those that are not.[16]

Conversely, there is no reason to suppose that biology

always exercises its determinations in the form of a negative coercion on the subject, as opposed to a liberating
impulse, or that it must impose itself in the form of a
simple unbrookable necessity. It is surely better viewed
as both limiting and empowering. Human biology is such
that we cannot fly unaided, exist on a diet of grass, survive
for more than limited periods without air or water, emit
or detect certain sounds or smells, and so on; but it is
also such as to have allowed us language, agriculture,
music-making, medicine, the development of a vast array
of skills whereby we have evaded or transcended purely
biologically imposed limits on our means of transport and
communication, enjoyment and survival (and one is not
here speaking simply of the achievements of 'scientific'
or 'developed' societies since it is equally pertinent to
consider those of other cultures in the light of these forms
of transcendence of nature). The specific constraints of
human biology will always pre-empt the development of
certain capacities that 'come naturally' to other beings.
But it is also in virtue of their particular biological evolution that human beings have developed quite exceptional
powers to intervene and deflect the course of nature. In
this sense we may speak of them as endowed with a
biology that has enabled them to escape the 'necessity'
of nature in a way denied to other creatures: to live
in ways that by comparison are extremely undetermined
by biology. But the correlate of this, of course, is their
over-determination by cultural modes and conventions
whose fixities and limitations on action can be just as
exacting as any imposed by nature. Those who are phobic
about allowing any reference to what nature 'proposes'
in their accounts of human society for fear of licensing
determinism might do well to consider the import of this
on their own preference for culturalist explanation. For
what culture 'deposes' has often proved so entrenched
and permanent in its effects as to constitute no less an

order of determination. Our developed powers over nature
have brought about a situation in which we are today far
more at the mercy of what culture enforces than subject to
biological dictate. Much of the famine, dysentery, blindness and other miseries afflicting the more impoverished
sectors of the world could be easily eradicated were it not
for the intransigence of the social forces responsible for
perpetuating their conditions of existence.

As far as sexuality is concerned, moreover, we might
note that it is very often easier to counter or alter what
is genetically determined than to disturb or transform
the codes and conventions of culture. As the Foucaultian
argument effectively recognizes, one can more readily alter
the body in order to bring it into conformity with existing ideals of gender appearance than change the cultural
prescriptions themselves. These remarks are not intended
to imply that we should accept such cultural enforcements
as inevitable givens, which would be precisely to succumb
to those forms of ideological naturalization of what is
socially instituted that the culturalists so rightly object
to. They are intended only to challenge the presumption
implicit in a good deal of constructivist argument that
what is culturally instituted is necessarily always more
temporary and readily manipulable than the givens of
biology – and always in some sense less regressive or
constricting. One can only successfully expose those reactionary cultural forces that have been falsely defended
as natural from a position that acknowledges the extent
to which these are themselves 'unnatural' impositions:
cultural dispositions that take too little account of the
exactions of natural needs and desires.

Clearly the 'violence' that has been done through
'nature' is not the effect of nature itself, however little
we may relish some of the forms of our subordination
to it (pain, illness, death); the problem lies in the
arbitrary and prejudicial use of the concept to police

and suppress specific forms of sexual practice and bodily behaviour that do not themselves do violence or injury to others or involve them in acts against their will. It is therefore paradoxical that those who are most concerned to pre-empt this prejudicial use should lend themselves to modes of thinking that collapse the distinction between an order of cultural determinations and those naturally given features (the capacity to experience pain or humiliation) that justify the condemnation of violence and explain our resistance to it. There may be certainly a case for eschewing the vocabulary of the 'natural' and the 'perverse' in view of the ways it has been used quite unjustifiably to repress and marginalize sexual practices that are no more problematic in terms of their potential for pleasure or pain than the 'norms' to which they are contrasted. But it would still be important to distinguish between what is consented to and what is not, what is mutually enjoyed or enjoyable and what is not. Even if we are reluctant to speak of rape, sexual torture or child abuse as 'unnatural', we would still want to appeal to biological and psychological properties in explaining a resistance to these forms of violence and a refusal to licence them.

Conclusion

I have suggested in this survey that the coherence of ecological and feminist and sexual politics, and the compatibility of their respective arguments, depends on the degree to which they are prepared to acknowledge and discriminate between a number of different conceptions of 'nature' or 'naturality' that they either explicitly or implicitly deploy. In conclusion, I shall here attempt to summarize the main implications.

A first implication is that a realist concept of nature is, whether it is avowedly admitted or not, presupposed to both kinds of argument, as designating those physical and physiological structures and processes to which we remain subject in all our cultural practices, whether it is the human subject or the non-human environment that is the primary site of these. But a more empirical concept of 'nature' and 'naturality' is also essential to both as a means of distinguishing between what is culturally processed and what is more literally 'constructed'; as a means, that is, of demarcating between the matter we transform, and the articles that we bring into being and that have existence only in virtue of that productive activity. Neither bodies (human or non-human), nor raw materials, nor wilderness, nor rural landscape are produced in this sense, and to that extent it is valid to refer to them as 'natural' entities and to recognize their dependency on causal laws and processes we cannot seek to overthrow. But to refer to them as 'natural' in this sense is not to imply that they have been unaffected by human culture, or to deny that they often acquire the form they do only in virtue of cultural activity.

A further implication is that, while we shall always have to live with the consequences of our cultural transformations (or perish as a result of them), nature does not, or only very minimally, determine the modes in which we respond to its limits and potentials. It may 'recommend' certain types of action, and it will always have its say in determining the effects of what we do, but it does not enforce a politics. Heterosexual relations, for example – which are often presented in contemporary feminist and gay writing as an arbitrary and coercive 'norm' of human sexual conduct – are a prescription of nature in the sense that they have been essential to the reproduction, and thus the history, of the species. But while biology has dictated that we cannot reproduce ourselves through same-sex relations, it has not dictated the political persecution of those relations, nor, given the persistence and extent of the preference experienced for these, has it ever given us any basis for presenting them as abnormal. Nor, one might add, has it given us any grounds for persecuting homosexuality on the basis of its non-procreative function.

Finally, we might note that just as it is mistaken to present the biology of human reproduction as if it had compelled the power relations and social institutions through which it has historically been organized, so it would be mistaken to describe natural desires or sexual promptings as directly forcing human beings into any particular form of sexual union. Human beings differ from other animals not only in the forms of their engagement in sexuality (which are irredeemably symbolic, orchestrated through fantasy, self-reflexive and consciously pursued for interests other than procreation), but also in the forms of their disengagement from it (willed self-restraint, celibacy, political separatism). It is moreover, in principle possible for us to attempt, as some feminists have suggested we might, to avoid or circumvent the heterosexual contacts involved in 'natural' reproduction. But this would certainly not be to escape the determination of biology. On the contrary, any such programme would demand the most extensive knowledge of biological law and process, and obedience to their dictate. The point is only that nature is not going to prevent the attempt to implement a project of this kind, if it were to prove a general political choice, and thus far, it may be said, nature does not determine our sexuality and sexual behaviour. The same goes for ecology, where nature will have its come back, as it were, on whatever we do or try to do, and will to some extent constrain what we *can* try on, but it will not set any but rather elastic limits on this; it will not specify how Promethean our ambitions can be, nor how foolish it may be always to seek to promote human welfare through technological manipulation. It will not, for example, inform us whether it is wise to think of 'terraforming' Mars, whether there will be any gain in human happiness were we to succeed in doing so, let alone whether it will have been morally right to have pursued it in that way.[17]

Indeed, it is the parallels here with contemporary gender debates that are more striking than the divergencies. For just as the real issue in dispute in the former is not the existence of biological processes, structures and regularities, but how far these do, or should be allowed to, determine and limit what we can be and experience as subjects, so the real and serious differences among the ecologists concern not the existence of nature as physical matter and process, but how we should harness and employ these powers, and in particular about what limits, if any, they do, or should be allowed to, set on human activity.[18] And in both cases, I think it has to be recognized that the debates only arise in the first place because nature is so relatively under-determining of human culture and choice of life-style.

But this is not to deny that there are needs that are universal and basic in the sense that their satisfaction is essential to the health and well-being of any human individual, or that suffering will be the inevitable consequence of the pursuit of policies that ignore these determinations of nature. Nor does it mean that we can do whatever we choose to the environment and still expect the planet or ourselves to survive and flourish, and the same is surely true in respect of gender and sexuality. Many arrangements in this area that were previously deemed to be necessary because 'naturally' dictated have now come to be regarded as merely matters of entrenched convention, and hence transformable, and there is no reason in principle why this process of reconceptualizing as norms of conduct what society earlier presented mistakenly as fiats of 'nature' should not continue to inform our thinking about sexuality and gender relations, prompting as it does so ongoing changes in the institutions through which we live these dimensions of selfhood. But it is one thing to recognize our political powers in this respect, and technical capacities to act on them, another to suppose that we could ever escape the constraints that biological and psychological nature will impose on what we can in fact enjoy or experience as practically feasible or morally acceptable. If the request to respect nature or to value its truth is construed in these terms, then it is perfectly valid; indeed without it, it would seem impossible even to begin to make those 'fundamental' distinctions between human nature and the nature destroyed by human culture, or between 'ecological' and 'ideological' conceptions of nature, that Dollimore rightly sees as being so important to disentangling the oppositions of contemporary theory around the concept of 'nature'.

Notes

1 Jonathan Dollimore, *Sexual Dissidence: Augustine to Wilde, Freud to Foucault* (Clarendon Press, Oxford, 1991), pp. 114–15.
2 Ibid., esp. chs 13–16 and bibliography; on the 'construction' of gay and lesbian identity, see Jeffrey Weeks, *Coming Out: Homosexual Politics in Britain, from the Nineteenth Century to the Present* (Quartet, London, 1977); *Sex, Politics and Society: The Regulation of Sexuality since 1800* (Longman, London, 1981); *Sexuality and its Discontents: Meaning, Myths and Modern Sexualities* (Routledge, London, 1985); *Sexuality* (Tavistock, London, 1986); David E. Greenberg, *The Construction of Homosexuality* (Chicago University Press, Chicago, 1988); Celia Kitzinger, *The Social Construction of Lesbianism* (Sage, London, 1987). For powerful attacks on the coercive 'norm' of heterosexuality, see Adrienne Rich, 'Compulsory Heterosexuality and Lesbian Existence' in *The Signs Reader*, ed. Elizabeth Abel and Emily K. Abel (University of Chicago Press, Chicago, 1983); Sheila Jeffreys, *Anticlimax* (The Women's Press, London, 1990); see also works cited in notes 6 and 8.
3 Michel Foucault, *The History of Sexuality: an Introduction*

(Penguin, Harmondsworth, 1978), p. 101; cf. Dollimore, *Sexual Dissidence*, pp. 225–7, 233–4; Kate Soper, 'Productive Contradictions' in *Up Against Foucault*, ed. Caroline Ramazanoglu (Routledge, London, 1993), pp. 33–5. My remarks here are not intended to imply that Foucault's work is exclusively responsible for the development of a 'social constructionist' approach to the history of homosexuality. While noting the 'spectacular' impact of the first volume of *The History of Sexuality* on gay studies, Jeffrey Weeks points out that his own, and other works adopting a 'constructionist' approach, preceded its appearance, and that 'it can now be seen that Foucault's *History* owes a great deal to work that was already going on independently of him' (see *Coming Out*, pp. xi–xii).

4 This is a very summary account of some of the key thematics of the more essentialist vein of ecofeminist argument. For a fuller sense, see *Healing the Wounds: the promise of ecofeminism*, ed. Judith Plant (Green Print, London, 1989); *Reweaving the World: the emergence of ecofeminism*, ed. Irene Diamond and Gloria Orenstein (Sierra Club Books, San Francisco, 1990); *The Politics of Women's Spirituality*, ed. Charlene Spretnak (Anchor, New York, 1982). Ecofeminism, it should be said, comprises a spectrum of philosophical and political positions not all of which would accept the more essentialist versions of the argument.

5 See Janet Biehl, *Rethinking Ecofeminist Politics* (South End Press, Boston, 1991), esp. pp. 1–28; Joan Cocks, 'Wordless Emotions: Some Critical Reflections on Radical Feminism', *Politics and Society* 13, pp. 27–57. For an assessment of the oppressive dimensions of the woman-nature association conducted from within an ecofeminist perspective, see Val Plumwood, *Feminism and the Mastery of Nature* (Routledge, London, 1993), ch. 1. See also Andrew Ross's reflections, *The Chicago Gangster Theory of Life* (Verso, London, 1994), pp. 220–30.

6 This is not to imply that all those committed to a 'deep' perspective would endorse these forms of argument. 'Deep' ecology comprises a spectrum of positions and includes many within its ranks who would reject this kind of extreme 'hands off' approach to nature. For a survey of 'deep' ecological perspectives and bibliography on these, see Robert Sylvan, 'A Critique of Deep Ecology', *Radical Philosophy* 40 (Summer 1985), pp. 5–12. See also the discussion and works cited on nature as 'intrinsic value' in chapter 8.

7   Cf. Val Plumwood, 'Woman, Humanity, Nature', *Radical Philosophy* 48 (Spring 1988).

8   Christine Delphy, *Close to Home: a Materialist Analysis of Women's Oppression* (University of Massachusetts Press, Amherst, 1984), p. 23. Cf. Monique Wittig, 'The Straight Mind', *Feminist Issues* (Summer 1980), pp. 103–11; 'One is Not Born a Woman', *Feminist Issues* (Fall 1981); 'The Category of Sex', *Feminist Issues* (Fall 1982); *The Lesbian Body* (Beacon Press, Boston, 1973). For a discussion of Delphy's and Wittig's argument, see Diana Fuss, *Essentially Speaking: Feminism, Nature and Difference* (Routledge, London, 1989), ch. 3.

9   Ibid., pp. 41–5. For some considerations of a more wide-ranging kind on sexuality and the 'authentic self' and the 'essentialism' of 'anti-essentialist' critiques in gender politics, see Dollimore, *Sexual Dissidence*, esp. parts 3, 7.

10 Judith Butler, *Gender Trouble: Feminism and the Subversion of Identity* (Routledge, London, 1990); cf. 'Variations of Sex and Gender' in *Feminism as Critique*, ed. Seyla Benhabib and Drusilla Cornell (Polity Press, Oxford, 1987), pp. 128–42; 'Gender Trouble' in *Feminism and Postmodernism*, ed. Linda Nicholson (Routledge, London 1990), pp. 324–40.

11 Though her most recent work, *Bodies that Matter: The Discursive Limits of Sex* (Routledge, London, 1993) offers a more considered view, and represents, Butler herself has very recently claimed, a shift of position on the materiality of the body. See her interview with *Radical Philosophy* 67 (Summer 1994), pp. 32–9.

12 Susan Bordo, 'Anorexia Nervosa: Psychopathology and the Crystallisation of Culture' in Irene Diamond and Lee Quinby (eds), *Feminism and Foucault: Reflections on Resistance* (Northwestern University Press, Boston. 1988), p. 90.

13 M. E. Bailey, 'Foucauldian feminism: Contesting bodies, sexuality and identity' in *Up Against Foucault*, ed. Ramazanoglu, pp. 106–7, esp. p. 101.

14 For further discussion of the 'realist' conception of nature, see chapter 5.

15 See Peter Wheale and Ruth McNally (eds), *The Bio-Revolution: Cornucopia or Pandora's Box?* (Pluto, London, 1990), part I, and their jointly authored paper on 'Environmental and Medical Bioethics in Late Modernity: Anthony Giddens, Genetic Engineering and the Postmodern State' in *Philosophy and the*

148   *Nature and Sexual Politics*

Natural Environment, ed. Robin Attfield and Andrew Belsey (Cambridge University Press, Cambridge, 1994). See also their *Genetic Engineering: Catastrophe or Utopia?* (Wheatsheaf, London, 1988).

16 This is a point developed in criticism of Judith Butler's performance theory of gender by Sarah Chatwin (unpublished Ph.D. thesis 'Habeas Corpus: theories of embodiment in the philosophy of Maurice Merleau-Ponty and contemporary feminism').

17 NASA is currently investing large sums in the research and development of a project to create the atmospheric conditions on Mars which might, in a matter of centuries, allow it to support life-forms of the kind found on earth. See report in *Geographical Magazine*, February 1993; *The Guardian*, 4 February 1993. For a discussion of the environmental ethics of the project, see Keekok Lee, 'Awe and Humility: Intrinsic Value in Nature. Beyond an Earthbound Environmental Ethic' in *Philosophy and the Natural Environment*.

18 For an example of this debate on the 'limits' of nature, see the exchange between Reiner Grundmann and Ted Benton in *New Left Review* (Benton, 'Marxism and Natural Limits', *New Left Review* 178 (November–December 1989); Grundmann's reply, *New Left Review* 187 (May–June 1991); Benton's reply to Grundmann, *New Left Review* 194 (July–August 1992).

5

NATURE AND 'NATURE'

In the previous chapter, I offered some illustration of the tension between the nature-conservationist ethic of ecology and the anti-naturalist impulse of culturalist theory; and I opened up some channels for rethinking this apparent conflict of perspectives. I here want to extend on my argument, by elaborating on the theoretical discriminations that I have suggested they both need to address more fully, though I shall be focusing here primarily on ecological discourse about nature.

Let me begin by expanding a little on the claims of anti-naturalist theory to ecological attention. As we have seen, the endorsement of nature as a site of truth and intrinsic value may easily proceed at the cost of proper recognition of the reactionary use to which these ideas have been put in the field of sexual politics. But since the forms of naturalization of the social that are criticized by feminist and gay theory have very standardly been used to legitimate other hierarchies and structures of oppression, notably those of class and racial difference, this point must be generalized into a caution against any too ready invocation of 'nature' as the victimized 'other' of human culture. Given how largely the appeal to the preservation of a 'natural' order of intrinsic worth has figured in the discourse of social conservatism, an uncritical ecological naturalism is always at risk of lending ideological support to those systems of domination that have played a major role in generating ecological crisis. This may seem an obvious point to make. But ecological critics of the atomizing and destructive effects of instrumental rationality need to be careful in redeploying the organicist imagery that has been such a mainstay of right-wing rhetoric. Romantic and aestheticizing approaches to nature have as readily lent themselves to the expression of reactionary sentiment as sustained the radical critique of industrialism,[1] and this means that left wing ecologists, however understandably keen they may be to re-seize this tradition of romanticism for their own purposes, are dealing with a problematic legacy.

We have also to be wary of the ways in which romantic ideology may serve as the cover for the continued exploitation of nature. However accurate it may be to portray our engagement with nature as 'anthropocentric', 'arrogant' and 'instrumental', it is the work of a culture that has constantly professed its esteem for nature. The societies that have most abused nature have also perennially applauded its ways over those of 'artifice', have long valued its health and integrity over the decadence of human contrivance, and today employ pastoral imagery as the most successful of conventions to enhance the profits on everything from margarine to motor-cars.

At the same time, ecological politics needs to be ever alert to the multiple dimensions and repercussions of its own social impact. Today, we are building 'virtual reality' zoos to preserve wildlife from the miseries of captivity, and eschewing nature's fur and flesh in favour of synthetic fibres and factory-made proteins; Japanese businessmen are seeking relief from the pressures of catering to a booming leisure industry in 'refresh capsules' where they can revel in the sounds and scents of 'nature';[2] heritage and nature conservancy have become themselves big business; green products are the latest capitalist growth area; the interests of thousands of human offspring are daily discounted as we monitor the habitats of other animal species. Meanwhile public support for any radically corrective ecological programme remains vanishingly small. These developments speak to complex and contradictory attitudes to 'nature' and our place within it, and indicate that we may be contributing to its destruction and pollution in the very name of its preservation. In an overall way, they suggest that an eco-politics will prove that much more incisive the more prepared it is to question its own discourse on 'nature'.

It is, however, one thing to argue that eco-politics must attend to culturalist criticisms of naturalist rhetoric; it is another to suppose that everything has been said about nature once we have remarked on its 'textuality' and its continually shifting signifier. It is true that we can make no distinction between the 'reality' of nature and its cultural representation that is not itself conceptual, but this does not justify the conclusion that there is no ontological distinction between the ideas we have of nature and that which the ideas are about: that since nature is only signified in human discourse, inverted commas 'nature' *is* nature, and we should therefore remove the inverted commas.

In short, it is not language that has a hole in its ozone layer; and the 'real' thing continues to be polluted and degraded even as we refine our deconstructive insights at the level of the signifier. Hence the inclination to respond to the insistence on the 'textuality' of nature as Johnson did to Berkeleyan idealism, by claiming to refute it with a straightforward realist kick, by pointing to the latest oil spill or figures on species extinction and saying, 'there's nature fouled and destroyed by human industry, and I refute your anti-naturalism thus'. This is an understandable response to those who would have us focus only on the play of the 'sign' of nature. But the straightforward realist kick is not only insensitive to the ideological representations of nature already discussed, but also fails to register the fact that an adequate response to anti-realism can only be conducted from a position which recognizes how difficult it is to refer to the landscape one is seeking to conserve simply as 'nature'. For if nature is conceptualized and valued, as it sometimes is in environmental philosophy, as that which is independent of human culture, then rather little of the environment corresponds to the concept: hardly anything we refer to as natural landscape *is* natural in this sense, and its supposed value might therefore be seen to be put in question. Even Cicero distinguished between an inherited non-human nature and a nature constructed through human activity, and concluded his survey of the forms taken by the latter by remarking that 'one may say that we seek with our human hands to create a second nature in the natural world.'[3] In our own time the human impact on the environment has been so extensive that there is an important sense in which it is correct to speak of 'nature' as itself a cultural product or construction.[4] Yet there is, of course, all the difference in the world between recognizing the truth of this and refusing to recognize the independent existence of the reality itself or the causal role played in its creation by processes that are not humanly created. It is one thing to recognize that much that is referred to as 'nature' takes the form it does only in virtue of human activity, another to suppose that this has no extra-discursive reality, or that there are no discriminations to be drawn between that which is and that which is not an effect of culture.

The distinctions in question are not, however, always clearly articulated within ecological argument, which is sometimes voiced in ways that obscure the difference between the 'nature' that is a product of human industry and historic in its formation, and the 'nature' that is theorized as prior to and independent of human activity. This tends to happen when green thinkers conceptualize nature and its 'intrinsic' value, in terms of its independence, while at the same time referring to the rural landscape as an illustration of 'nature' in this sense. It is also evident in some of the arguments around the pros and cons of 'restoring' nature. For example, in defence of his claim that restored nature is always less than genuine nature and therefore depleted in value, Robert Goodin cites the objections that protesters made to the proposal to lease a National Trust property at Bradenham in Buckingham-shire for use as a NATO bunker. Since the bunker would have remained underground, the visual aspects of the site would have remained unchanged. Yet the protesters complained that their appreciation of the area would have been lessened by the knowledge that there was a bunker underneath it.[5] Now there were very good reasons to oppose the bunker, including this one, but Goodin's presentation of this particular objection in support of his value theory trades on the mistaken intimation that the site proposed for the bunker was pristine nature, when in fact, of course, it was a landscape already thoroughly worked over by human hand – and, indeed, if we are judging only by the number of human interventions that had gone into its creation, might have to count as more 'artificial' than some built environments. Goodin is here reliant on an 'ordinary' intuition that a piece of country estate counts as 'nature' in a way that, say, Los Angeles does not, even though in terms of his own theory of nature it is not at all obvious that it ought to be allowed to do so. It is not that Goodin is wrong to invoke his 'intuition', but rather that it is the kind of intuition that is very difficult to square with the fundamental intuition of his *theory* of nature – namely that this be conceptualized as that which is independent of human process. Something similar applies in John Passmore's case, too, since despite his professed restriction of the term 'nature' to that which is 'human neither in it itself nor in its origins',[6] much of his – very illuminating – argument concerning the conservation and preservation of 'nature' is referring to an environment that only exists in the form it does as a consequence of human activity and to which in that sense it owes its 'origins'.

Indeed, it is not at all clear what it is that is being said to be independent of human activity in some of these arguments, or whether nature so conceived is something of which there can be said to be immediate experience. Wilderness, we might allow, does give us an *experience* of nature in this sense (though some have disputed whether there are any parts of the planet that are today entirely free of the impact of human industry). But clearly much of the experience of the countryside (especially in Western Europe) is of a humanly modified environment, and the 'nature' it instantiates that may be said to be independent of human activity would seem to refer us to *that which has been modified* and is therefore not the object of direct perception or evaluation. It would seem, that is, to refer to properties and processes that are indeed independent in the sense that they are not humanly created but only humanly managed, but that are certainly conceptually distinct from the surface forms of the environment to which they give rise as a consequence of that management. In fact a distinction of this kind seems equally applicable in the case of wilderness, which differs from the cultivated landscape not in virtue of the greater independence of the natural processes that have gone into its making, but in virtue of the fact that humanity had no hand in shaping their outcome. But if it is nature at this level – nature conceived as causal process – that the ecologists have in mind when they speak of the 'independence' of nature, then it is not clear that this is the kind of thing we can be said to 'destroy' or can be called upon to value and conserve. For nature in this sense is permanently at work in the world and an indispensable condition of every possible kind of human practice however destructive of the environment; indeed, it is also at work within ourselves and thus cannot be viewed as exclusive to the non-human world, or identified with some separable realm of 'natural' entities that are thought of as valuable in virtue of their separation and independence of humanity.

Ecological Discourses of Nature

At any rate, it would seem important to recognize the multiple roles which 'nature' can be called upon to play in ecological discussion, and notably to distinguish between three very differing concepts it may be drawing upon. In line with the conceptual distinctions sketched in the previous chapter, I shall refer to these as the 'metaphysical', the 'realist' and the 'lay' (or 'surface') ideas of nature.

1 Employed as a metaphysical concept, which it mainly is in the argument of philosophy, 'nature' is the concept through which humanity thinks its difference and specificity. It is the concept of the non-human, even if, as we have seen, the absoluteness of the humanity–nature demarcation has been disputed, and our ideas about what falls to the side of 'nature' have been continuously revised in the light of changing perceptions of what counts as 'human'. But in a formal sense, the logic of 'nature' as that which is opposed to the 'human' or the 'cultural' is presupposed to any debates about the interpretations to be placed on the distinction and the content to be given to the ideas. One is invoking the metaphysical concept in the very posing of the question of humanity's relation to nature.

2 Employed as a realist concept, 'nature' refers to the structures, processes and causal powers that are constantly operative within the physical world, that provide the objects of study of the natural sciences, and

condition the possible forms of human intervention in biology or interaction with the environment. It is the nature to whose laws we are always subject, even as we harness them to human purposes, and whose processes we can neither escape nor destroy.

3   Employed as a 'lay' or 'surface' concept, as it is in much everyday, literary and theoretical discourse, 'nature' is used in reference to ordinarily observable features of the world: the 'natural' as opposed to the urban or industrial environment ('landscape', 'wilderness', 'countryside', 'rurality'), animals, domestic and wild, the physical body in space and raw materials. This is the nature of immediate experience and aesthetic appreciation; the nature we have destroyed and polluted and are asked to conserve and preserve.

I submit that when the Green Movement speaks of nature, it is most commonly in this third 'lay' or 'surface' sense: it is referring to nature as wildlife, raw materials, the non-urban environment, and thus to a 'nature' that has been affected in certain respects by human occupancy of the planet, and in some cases acquired its form only in virtue of human cultural activity. But when it appeals to humanity to preserve nature or make use of it in sustainable ways, it is also of course employing the idea in a metaphysical sense to designate an object in relation to a subject (humanity), with the presumption being that subject and object are clearly differentiable and logically distinct. At the same time, by drawing attention to human transformation (destruction, wastage, pollution, manipulation, instrumental use of) nature, it is, at least implicitly, invoking the realist idea of nature, and referring us to structures and processes that are common to all organic and inorganic entities, human beings included. Through the metaphysical concept, then, it refers to that realm of being that is differentiated from and opposed to the being of humanity, through the realist concept to nature as causal process and through the lay concept to nature as a directly experienced set of phenomena. I shall not, however, attempt to expound these concepts any further in isolation from each other, since they are interlocking, and getting clear about the one will necessarily depend on establishing the meaning of the other.

In the first instance it is important to note the conceptual nature of the distinction between 'realist' and 'surface' nature, which is not intended to imply that these are separable dimensions, nor that the one is any more 'real' or more properly thought of as 'nature' than the other. The distinction rather (and I am here drawing on the work of Roy Bhaskar, and on Ted Benton's employment of Bhaskar's theory in developing his own ecological argument)[7] is between two aspects of a complex and ontologically stratified whole. The 'realist' concept is used in reference to those 'deep structures' of physicality and its causality whose processes are constantly at work in the world, the 'surface' concept in reference to the empirically observable 'nature' that is continually transformed as a consequence of the operation of these causal powers. The contrast here is between the nature that is presupposed as a permanent ground of all ecological activity and environmental change, and its historically changing surface effects, whether these be naturally precipitated (the earthquake or volcanic eruption) or humanly engineered (the ancient barrow or nuclear bunker). Nature is invoked in the realist sense not to discriminate between human and non-human being, but as the concept of that which is common to all animate and inanimate entities, and whose particular laws and processes are the precondition and constraint upon all technological activity, however ambitious (whether, for example, it be genetic engineering, the creation of new substances and energy sources, attempted manipulations of climatic conditions or gargantuan schemes to readjust to the ecological effects of earlier manipulations).[8]

An observance of a distinction of this kind between 'deep' and 'surface' levels of nature is, as I have already suggested in the previous chapter, indispensable to the coherence of ecological argument. Without it, at any rate, it would seem difficult to make sense either of the notion of our 'instrumental' use of nature (which implies a nonchalant and myopic harnessing of its causal powers with a view solely to the advancement of human interests), or of the prescription to 'conserve' nature (which implies the need for us to change our forms of intervention in those causal powers). In short, it is only if we recognize a distinction of this kind that we can discriminate in the way required by green politics between what is and is not changed when human beings modify nature. As Ted Benton has put it:

> Factories, railways, telegraphic cables, hedgerows, fields and so on all bear the imprint of this restless human activity of shaping, moulding, rearranging things to suit our purposes. True, some of the changes wrought go deeper than this. Factories may be made of brick or stone, hedgerows of naturally-occurring species of tree and shrub, all of which have fairly obvious immediate or mediate sources in nature, given prior to and independently of human activity. However, there are also plastics, selectively bred or genetically engineered organisms, and so on. Humans create new kinds of substance and in doing so do not *merely* 'trigger' or 'regulate' causal mechanisms already present in nature. But my claim is that no matter how 'deep' we go into the structure of the materials and beings with which we work, it remains the case that the transformations both *presuppose* the causal constancy of structure and causal powers at a *deeper* structural level and are limited by the nature of that deeper-level structure.[9]

To accept this realist perspective, however, essential though it is to the coherence of ecological politics, is not in itself to take up a normative position towards nature (to specify what attitudes we should ideally adopt towards it or how best to conduct ourselves in our interactions with it). Nature in the realist sense is, as Benton himself suggests, essentially a theoretical-explanatory concept, which can tell us about the causes of problems in certain relations to nature and the conceptual coherence of envisioned alternatives, but does not tell us what is desirable in the way of comportment towards it.[10] It is true that nature in the realist sense sets certain limits on what we can do, or even try to do, and we must observe these on pain either of looking very foolish (as did Canute) or else perishing in the effort to transcend them. But since the elasticity of these limits is very much in dispute even among the ecologists themselves,[11] their existence does not guide in any but the broadest sense the policies we should adopt to the natural world. Indeed, since nature conceived as deep level structure has been a condition of all practices hitherto adopted, including those most condemned by green politics, we must conclude that none of the normative questions raised by the latter are to be settled *simply* by reference to the limits imposed by nature in the realist sense. In other words, there is a vast range of options open to human beings in this respect, all of them having divergent consequences on the planetary eco-system. Nature conceived as a complex of causal powers and structures clearly has its say in determining these consequences, and many of these, including some of the most calamitous from an ecological point of view, are unintended effects of the limits and conditions it imposes. We must observe these conditions if we wish to avoid such calamities and to preserve nature conceived as a set of resources and surface environment, but we shall not 'destroy' nature at this level if we fail to do so. Nature at this level is indifferent to our choices, will

persist in the midst of environmental destruction, and will
outlast the death of all planetary life.

Nature, then, in this conception is not that which we
are being asked to 'conserve' or towards which we have
attitudes of the kind that enter into moral and aesthetic
evaluations. Where ecology is associated with a set of
political demands and requires us to preserve rather than
destroy nature, or to rethink our attitudes towards it, it
is drawing on the other conceptions to which I have
drawn attention. The complexities of the 'lay' or 'surface'
concept and some of their implications for the politics of
environmentalism form the topic of the following chapter.
For the remainder of this one, I propose to consider the
implications for ecological politics of the answers given to
the questions concerning the humanity–nature distinction
that are raised through the 'metaphysical' concept.

Ecology and Metaphysics

I have consistently argued that there can be no ecological prescription that does not presuppose a demarcation
between humanity and nature. Unless human beings are
differentiated from other organic and inorganic forms of
being, they can be made no more liable for the effects
of their occupancy of the eco-system than can any other
species, and it would make no more sense to call upon
them to desist from 'destroying' nature than to call upon
cats to stop killing birds. Since any eco-politics, however
dismissive of the superiority of *homo sapiens* over other
species, accords humanity responsibilities for nature, it
presumes the possession by human beings of attributes
that set them apart from all other forms of life.

We may reformulate this point in terms of the reliance
of eco-politics (however tacitly) on a non-reductionist
approach to human 'being': the species-specificity of

humanity must be conceptually distinguished and observed as a condition of imputing ecological accountability. But since our species-specific attributes may be regarded either as making us different in kind from the rest of nature or as marking only a difference of degree within an essential continuity of being, it is clear that anti-reductionism can be defended from either perspective. Specifically human needs, capacities and modes of living may be deemed such as to render implausible any attempt to explain them by analogy with those of other animals; or they may be thought explicable only by reference to what is commonly shared between human beings and other creatures. In short, an anti-reductionist approach to human 'being' can be professed from either an anti-naturalist or a naturalist perspective.

It is therefore not surprising that the key debate among those ecological theorists who have addressed these metaphysical issues concerns not anti-reductionism itself, but naturalism, and specifically the extent to which the latter is essential to the adoption of sound ecologial principles. Can one, as it were, be green without being anti-dualist? Now it may be said that the question is posed too baldly since so much depends on what is meant by being 'green' and what is meant by being 'dualist'. But if we treat it loosely as asking whether people can subscribe to ecological critiques of human abuse of nature while insisting upon our ontological difference, then it would seem that on the whole the argument of the ecological movement has been in the negative. Many green thinkers, that is, have tended to regard metaphysical naturalism as the obvious ally of their cause, and rejected dualism as inherently un-eco-friendly and even incompatible with support for their objectives. In other words, while the emphasis on our difference is thought to license an instrumental and destructive use of nature as mere means to human ends, the emphasis on our continuity and communality with

other species is presumed to encourage a more proper
respect and preservative instinct for nature. The essential
point at issue here has sometimes been expressed in terms
of the conflict between ecology and 'humanism'. As Tim
Hayward has put it:

> It is widely assumed by ecologistic writers, that humanism
> must be anti-ecological, or 'speciesist', due to an associa-
> tion of ideas which runs something like this: in starting
> from perceptions of the distinctiveness of human beings,
> humanists overemphasise their uniqueness vis-à-vis the
> rest of nature, and this leads them to see humans as
> apart from rather than a part of nature: a corollary of
> this is to view humans as ends in themselves, and the
> rest of nature as means only; this in turn serves as a
> legitimation for the Promethean project of 'mastering'
> nature.[12]

Hayward himself contests the assumption that 'humanist' and ecological agendas are in this sense opposed, while
at the same time arguing against naturalist attempts to
reconcile these: recognition of the ontological duality of
human and animal being, he suggests, is not necessarily
inimical to ecological objectives, and may be important to
their promotion in ways that respect the quality and distinctiveness of human needs and capacities. It is from this
perspective that he questions Ted Benton's defence of a
'non-reductive naturalism' as providing the more coherent
basis from which to pursue an eco-socialist programme: a
programme, that is, wherein social justice and the pursuit
of human self-realization can be rendered consistent with
natural limits on resource consumption and due regard for
the needs of other creatures.[13] Hayward suggests, in fact,
that Benton is seeking a synthesis of environmentalism's
normative anti-humanism with a Marxism that is understood as a theoretical anti-humanism. But since Benton
would want to defend his position as fully consistent

with a certain conception of 'humanism', this may be to invoke a prejudicial vocabulary. What is essentially at issue between them, one may argue, is the construction to be placed on 'humanism', and whether this does or does not preclude naturalist accounts of human formation and well-being.

Benton does not deny that there are 'self-realization' needs that appear peculiar to human beings as self-conscious and historical beings. But he associates dualism with a failure to respect the relative sophistication and complexity of the mental and social life of other species, and suggests that it often goes together with an imperializing disdain for animality and ecological co-existence. He would claim, in contrast, firstly, that there are many human needs which are, in fact, held in common with other animals, and that these can best be analysed by viewing them as specific modes of doing what other animals also do; and secondly, that those ('self-realization') needs that are wholly particular to human beings, and resistant to explanation in terms of a clearly perceptible cross-species need, are nonetheless illuminated by viewing them as derived from attributes or requirements common to both humans and non-humans. It is only a naturalistic approach of this type, he argues, that 'begins with the common predicament of natural beings and moves from that basis to render intelligible their specific differences in constitution, structure and mode of life', that can provide a satisfactory account of the *differentia specifica* whether of human beings or of any other living creature.[14] Thus, not only in respect of human activity relating to physical reproduction and gratification, but even in the case of 'spiritual' or 'cultural' pursuits, he suggests that the specification of the distinctively human 'proceeds not by identifying a further *sui generis* class of attributes or needs possessed only by humans, but, rather, by identifying the species-specific ways in which humans exhibit attributes

or meet needs which they share with other species'.[15]
Cognitive, aesthetic and normative capacities and needs
are thus to be viewed as 'in some sense consequential
upon those needs which are common to natural beings,
or upon the species-specific ways in which those common
needs are met'.[16]

In the absence of any developed application of this
naturalist programme (and Benton acknowledges it needs
much further elaboration),[17] it is difficult to judge of
the extent to which it can sustain its claim to be 'non-
reductive' while remaining genuinely informative. My own
sense is that Benton's argument may be reliant on an
inherently problematic distinction between two types of
human need or activity: those (relating to nutrition, reproduction etc.) whose specific modes are said to be explicable by reference to what other animals also do, and
those ('spiritual' or 'cultural') needs which are said to be
consequential upon those specific modes. At any rate, it
seems to me to be highly questionable whether the specific
modes in which human beings gratify physical needs can
be understood without invoking precisely those 'spiritual'
dispositions which are said to be 'in some sense' emergent
or derivable from them. In other words, what distinguishes
the specifically human mode of gratification of needs held
in common with other creatures is the aesthetic and symbolic dimension itself, and one must question whether a
non-reductive naturalism of the kind defended by Benton
can fully respect this differentiation without falling into
circularity.

A further – clearly related – problem is that Benton's
claim that 'spiritual' capacities are to be viewed as 'in
some sense' consequential upon other commonly shared
'animal' needs is altogether too evasive. For unless we are
told more precisely in what sense this is, it is impossible
to determine whether the position held is indeed non-
reductive or not. As Hayward points out:

If 'in some sense consequential' is to mean something more than the uncontroversial point that certain basic biological needs (e.g. eating) have to be satisfied before other (cultural) needs (e.g. composing symphonies) can be satisfied, or even arise, then it might be interpreted in one or other of the following ways. (a) The fulfilment of a 'higher' (or, as Benton calls it, 'supervenient') need is *eo ipso* the fulfilment of a 'more fundamental' need – e.g. a kind of sublimation: if so, then presumably the basic need could also be directly fulfilled without such a mediation; in which case, though, there would be nothing of the 'higher' need which really has the compelling quality of a 'need' at all. (b) If, on the other hand, it is consequent on the fulfilment of basic needs that higher needs arise, *as qualitatively new needs*, then it would not appear to be possible to explain the latter in terms of the former, since they would no longer be specific ways of meeting some more general need, but entirely irreducible, 'autonomous' needs.[18]

Since the first of these interpretations is reductionist, and the second dualist, neither, it seems, can be what Benton intends. Nor, it seems, can Benton mean that human needs can always be analysed as developed or elaborated forms of animal needs, or if he does, it is surely equally challengeable. In the first place, this carries the – highly contentious – implication that all human skills or powers are in some sense 'needed' or meeting needs. Benton himself explicitly rejects any crude biologism of the kind that might invite us to view, say, nuclear arsenals as the 'satisfiers' of an elaborated version of a porcupine's need for its quills, and he is surely right to do so. But anyone who is understandably resistant to that line of interpretation is surely opposed to it precisely because, by confusing properties that are biologically endowed and transmitted with culturally acquired capacities, it invites us to think of such capacities (e.g. to wage nuclear war) as

if they were essential attributes of human species existence. Perhaps, then, as Hayward suggests, what Benton
has in mind is a view of distinctively human needs as
emergent properties of needs shared with other animals: as
'complex needs which retain elements of more basic simple
needs, but also incorporate a further "higher" element
such that the whole need is something more than the sum
of its parts – an emergent need which is neither reducible
to the simple basic need nor autonomous of it'.[19] But as
Hayward points out, this in effect confounds needs with
'emergent powers' or capacities, which is not at all what
Benton wants, since his whole point is that human beings
have developed many 'powers' to do things (such as build
nuclear arsenals) that go against their needs.

The problem with the case put forward by Benton is that
in its argument for *naturalism* it seeks to explain everything that human beings do as consequential upon needs
held in common with other animals, and this invites us to
view and accept as 'in some sense' natural all of humanity's various (and often extremely ecologically destructive)
ways of doing things. But in order to preserve himself
from *reductionism*, Benton must invoke, if only implicitly, a prior evaluation of human ways of doing things
that distinguishes between their more or less 'naturally
needed' quality – and the effect of this is to render those
modes of doing things that are deemed not needed, or
'falsely' needed, unamenable to explanation in terms of
his naturalist theory. I am thus substantially in agreement
with Hayward's point that

> Benton expects more from a theory of needs than it
> will be able to yield, and is seeking to hold together
> an unsustainable set of claims: that the development of
> human species powers gives rise to new needs; that only
> some of those needs are 'real', and that a naturalistic
> account of how powers develop new needs will tell us
> which of these are *really* needs. The question this leaves

us with is how any (normative) distinction between real and apparent needs can be generated from an account which would show that *all* new needs are produced by the development of species powers.[20]

Decisions about how we should comport ourselves, whether in our relations to each other or to nature, necessarily involve evaluation of the priority to be accorded to differing needs, capacities and forms in which human beings have pursued 'self-realization', and cannot be derived directly from some supposedly wholly objective knowledge we could in principle attain about the 'truth' of our needs. We may argue that there are some needs that ought to be universally met precisely because they are naturally dictated requirements of health and survival.[21] But we can do so only by appealing to the justice of equally providing for needs that are common to us all.

There is a further, more specifically ecological problem, so it seems to me, in the assumption that there is an objectively cognizable set of 'truly' human needs that we have in virtue of our common species-being, namely that it might invite us to suppose that these are necessarily compatible with what nature can furnish, and that we have only to get clear about the former (hence to dispense with 'false' needs) for ecological harmony to be restored. But this is surely to look at the problem from the wrong end on, and for a naturalistic philosopher might seem tantamount to arguing that the dinosaur became extinct through an excess of 'false' needs. Even if there were agreement on what is 'truly' needed, and a reorganization of production with a view to ensuring its universal satisfaction, there can be no guarantee of an indefinite fit between that which is established as collectively required as a condition of survival and flourishing and the provisioning of nature. It may well be the case that a certain level of material provisioning for everyone, both now and in the future, is consistent with indefinite ecological sustainability.

But nature is not bound to deliver even on a norm of 'basic need' satisfaction, and how far it could, even in principle do so, depends on a number of relatively unpredictable variables (rates of human population growth, the technical potential for continuously enhancing the efficiency in the use of existing resources and energy forms, the rate and extent of pollution control and of new resources development, etc.).[22] Even less in the case of 'flourishing' can we proceed as if we could determine in some objective sense what provision, over and above basic need satisfaction, we would need in order to ensure it, or suppose that nature will automatically prove accommodating.

The point, surely, is that any ecological politics involves a choice of what – and whose – needs or preferences are going to be satisfied in the light of the available knowledge of ecological constraints. 'Flourishing' is what we ought to be re-thinking in the light of current and likely future resources; it is not an *a priori* given of human nature whose 'true' needs nature can be expected to fulfil. Meeting ecological constraints may require us, quite possibly, to sacrifice or severely restrict some sources of gratification and self-realization that it seems very difficult simply to dismiss as 'false' (very swift and flexible means of transport, for example). It will almost certainly require us to be imaginative and undogmatic in our attitudes to what we can enjoy: to open ourselves to the possibilities of an 'alternative hedonism' and to modes of living and self-fulfilment very different from those associated with our current assumptions about 'flourishing'. Openness of this kind, I suggest, is not necessarily encouraged by the adoption of a theoretical perspective that tends to discount the validity of subjective experience (and the important, if never exclusive, role it must be accorded in legitimating any 'politics of need') in favour of objective pronouncements on what is or is not a 'genuine' requirement of a 'flourishing' existence. Rather than adopt a position that implies that there can be a decisive authority on needs, we should recognize the extent to which human beings can be said to acquire 'new needs' in ceasing to experience old ones. Obviously, 'human nature' is not indefinitely malleable at this level, and we can certainly question the propriety of many forms of current consumption from the standpoint of their impact on the environment and the universal satisfaction of 'basic' needs. But to assume too much fixity in what we need as a condition of 'flourishing' would, in the end, be to undermine the demand that we should accommodate our consumption to the limits imposed by nature. At any rate, it would appear difficult on that basis to develop a compelling hedonist case for doing so.

Finally, let us note (though my argument here is in no sense directed against Benton's form of naturalism) that even if there are some who feel that they cannot be said to 'flourish' in a world where others are starving – that their 'flourishing' depends on everyone else having the means to do so – we can hardly claim a universal consent to this conception of 'flourishing'. In practice, as we know, the 'coat' of 'flourishing' can be cut in many differing ways, depending on who is in charge of the tailoring and what their priorities are. The fact that resources are limited no more determines who will be made to feel the pinch than the universality of the need for food ensures its satisfaction. The attempt to accommodate ecological crisis, in short, can be made in a variety of ways: capitalist, socialist, authoritarian, fascist, all of them in contestation over what it means for human beings to 'flourish' (which means also over the issue whether some, more than others, should be allowed to do so).

To denounce humanism as a form of speciesism that is automatically bad for the rest of nature is falsely to universalize a species that is profoundly divided against itself on

these kinds of issue. Many of its members are not at all
convinced of the 'special' status of the others, and some
of them will happily spend a good deal more respecting
the needs of their polo pony in a week than an African
peasant earns in a year. Of course, this latter point is itself
'speciesist' in the sense that it implies that the African
peasant deserves as good or better than the polo pony.
But this in itself only serves to highlight how central value
issues of this kind are to ecological politics.

Humans and Animals

More generally – though my points here apply essentially
only to the more reductive ('naked ape') forms of naturalism[23] – we may argue that attempts to account for human
in terms of animal behaviour are vulnerable to the charge
of being speculative and hence unverifiable. It is always
open to one defending this position to speculate on the
ways in which human 'needs' for poetry and pornography,
casinos and Catholicism, archaeology and astronomy are
'built upon' or emergent out of more 'animal' types of
need, but it is only if we are already disposed to overlook
critical differences between symbolic and non-symbolic
modes of being in the world that we shall be inclined
to accept the account as uncontroversially informative;
and even then, it can always be challenged by an alternative naturalist explanation of the putative line of connection between the human and the non-human. This
is because what we map back onto 'nature' as proto-
typical of humanly elaborated needs or dispositions is
necessarily to some degree a projection of our own self-
understanding, and of the meanings attributed to our
specific ways of doing things. There are ecologists, as we
have seen, who are prone to accuse dualists of an anthropocentric arrogance in the emphasis they place on human

superiority. But there may also be something dubiously anthropocentric about their own readiness to assume that human needs, desires and capacities give us a direct access to knowledge of their 'analogues' in the worlds and life-styles of other species. It may be that we do not know as much about the meaning of animal modes of comportment as some naturalist accounts assume that we do. Perhaps the more Kantian approach, which argues that we cannot know what it would be for other creatures to consider themselves subjectively as ends, is less arrogantly humanist than is sometimes supposed, since it accepts, as Peter Strawson has put it, that for lack of the words to say what it is to be without them, 'we must in this matter be content with knowing ourselves.'[24]

In any case, it would seem important to distinguish between the 'arrogance' of a humanism that appeals to human difference in order to justify the maltreatment of animals and the 'humanist' defence of specifically human forms of self-fulfilment. It is one thing to 'boast' of our rights over animals, another to subscribe to the force of Hamlet's point, when he asks:

> What is a man,
> If his chief good and market of his time
> Be but to sleep and feed? A beast, no more.
> Sure he that made us with such large discourse,
> Looking before and after, gave us not
> That capability and godlike reason
> To fust in us unused.[25]

Admittedly, to our environmentally attuned ears, Hamlet's protestation may seem somewhat insensitive to the beast's ends, but its presumptions about the distinctive qualities of a human life are surely ones we want to respect – and can respect without in any sense endorsing the abuse of animals. There is a confusion, I think, in supposing that in any 'vaunting' of the human over the animal mode of existence we are somehow doing an injustice to the latter or at risk of licensing indifference to animal suffering.

Moreover, we should be wary of the 'cruelty' that may be lurking in the 'kindness' of attempting to give voice to the 'subjective ends' of other animals. Projects such as that to extend the 'community of equals' to include the great apes[26] are certainly well-intentioned, but the bonds they seek to cement are arguably too little respectful of the quality of ape life and the ways in which it must be allowed to differ from our own. We should certainly protect apes from physical and mental cruelty as far as it is in our power, but whether the right way to go about it is to attempt to include them within a community in which they would necessarily seem to have to figure as a class of 'sub-humans' or 'second-class citizens' is altogether more dubious. Nor does it seem at all appropriate to claim in justification of such a project that rights should be granted to great apes on the same grounds we accord them to human imbeciles. We regard human beings who are too damaged to respect rights or to claim them for themselves as nonetheless possessing them in recognition of their potential to claim them had they met with less misfortune. To argue that fully flourishing animals, who in their normal state have no more capacity than the least self-realized human being to appreciate the meaning of a system of rights and obligations, should be accepted within the human moral community, is to overlook some fundamental and critical conceptual barriers; and, indeed, to ignore them at risk of abusing both members of our own species and failing to protect other species from misguided and potentially harmful forms of protection. For damaged human beings should no more be regarded as comparable to flourishing apes than should flourishing apes be exposed to the possible forms of maltreatment that might be invited by their legitimation as in some sense human 'equals'. To be sensitive in this area is precisely not to seek to overcome these conceptual barriers or to undermine our intuitive respect for them, but rather to be as open as possible to the implications for non-human nature of the human forms of sensibility with which we are bound to approach it.

Of course, the Kantian line can be used to support assumptions about animal nature that are no less crass than those that the theorists of the 'naked ape' have offered about human nature. I would strongly dissent from any attempt to bend such arguments in support of an approach to other sentient creatures that denied their capacity for pleasure and pain. Nor am I implying that there is something inherently misconceived or pre-sumptuous in the attempt to speak 'on behalf' of other animals. The point is not that we should dispense with human interpretations of their needs (an injunction that it would in any case be impossible to fulfil), and advocates of animal liberation are quite right to highlight the ways in which cruelty or indifference to the consequences of our actions towards other creatures is licensed by particular constructions of human 'needs' or 'identity'. The point is rather that in any understanding we bring to other animals we need to be aware of the limits of our understanding;[27] our very empathy with them requires us, as it were, to respect their difference from us and the ways this may constrain our capacity to 'communicate' on their behalf. To 'think' from their position is, as Derek Mahon suggests in his poem, *Man and Bird*,[28] to accept a certain inability to do so:

> All fly away at my approach
> As they have done time out of mind,
> And hide in the thicker leaves to watch
> The shadowy ingress of mankind.
>
> My whistle-talk fails to disarm
> Presuppositions of ill-will;

Although they rarely come to harm
The ancient fear is in them still.

Which irritates my *amour propre*
As an enlightened alien
And renders yet more wide the gap
From their world to the world of men.

So perhaps they have something after all –
Either we shoot them out of hand
Or parody them with a bird-call
Neither of us can understand.

Considerations of this kind do not imply that we should give up on all attempts to think across the 'gap' between the world of animals and the 'world of men'. To conceive of oneself as an 'enlightened alien' doomed to parodic whistling might precisely count as one such attempt. Nor do they imply that we should view our 'spiritual' needs or aesthetic, cognitive and moral capacities in wholly idealist terms as a supernatural endowment from the deity. To recognize what is exclusive to *homo sapiens* is not to reject evolutionary theory or to deny the particular determinations exercised by biology on what human beings can be or do. But it does mean recognizing that there are indeed features (language, reflexivity and evaluation, a vast excess of learnt over inherited skills, knowledge of mortality, an immense diversity of views within the species as to *how* best to do things) that pertain only to human cultures; and that reductive naturalist accounts will always be open to the objection that, by seeking to explain these by reference to other animals, they fail to engage with their species-specificity.

It also means recognizing that the human predicament is sufficiently different from that of any other living creature to make it implausible to suppose that metaphysical naturalism is the automatic ally of ecology, dualism (or 'humanism') its obvious enemy. For if human beings (or significant numbers of them) do need to change their patterns of relating with the rest of nature, reminding them of what they share with other animals, who are incapable of any deliberated alteration of their ways, seems no more obviously persuasive than does the insistence on their difference. It is difficult to see why 'humanists' should necessarily be indifferent to the fate of non-human nature, or prove incapable of advancing its cause. Nor does there seem any reason to suppose that naturalism will guarantee good human relations or necessarily help to mitigate ecologically damaging forms of social exploitation.

The essential point here is that the relations between the adoption of a particular ontological outlook, and the attitudes one holds towards the conservation of nature, are much more tenuous than some ecologists seem to suppose; and no ecological set of prescriptions automatically follows from our putting the ontological knife in at one point rather than another. Indeed I would want to emphasize, in support of this point, that the forms of sensibility towards ourselves and other animals that I have here been advocating seem to me to be as readily endorsable from the 'non-reductive naturalist' position advanced by Benton as they do from the kind of 'dualism' defended by Hayward. Both the dualist and anti-dualist may be equally sensitive to the cruelties or malpractices that may be justified on the basis of their respective positions, or, in other words, may bring very similar intuitions or feelings to bear in their judgements about human relations to nature, despite their differences of ontological commitment. In a sense what this points to, in fact, is the limitations of presenting our feelings for nature as if they were solely determined by our theories of it, since our theories are in an important sense only as good as the sensibilities we bring to their interpretation and the constructions we place upon their implications for practice. We do not, as it were, first decide whether humans are or are not

quite distinct from animals and then adjust our feelings
and practices accordingly. We develop or respond to the
theories in the light of the feelings we feel (or fail to
feel) towards nature, and thus far it may be said that
specific ontological commitments do not govern, even
though they can exercise a considerable influence, upon
ecological responses.[29]

Moreover, whether we view our species-specific characteristics as rendering us distinct from the rest of nature, or
as participant in its form of being, though in ways that also
'in some sense' divide us from it, we still have to decide
what our view implies for the particular programmes we
should adopt towards the natural realm (which means
deciding what value we place on our own 'special' status
in regard to it; to what extent nature should be preserved
primarily for its 'intrinsic' qualities, to what extent it
should be preserved because of our human dependencies
and interests; to what extent our interests can be claimed
to include an interest in the preservation of the 'intrinsic'
worth of nature, and so forth).

The adoption of a naturalist metaphysics, I would argue,
is no more obviously bound to generate progressive policies
on these issues than is dualism bound to remain trapped
within those forms of instrumental rationality that have
made them so pressing. Since contrary political ideologies
can be constructed upon both dualist and non-dualist
positions, the commitment to either may be said to be less
critical to the practices of the Green Movement than the
evaluative interpretations that are brought to these differing perspectives on the nature–culture, nature–humanity,
divides.

Notes

1 Cf. Raymond Williams, *Culture and Society* (Hogarth, London, 1987), p. 229f; Terry Eagleton, *The Ideology of the Aesthetic* (Blackwell, Oxford, 1990), pp. 60–1. See also the essays collected in Robert Colls and Philip Dodd (eds), *Englishness: Politics and Culture 1880–1920* (Croom Helm, Beckenham, 1987).

2 See Gavan McCormack, 'The Price of Affluence: the Political Economy of Japanese Leisure', *New Left Review* 188 (July–August, 1991), pp. 121–34 (the 'refresh capsules' and other hi-tech stress relief facilities are described on p. 123).

3 Cicero, *De Natura Deorum*, II, 151–2; see Neil Smith, *Uneven Development* (Blackwell, Oxford, 1984), pp. 45–6.

4 Notably in the work by Neil Smith cited above; in Ed Soja, *Postmodern Geographies: the Reassertion of Space in Critical Social Theory* (Verso, London, 1989); David Harvey, *The Condition of Postmodernity* (Blackwell, Oxford, 1989); Doreen Massey, *Spatial Divisions of Labour* (Macmillan, Basingstoke, 1984); cf. Henri Lefebvre, *The Production of Space*, trans. D. Nicholson-Smith (Blackwell, Oxford, 1991); Alexander Wilson, *The Culture of Nature* (Blackwell, Oxford, 1991).

5 Robert Goodin, *Green Political Theory* (Polity, Oxford, 1992), p. 32.

6 John Passmore, *Man's Responsibility for Nature*, 2nd edn (Duckworth, London, 1980), p. 207.

7 Roy Bhaskar, *A Realist Theory of Science* (Harvester Press, Hassocks, 1978); *The Possibility of Naturalism* (Harvester Press, Brighton, 1979); *Reclaiming Reality* (Verso, London, 1980); *Dialectic, The Pulse of Freedom* (Verso, London, 993); Andrew Collier offers a valuable introduction to Bhaskar's work in *Critical Realism: an Introduction to Roy Bhaskar's Philosophy* (Verso, London, 1994). For Benton's ecological development of a 'realist' theory, see 'Marxism and Natural Limits', *New Left Review* 178 (November–December, 1989), pp. 51–86 (now reprinted in *Socialism and the Limits of Liberalism*, ed. Peter Osborne (Verso, London, 1990), and 'Ecology, Socialism and the Mastery of Nature: a Reply to Reiner Grundmann', *New Left Review* 194 (July–August 1992), pp. 55–74. See also *Natural Relations* (Verso, London, 1993).

8 Ibid., p. 66f.

9 Ibid., p. 66.

10 Ibid., p. 58–9; cf. Benton's point that 'to recognize the "eco-logical facts of life", so to speak, is quite different from taking a certain view of how nature works as morally prescriptive.' (p. 69).

11 This is the important issue of dispute between Reiner Grundmann and Benton, the former (in his reply to Benton's 'Marxism and Natural Limits' in *New Left Review* 187 (May–June, 1991), pp. 103–20; and cf. his book on *Marxism and Ecology* (Clarendon, Oxford, 1991) emphasizing the almost indefinite technical possibilities for overcoming naturally imposed barriers on our powers to transform and 'master' nature, the latter insisting that the 'idea of a limitless mastery, the project of "controlling all natural and social processes" is literally unthinkable' ('Ecology, Socialism and the Mastery of Nature', p. 67).

12 Tim Hayward, 'Ecology and Human Emancipation', *Radical Philosophy* 62 (Autumn 1992), p. 12.

13 Hayward in particular takes issue with two articles by Benton: 'Humanism = Speciesism? Marx on Humans and Animals', *Radical Philosophy* 50 (Autumn 1988), pp. 4–18, in which Benton offers his view of naturalism as a corrective to the dualist tendencies of Marx's argument on nature in the 1844 Manuscripts; and 'On the Limits of Malleability', *Capitalism, Nature, Socialism* 4 (1990), pp. 68–71, in which Benton offers some criticisms of Richard Lichtman's account of human nature in an article in the same issue of *Capitalism, Nature, Socialism*. Cf. John O'Neill's discussion of how far Marx's approach to nature in his early work may be said to be 'eco-friendly' in 'Humanism and Nature', *Radical Philosophy* 66 (Spring 1994), pp. 21–9. O'Neill concludes that there are indeed central components of Marx's early thought that lend themselves to an 'anthropocentric humanism', and thus cannot be incorporated into defensible ecological political theory. But he also argues that the aspects of Marx's argument that most need to be rejected (notably his view of nature as 'man's inorganic body') are also those that have often been thought by greens to be closest in spirit to their own concerns.

14 Benton, 'Humanism = Speciesism ?', p. 13; cf. *Natural Relations*, pp. 54–7.

15 Ibid., p. 54.

16 Ibid., p. 56.

17 It is, he argues, no more than 'a very open-ended promissory note', see *Natural Relations*, p. 56.

18 Hayward, 'Ecology and Human Emancipation', p. 8.

19 Ibid.

20 Ibid.

21 For a very forceful case in defence of this, see Len Doyal and Ian Gough, *A Theory of Human Need* (Macmillan, London, 1991).

22 These points are developed further in the last section of my review of Doyal and Gough, *A Theory of Human Need*, *New Left Review* 197 (January–February 1993), pp. 113–28; see also Doyal's response, *New Left Review* 200 (July–August 1993).

23 See, for example, the works cited in note 18, ch. 2.

24 Peter Strawson, *Bounds of Sense* (Methuen, London, 1966), p. 273; cf. Hayward, 'Ecology and Human Emancipation', p. 10.

25 Shakespeare, *Hamlet*, IV. iv.

26 Cf. Paola Cavalieri and Peter Singer (eds), *The Great Ape Project: Equality beyond humanity*, (Fourth Estate, June 1993), whose 'Declaration on the Great Apes' calls for 'the extension of the community of equals to include all great apes: human beings, chimpanzees, gorillas and orang-utans' and defines the 'community of equals' as 'the moral community within which we accept certain basic moral principles or rights as governing our relations with each other and enforceable by law'.

27 For Benton's discussion of the implications of this point, see *Natural Relations*, pp. 162–5, 212–15.

28 From *Four Walks in the Country Near Saint-Brieuc*, in Derek Mahon, *Selected Poems* (Penguin, Harmondsworth, 1991), p. 16.

29 Cf. Michael Reid's emphasis on the primacy of empathetic feeling over discursive reasoning in determining our responses to the suffering of animals ('The Call of Nature', *Radical Philosophy* 64 (Summer 1993), pp. 13–18), though Reid, it seems to me, bends the stick too far in the other direction, and does not give due recognition to the important role that theory and discursive reasoning can play in changing the quality of our 'immediate' affective responses to the world.

6

THE SPACE AND TIME
OF NATURE

To turn now to what I have termed the 'lay' idea of nature: nature as a domain of of observable phenomena and directly tangible forms. This is the nature we feel for: the nature we love and revere, by which we are inspired, and with which we commune. It is also the nature we have lost, polluted and destroyed, and which we are ever more insistently enjoined by the ecologists to conserve or preserve.[1] It is, then, the concept of nature that figures most prominently in environmental politics, but also that invoked in aesthetic judgement and in commentary on nature in a wide range of academic disciplines and cultural forms. It is, in short, to nature in this sense that evaluative discourses most typically refer. The physicist or chemist or biologist may be fascinated by the workings of nature in the realist sense and claim an aesthetic appreciation of them, but it is more usually in respect of nature as an empirical domain or 'surface' environment (nature as landscape, wilderness, plant and animal life) that we can be said to have feelings of love or disdain, respect or indifference. Expressions of sentiment of this kind, whether or not deployed in support of ecological causes, typically refer to the tranquillity, beauty and sublimity of the river or the mountain, not to the intricacies of their atomic particles; to the charms of wildlife, not to its physiological structure. This is not to deny the aesthetic attractions of nature placed under the microscope. Nor is it to suppose that the nature in question has some determinate scale or magnitude. As Adorno points out, 'any fragment of nature can acquire an inner glow of beauty'.[2] The essential point is that we are talking about nature as *appearance*, and usually of nature as it appears in everyday experience (even though, of course, such 'everyday' experience is culturally and historically specific). The nature of aesthetic and moral judgement is that which is normally encountered in human experience, whether the experience be had from car, train or aeroplane window, while pony-trekking or ploughing, on a safari expedition or a country walk, while targeting a grouse or surveying the panorama.

If I have previously referred to this sense of nature as 'lay' or 'loose', this is partly in acknowledgement of the range and diversity of phenomena to which it can refer. For nature here can include within its compass both the worked and unworked environment, the 'virginal' territory and the 'cultural landscape'.[3] It embraces both bred and unbred animals, both the nature reserve and the unprotected 'wild', the sylvan glade and the impenetrable jungle. Moreover, though the concept itself may be held in common, the discourses invoking it range from geography to Georgian poetry, from Coleridge to Catherine Cookson, from horticultural science to advertising exhortation. A shared idea of nature may be at work in the productions of both Heidegger and the Heineken copy-writer, Adorno and Walt Disney, even as the form and content and purposes of their discourses diverge profoundly. Science and literature, high-brow and popular culture, philosophical critique and advertisement jingles all make use of, and appeal to, a certain set of intuitions by which we collectively assess the environment and its entities in terms of their 'natural' or relatively 'natural' status.

The idea, then, is discriminatory in some sense. But, as

we have several times noted, it hardly conforms to any definition of nature as that which excludes the presence or effects of *homo sapiens*. Nature, as it appears in the Yorkshire Dales or Sussex Downs, the Tuscany hillside or Canadian Prairies, is a product of human cultivation, often over centuries, and would be very different without the impact of that management. It also includes within its compass many human constructions, from the stone walls enclosing the field system to the laid out paths of the nature reserve, from the dolmen to the folly on the country estate. In view of this, David Harvey has suggested that 'the distinction between the built environments of cities and the humanly modified environments of rural and even remote regions then appears arbitrary except as a par-ticular manifestation of a rather long-standing ideological distinction between the country and the city'.[4] But while the distinction between the country and the city may, in a sense, be arbitrary, and has certainly proved the vehicle of much ideological misrepresentation, it also indicates, as Raymond Williams has put it, 'some permanent, or effectively permanent, need'.[5]

In line with this, I would suggest that while 'ordinary' discourse about 'nature' may be less than precise, it is also speaking to sentiments that it is as mistaken to overlook as it is to ignore the ideologies they generate. At any rate, it is in this spirit that I propose to proceed here. My aim is not to recommend a more exact use of language, but rather to explore the implications of the one we have – the very ambiguity of which may be just as significant from an ecological point of view as more rigorous theoretical insights on the nature of 'nature'.

A first point to note is that, although the key demarca-tion is between the country and the city, this is not the whole of the story. A nuclear power station is regarded as an unnatural excrescence upon the countryside however remotely sited within it, whereas a complex reservoir system, such as the Elan Valley, is deemed to be much more part of the natural landscape, and even an attraction of it.[6] A rural village, its church and farmhouses, will be more readily viewed as part of the countryside than an isolated factory, even though the buildings of the latter may cover a smaller area than the former. A field system is 'natural' in a way that an air-strip is not, even though both are the work of human transformation of the land and include within them imported human constructions. Ancient earth-works, ruins and monuments, even the disused quarry or slag-heap, can figure as components of rural scenery in a way that the contemporary land-fill site or junk-heap cannot.

All this implies that the criteria at work in this idea of 'naturality' are complex and involve something more than a straightforward distinction between the built and unbuilt environment. But what else exactly? One plausible suggestion might be that the distinction is never simply one between two types of space considered in abstraction from the use to which they are put and the purposes they serve. We view the countryside as relatively 'natural' in virtue of its differing socio-economic function: where the urban is the zone of industry and commerce, the rural is the zone of agricultural and eco-regulatory activities. Implicit here seems to be a criterion of function whereby environments are regarded as more or less natural according to the type of needs that their human transformation is designed to accommodate, the countryside being associated with more 'primary' or 'basic' forms of consumption, the urban with the servicing of more historically developed or luxury requirements. In support of this, it might be claimed that the eco-regulatory activities which issue in the 'natural' landscape (the care of the soil and live-stock, forestry, the management of wet-lands, etc.) are essentially reproductive rather than productive of new commodities, and their functioning itself depends on the consumption of resources that they themselves directly serve to replenish. They thus contribute to a cyclical rather than linear and exponential productivity: the air-strip, for example, is less 'natural' than the field system because its purpose is to provide for the consumption of air-flight, which itself consumes raw materials it has no direct role in creating, whereas agricultural use of land employs resources that it also directly produces and sustains.

But while considerations of this kind no doubt have some part to play in shaping conceptions of 'nature', they offer no more clear-cut guidance on this than the broad-brush distinction between the built and unbuilt environment. Indeed, it might be argued that none of the antitheses on which they draw – between 'basic' and 'developed' needs; between object production and eco-regulatory activity; between industry and agriculture – have theoretical precision and may even confuse rather than clarify the issue. Food may count as a 'basic' need in a way that air-flight does not, but it is produced in both fields and factories and tailored in both cases to specific and historically developed dietary requirements. In any case, other needs with equal claims to be counted as 'basic' (notably for shelter) are served primarily by the built environment, and luxury production is by no means an exclusively urban activity. The champagne vineyard is scarcely less involved in luxury production than the factory producing needles, nor can the culture of orchids be said to be more 'basically' needed than the fabrication of saucepans. Contemporary agriculture is very energy consuming and dependent on inputs from outside its own systems. We may note, too, that the ancient barrow is no more 'natural' in terms of function than the urban cemetery, the water-mill no more than the power-station, the ruined fortress no more than the nuclear bunker. The purpose, then, to which a space is put is certainly a factor in determining judgements on its 'naturality', but there is little consistency in its application as criterion, and it is but one of a number of considerations that are brought to bear in these decisions.

Henri Lefebvre has suggested that 'The more a space partakes of nature, the less it enters into the social relations of production', and implies that, by reason of the ambivalence we may feel about the degree of such 'entry', judgements on certain 'spaces' are inherently problematic:

> Take national or regional 'nature parks', for instance; it is not at all easy to decide whether such places are natural or artificial. The fact is that the once prevalent characteristic 'natural' has grown indistinct and become a subordinate feature.[7]

Or again, of a peasant dwelling he writes that it:

> ... remains, to a greater or lesser degree, part of nature. It is an object intermediate between work and product, between nature and labour, between the realm of symbols and the realm of signs. Does it engender a space? Yes. Is that space natural or cultural? Is it immediate or mediated – and, if the latter, mediated by whom to what purpose? Is it given or artificial? The answer to such questions must be: 'Both'. The answer is ambiguous because the questions are too simple: between 'nature' and 'culture', or between work and product, complex relationships (mediations) already obtain. The same goes for time and for the 'object' in space.[8]

Certainly, the questions are too simple, and by reason of the complexity of the mediations that Lefebvre notes. But if he hesitates to pronounce on the naturality of the nature reserve or peasant dwelling, he does not hesitate in his selection of these as the relevant sites of ambiguity. How far is this selection explicable by reference to his own criteria of their respective degree of entry into the social relations of production? Here the answer must depend on how we construe these relations. If we are speaking of the relations of capitalist modernity, then certainly the peasant dwelling might be said to be less imbricated. But it is far less clear that this is true of the 'nature reserve', which is a prime asset of the contemporary eco-tourist industry, and no less inserted within capitalist relations of production than the airport. If, on the other hand, 'social relations of production' is here being deployed without historical specificity, it is not clear why the ambiguously 'natural' status of the peasant dwelling is accountable to its 'lesser' entry. For it surely entered just as fully into the social relations of feudalism as the hyper-market does into the relations of the contemporary market economy. One can agree, therefore, with Lefebvre that the question, 'Is it natural or cultural?', is too simply posed in respect of either of his examples, while at the same time feeling that their degree of entry into the social relations of production cannot suffice to explain his (and our own) sense that these are indeed very pertinent items for the query.

All the same, Lefebvre's appreciation of the difficulties attaching to judgements of this kind is very much to the point; as is his recognition of the complex spatial and temporal mediations that are implicitly acknowledged and explicitly erased in the discriminations we make between the natural and the cultural. In some cases, these judgements would seem to have more to do with the qualities of a given space. The nature reserve may be just as much caught up in relations of modernity as the airport and equally serving contemporary needs. But qua space, it differs in multiple ways: in appearance, in function, in the degree and quality of the physical transformations involved in its making, and so on. In other cases, the judgement has been determined less by factors of this kind than by temporal considerations: if the peasant dwelling is judged more 'natural' than the modern house, this is not so much because of a difference of function, or because it is any less an 'artificial' construction, but rather in virtue of its greater age and obsolescence.

Temporal and spatial factors, however, cannot really be regarded as separable here, for what underlies any inclination to view the peasant dwelling as more 'natural' in virtue of its age or disuse is a tacit recognition of the pre-givenness of the feudal production of space to the social relations of capitalism. To the culture of the high-rise block and supermarket, the peasant house figures as a 'natural' residue of the ground upon which capitalist relations set to work, erasing as they did so the social relations within which it was experienced as contemporary 'cultural' product rather than natural legacy. The feudal peasant may, similarly, have looked upon the barrows and other earthworks of antiquity as more directly belonging to the rural surround than the transformations of the landscape wrought by contemporary human labour. The legacy of an earlier culture appears more 'natural', one may say, because it is a legacy – a fact not without its bearing on the rhetoric and politics of environmental preservation.

Much of the complexity of the 'lay' conception of nature derives, then, from the fact that it is used as a spatial and as a temporal marker: both to distinguish between the grey and the green, without any eye to their age or degree of disuse; but also as a way of thinking the relations of the older to the newer. Nature, in this conception, is both a present space and an absent – already lost – time/space: a retreat or place of return, to which we 'go' or 'get' back, in a quest not only for a more originary, untouched space, but also for a *temps perdu*; or perhaps, more accurately, for a time that never was, a time prior to history and culture. Getting back to 'nature' is, in this sense, as much about getting out of time, or away from 'progress', as it is about getting into wilderness. The idea is expressive, we might say, of a desire not only to get close to the land, but also to retreat from culture – in other words, from a present which is always viewed as unprecedentedly further distanced from a supposedly pre-cultural point of origin. The 'natural' is thus conceived conjointly in terms of propinquity to the space of 'nature' (rurality, wilderness), and in terms of a temporal dynamic of relative distance from an always more 'historical' or more 'cultural' present. This double articulation of spatial and temporal conceptions is of the essence of the deployment of 'nature' as a normative idea, and very manifest in the eulogizing representations of the pastoral tradition, where rurality figures not only a more desirable type of space, but also a more fortunate moment in time.

On the Escalator

Raymond Williams has attempted to capture the inherent relativism of the nostalgia for a lost time/space of nature in his image of the 'escalator' of pastoral writing. No matter how far back we trace the documentation of the land we always come upon a lament for a destruction of a more 'natural' way of life of the immediate past. In English letters, for example, the demise of 'Old England' has always, it appears, just happened. The claim of a contemporary country book that 'A way of life that has come down to us from the days of Virgil has suddenly ended' prompts Williams to recall George Sturt writing in 1911 of rural England as 'dying out now', and from then onwards:

> . . . what seemed like an escalator began to move. Sturt traced this ending to two periods: enclosures after 1861 and residential settlement after 1900. Yet this at once

takes us into the period of Thomas Hardy's novels, written between 1871 and 1896 and referring back to rural England since the 1830s. And had not critics insisted that it was here, in Hardy, that we found the record of the great climacteric change in rural life: the disturbance and destruction of what one writer has called the 'timeless rhythm of agriculture and the seasons'? And that was also the period of Richard Jefferies looking back from the 1870s to the 'old Hodge', and saying that there had been more change in rural England in the previous half-century – that is, since the 1820s – than in any previous time. And wasn't George Eliot in *Mill on the Floss* (1860) and in *Felix Holt* (1866) looking back, similarly, to the old rural England of the 1820s and early 1830s?[9]

And thereafter the escalator moves without pause: by way of Cobbett, John Clare, Crabbe and Goldsmith back to the 1750s; from thence to Philip Massinger's regrets for the corruption of an older rural civilization; from there to a similar lament in Thomas More's *Utopia* of 1516. Does the escalator stop, asks Williams, when we reach

> the timeless rhythm in Domesday, when four men out of five are villeins, bordars, cotters or slaves? Or in a free Saxon world before what was later seen as the Norman rape and yoke? In a Celtic world, before the Saxons came up the rivers? In an Iberian world, before the Celts came, with their gilded barbarism?[10]

And if not there, then where, if not in Eden or Arcadia, for it certainly has not stopped in Virgil, whose pastoral contrast is between the pleasures of rural settlement and the threat of loss and eviction? And who can echo in his *Georgics* the yearning of Hesiod long before him for the Golden Age of a land that farms itself before the 'iron time' of labour and hardship?

There has always been, it would seem, a Golden Age, a prelapsarian time–space of 'nature', whether conceived in directly mythical–theological terms as an absolute origin in Eden or Arcadia, or more mundanely and historically, as the utopia of the erstwhile rural stability that has been 'displaced' by modernity: an 'old country' or 'more natural way of life' that encroaches ever forward in memory like a green tide on the heels of the present. Often enough, moreover, the Arcadian image of a 'naturally' abundant land directly serves to reinforce the social message, and the older order that is to be preserved from the corruption of modernity is imbued with the mythic qualities of the pre-historic 'unworked' nature. In the country-house poems of Ben Jonson and Thomas Carew, the estates of Penshurst and Saxham are celebrated as bulwarks of a more natural social order, whose stability is rewarded by the bounty of nature itself. At Penshurst, as Jonson has it, the estate

> To crowne thy open table, doth provide
> the purpled pheasant with the speckled side:
> The painted partrich lyes in every field
> And, for thy messe, is willing to be kill'd.

At Saxham, it is not only pheasant, partridge and lark that are volunteers for the table, but also

> The willing Oxe, of himselfe came
> Home to the slaughter, with the Lamb,
> And every beast did thither bring
> Himself to be an offering.
> The scalie herd, more pleasure took
> Bath'd in the dish than in the brook.

In all this, the poet-guest makes use of conventional associations of Christian and classical myth to express his gratitude for the hospitality of his host by presenting the provident land and old world virtues of the latter as an Eden before the fall and curse of labour. Of course, this is a conceit, and in a sense no one is taken in by it. What is interesting about it is the desire it plays on to abstract from the human labour and animal suffering that has actually supplied the table.[11]

Wherever we stop on the escalator, in fact, we encounter idylls and hymns on the rural retreat, which work on the reader's wishfulness in this respect by selecting out all those features that might detract from the idea of a purely 'natural' order. Anything unsettling to the sense of a timeless and spontaneously generated political and moral economy is expunged or glossed over: both the uglier and more painful aspects of its production of the land and its livestock, and the relations of ownership responsible for the surface appearance of the countryside, its enclosures and country estates, grouse moors and feudal hamlets.

In the most idealized versions of the pastoral, the reliance of the leisured landowner on the sweat and toil of the agricultural labourer is obscured by the displacement of idleness itself: shepherds and shepherdesses while away the day pursuing bucolic amours, yokels are permanently merry with pipe and tankard at the tavern doorway, the hay has always just been made, and lads and lasses enjoy an endless May Day on the village green. In the literature, as in the landscape painting of this pastoral tradition, the 'nature' that is being portrayed is not only itself a cultural product, but one whose reality as cultural form is distorted by a representation that selects only what it wishes to observe, and which is very often functioning as a form of expiation for, or repression of, the actual history of the land.

This wishful denial of the historic and less congenial aspects of rural existence is discernible even in writing and painting that would precisely have us note the 'reality' of the country labourer's or the peasant's lot, insofar as they imbue this with the virtues of the 'earth' and its 'simple life' and assign the worker to some timeless mode of rural existence. Heidegger's attempt to determine the 'being' of

Van Gogh's painting of the peasant boots is working with a very different conception of nature than that which is celebrated in Poussin or Claude Lorrain; the tribute to the careworn labourer in his cot is markedly different from the eulogy on the country house; the Lyrical Ballads treat of rurality in a very different mode from Jonson or Marvell; the poetry of Edward Thomas is not that of Theocritus. Yet all these may yet contribute to a 'version of history which succeeds in cancelling history', and to a merging of all conditions and periods of agricultural labour within a single image of rustic 'simplicity'.[12] Indeed, even where the work is most directly registering the actual complexity and disruption of country existence, and is centrally engaged with the rhythms of change and their social impact, the disposition to overlook these is evident in the failure of critical appreciation of this very sensibility. Such was Hardy's fate at the hands of those readers who took Wessex to their heart as a 'rural haven from contemporary life', and could celebrate his writing only as a record of 'Old England' and the cyclical reproduction of Dorset village life.[13]

Patriotic Greenery and the Market Garden

It is, of course, not only in art and literature (and its criticism) that 'nature' serves to cancel history. The device is a favourite of politicians, a standard trope of patriotic sentiment and a mainstay of heritage rhetoric. Nor are we speaking here of exclusively Conservative representations, since the Socialist tradition, at least in England, has also lent itself to this form of idealization of rurality. In this context, however, it is important to distinguish between the more grotesque and sentimental forms of its expression and the more considered and powerful critiques of the impact of industrialism on the English countryside, whether from the Right or the Left. As an organicist defendant of the importance of class hierarchy to the maintenance of cultural integrity, T. S. Eliot can hardly be placed within the tradition of political radicalism associated with Blake, Shelley, Hazlitt, William Morris and E. P. Thompson. Yet Eliot's expression of concern with the 'deformation of humanity by unregulated industrialism'[14] is much closer in tone and import to Blake's imaging of the 'satanic' corruption of the land than it is to the sort of conservatism voiced in George Bartram's paean to:

> Old England, gracious wielder of the spell
> Of pastoral beauty, janitress benign,
> Of green Arcadian temples, matron-belle
> Robed rich of rustic glory, it is well
> Yea, past all boasting to by thine son.[15]

We must also distinguish between an essentially conservative celebration of the supposedly eternal rurality of the land, and the left-wing challenge to the entrepreneurial 'patriotism' that has led to the destruction of the countryside and the horrors of industrialism. In the one case, 'patriotic greenery' is deployed to confirm the 'harmony' and well-being of the status quo of class division and private ownership; in the other, existing conceptions of the national 'good' are contested through a revolutionary vision of an alternative order wherein both humanity and nature are freed from oppression. Even where the ideal of 'rural England' is voiced in the most banal and absurd terms, we can detect a trace of this difference of project across the political divide. Stanley Baldwin's fulsome rhetoric speaks of what is and will always be:

> The sounds of England, the tinkle of the hammer on the anvil in the country smithy, the corncrake on a dewy morning, the sound of the scythe against the whetstone, and the sight of the plough team coming over the brow of the hill, the sight that has been seen in England since

England was a land, and may be seen in England long
after the Empire has perished and every works in England
has ceased to function, for centuries the one eternal sight
of England . . . [16]

In the fancy of the Labour Leader, George Lansbury, it
is at least a question of revivifying these immortal features
of the landscape:

I just long to see a start made on this job of reclaiming,
recreating rural England, I can see the village greens with
the Maypoles again erected and the boys and girls, young
men and maidens, all joining in the mirth and foll of May
Day.[17]

Invocations of the rural 'identity' of the nation, we need
hardly add, have been put to even more nakedly propagandist purposes in time of war, most notoriously in Nazi
Germany, whose folk-values were echoed in the imagery
of English fascism. But this propaganda was itself contested through the projection of an 'authentically' pastoral
England, and recruitment in the war was heavily reliant on
an identification of the 'homeland' with the countryside.[18]
More insistent in recent times has been the commercial
recourse to the 'rural imaginary', in order to reconcile us
to the activities of multinational companies and to solicit
our custom for their commodities. Today, it is the marketing rather than the political propagandist potential of
nature that is more exploited, and the clichés of nationalist
rhetoric have become the eco-lect of the advertising copy-
writer. Margarine comes to us from dew-bedecked pas-
tures, cider from the age-old orchards of country hamlets,
whisky out of Scottish burns (or Irish mists), mineral water
direct from a Samuel Palmer landscape. The plough is still
sometimes to be seen coming over the brow of the cereal
packet, and the motor-car is almost always somewhere on
the way back to nature. The rural provenance or 'natural'
properties of commodities is now one of their most vital

merchandizing features, and there is a whole range of products on the market today that cannot be offered for consumption without nature's imprimatur. Here, too, the pastoral imagery is being deployed in its customary role to screen out the actual conditions of production and protect the consumer from a too direct confrontation with the facts of modern industrial process. This too, one may argue, like much of the literature of the rural, involves a conceit, and no one perhaps is really fooled. But that commerce can trade on 'nature' in this way bears witness to a widespread interest in not confronting the truth of its actual exploitation. The copy-writer plays upon and panders to the consumers' interest in sustaining a certain self-deception about the 'badness' for the environment of the 'goods' on the market.

It may be objected that the marketing of 'greenery' has not so much constructed the obsession with 'natural' products as followed in response to a growing public concern over ecological degradation. This is perfectly true, and there is no reason to dispute that it is the actual 'loss' and pollution of nature that has motivated the demand for a less contaminated consumption, which has in turn prompted the 'green' merchandising of production. Cosmetic though the manufacturing response has been in many cases, there has been some shift to more eco-friendly methods of production, and certainly to the production of more 'additive-free' goods. Nor should we underestimate the transformation of the climate of thinking to which advertisement is now responding. It is quite unthinkable today that a garden spray could be promoted, as it was in the early 1950s, with a picture of mother, father and small child, each equipped with a suitably sized siphon, and all of them wreathing themselves in clouds of pesticide in their eager assault upon the greenfly.[19]

But what is at issue here, as it is more generally with the recourse to ideology of the rural, is the post mortem quality of the appeal of 'nature': that it is most forcefully felt only in the wake of its destruction. For there is a definite correlation between the erosion of the countryside and the 'pulling power' of rural ideology. To put the point rather crudely we may say that a certain idea of 'nature' becomes more desirable, and the desire for it more manipulable, as the reality it conceptualizes is diminished and degraded. In this sense, the phony or merely cosmetic character of much that is offered up as authentic 'nature' cannot be considered in abstraction from the realities of technological domination and urbanization to which it is responding; and while it is a comparatively easy critical task to expose the phoniness, it is much harder to find a political language in which to register both the illusions *and* the truth that attach to the idea of the 'loss of nature'.

Preserving the Legacy

Several commentators have pointed out in the case of England in particular how dramatic a correspondence there has been between the encouragement of the idea of the nation as essentially rural and its actual falsification by the growth of the cities and the encroachment of suburbia. As Williams puts it, by the end of the nineteenth century, rural Britain 'was subsidiary, and knew it was subsidiary'. Yet:

> so much of the past of the country, its feelings and its literature, was involved with rural experience, and so many of its ideas of how to live well, from the style of the country-house to the simplicity of the cottage, persisted and even strengthened, that there is an almost inverse proportion in the twentieth century, between the relative importance of the rural working economy and the cultural importance of rural ideas.[20]

The point, no doubt, can be over-stated, and may be skewed by focusing too exclusively on the celebrations of rural rather than urban existence. It can also be used too undialectically, as it arguably is by Martin Wiener in his tracing of the decline of the 'industrial spirit' to the nostalgic obsession with rustic values. Wiener is so insistent on the British loathing for industrial and mercantile pursuits that it is difficult on his account to see how there could have been any consequences of entrepreneurial activity post-1850 to have been regretted in the first place.[21] All the same, the general point, that the rural ideal has tended to gain its hold on the imagination correlatively with the erosion of the countryside, is surely well taken and is possibly the most relevant factor in the appreciation – and the critique – of contemporary environmentalist attitudes.

However, no serious analysis of environmentalism can stop short at the exposure of the ideological mismatch between the rural 'imaginary' and the reality of the modern industrial nation, even less be content with sneering at its deluded romanticism. Granted the truth of everything that Williams has to tell us about the retro-dynamic of the 'escalator',[22] the fact remains that the regret (or preservationist impulse) comes into play against a continuous destruction of the 'natural' landscape and its buildings; and that this has proceeded at such an accelerated pace in recent history that it constitutes a sufficient difference in scale and degree to anything preceding the Industrial Revolution to count as a difference in kind. Contemporary concerns over the 'loss of nature' may share in a structure of feeling with More or Cobbett, Marvell or Crabbe, even Virgil and Hesiod, but they relate to material transformations of the landscape and forms of ecological pollution and depletion of a very different order from anything that any of these earlier 'preservationists' encountered.

The immensely accelerated rate of natural resource exploitation, and its environmental impact, in the period after industrialization has been extensively documented and widely discussed. Suffice it to note here that in the decades of 'Fordist' modernization more energy has been consumed than in the whole of previous human history.[23] Over the same period, the scale and constituency of the concern with preservation of environment and wildlife has also significantly altered. Membership of the Society for the Protection of Birds increased by 539 per cent during the period 1971–85; of the National Trust by 505 per cent; of the Royal Society for Nature Conservancy by 281 per cent; and of Friends of the Earth by 2,850 per cent.[24] Greenpeace UK, founded in the early eighties, now has more members than any political party in the UK. It would perhaps be mistaken for the commentator on any past expressions of regret for the loss of a rural order to treat these only as the ideological vehicle of a defence of hierarchy or resistance to progress at the expense of recognizing the love of nature by which they were more consciously motivated. In our own time, when we face ecological degradation on a calamitous scale, it would be even more inappropriate to adopt a purely cynical approach to the preservationists and lovers of the countryside. For the alarm here speaks to real concern over real losses, and is rooted in aesthetic and moral feelings that we ignore only at the cost of undermining some of the most important sources of legitimation for *any* form of ecological prescription. By comparison with the revolutionary shifts in the methods of production and the quality of consumption that will be necessary to halt and reverse ecological degradation, some environmentalist campaigns may seem 'shallow' or narrowly focused. But they are motivated by forms of concern that will also be important to the promotion of the more radical programmes demanded, and which it would therefore be mistaken to disregard. Even in the case of the currently booming heritage 'industry', which has been a justifiable target of much sarcastic comment, something of the same sensibility should be brought to bear. For even as heritage trades on an over simple retrospection responsible for much 'bogus history',[25] it reflects genuine insecurities about the present that cannot be dismissed as ecologically irrelevant.

It has been suggested that heritage is to 'cultural' preservation what environmentalism is to the preservation of 'nature'. '"Heritage," says John Urry, prioritizes "culture" over a particular construction of "nature" and "natural desires".'[26] Up to a point, one may agree, but in the light of our earlier comments about 'nature' as temporal eraser, one might also claim that heritage is directed towards the encapsulation of 'nature' conceived as the less culturally developed past, much as environmentalism is directed toward its spatial perpetuation as countryside; that it is about saving what is more 'natural' by stopping the clock, rather than checking the urban encroachment.

Now there is no doubt that this does lend itself to some very bogus constructions of history, notably through the emphasis that has been placed by the purveyors of heritage on the preservation of the past *as if* it were the present. In the case of the country house, in particular (the most popular of the heritage attractions), the aim, it has been said, is to sell this not as museum, but as 'living organism'. Or, as one interior decorator has put it, to make the vacated country seat 'look like one where the family has just gone out for the afternoon'.[27] In the process, the fantasy of the visitor's personal occupation of the premises is the more directly encouraged, and becomes an important element in the fiction that the country house is a 'common property' belonging to us all – and thus in projecting an image of the past as less socially divisive or even as more 'naturally' harmonious. As Roy Strong has put it: 'the ravished eyes stir the heart to emotion, for in a sense the historic houses of this country belong to everybody, or at least everybody who cares about this country and its traditions'. In a sense, yes, which, as Robert Hewison is right to protest, elides private ownership 'into a vague conception of public trusteeship. By a mystical process of identification, the country house becomes the nation, and love of one's country makes obligatory a love of the country house'.[28] Those who have been locked out and confined, at best, to suburbia, are here seduced into collusion with the powers of exclusion themselves, in short, into the allowing the owner 'to continue his life very much as before, and without the financial burden of maintaining the house in which he lived'.[29]

Other dimensions of the heritage industry, noted by Hewison, may be less exploitative but equally, if not more, mythical in the history they project: the Beamish Open Air Museum 'colliery' that never existed; or the award winning village of Alcester, of which the architect from the Department of the Environment wrote: 'We have created the village we should like to see; not preserved that which was in fact there'.[30] In these cases, and many others, it is precisely not a matter of preservation but of recreation through the gaze of the modern rural retrospect: the 'conservation' of an imaginary past.

Not all forms of heritage conservation, however, are equally spurious, and as John Urry points out, one should avoid conflating blatant 'artefactual' history with restorations that can claim at least a 'semi-scholarly' status.[31] In any case, as suggested earlier, it is one thing to expose the myth-making, another to dimiss the impulse to environmental and heritage preservation as unwarranted or irrational, since it speaks to an altogether justifiable alarm about the ecologically destructive and deracinating effects of modernity and its continuous incursions upon 'an older way of life'. We must also surely, in this connection, endorse Williams's point about the 'permanent or effectively permanent' need for the contrast between the country and the city, which, as he says, despite the cultural relativity of its expression, 'is one of the major forms in which we become conscious of a central part of our experience and of the crises of our society'.[32]

The desire to preserve or return to the time/space of the rural order is not in this sense to be viewed as merely whimsical or nostalgic, but as an inevitable element of the response to modernity and the accelerated pace of environmental transformation. A present that is too quick to eradicate its past may cease in effect to be experienceable as present, and we may regard the yearning for the past, even to the point of artificially recreating it, as a bid to discover a time *of* and *for* experience. The snide references to an 'antique self-image', to a 'Britain in semi-retirement', and so forth,[33] are all very well, but in their implication that 'nostalgia' is a sentimental indulgence, they themselves offer an extremely partial, and in its own way deluded, account of what it is to be alive in the present. In this connection, one might note the force of Adorno's appraisal:

> As long as the face of the earth keeps being ravished by utilitarian pseudo-progress, it will turn out to be impossible to disabuse human intelligence of the notion that, despite all the evidence to the contrary, the pre-modern world was better and more humane, its backwardness notwithstanding. Rationalization has yet to become rational; the universal system of mediations has yet to generate a livable life. In this situation the traces of an old immediacy, no matter how outdated and questionable they may be (...) are legitimate in view of the outright denial of gratification by the present state of things. (...) While it is true that nowadays an aesthetic relationship to the past is liable to be poisoned by an alliance with reactionary tendencies, the opposite standpoint of an ahistorical aesthetic consciousness that

brushes the dimension of the past into the gutter as so much rubbish is even worse. There is no beauty without historical remembrance.[34]

This is not to deny the tendency of much 'heritage' provision to obscure what it would be ecologically useful to have revealed: the history of the relations between country and city; the history of the tensions between the preservation of 'nature' and the advance of more progressive social relations; the history of the interconnection between class privilege and the destruction of the environment. Moreover, there is reason to believe that these histories might well prove more poignant than the more illusory and artefactual variants. As Williams has aptly said of the writing of the pastoral tradition, 'The irony is that the real rural history would support so much more of the real observation, the authentic feeling, that these writers keep alive.'[35] Nor is it a question of simply revealing the hidden history of the confiscations and disruptions that have gone into the making of the 'timeless' and settled order of the countryside. We should be alert, too, to their implications for the contemporary project of rural preservation. As noted, the policies of the National Trust (originally established in 1865 to preserve public access to the country) have been criticized for being directed as much to the protection of private landowners and their properties as to the conservation of rural space. The other side of this story is that local authorities who are keenly concerned to preserve the countryside as a public amenity are constantly up against the exorbitant costs of doing so. Preserving what Roy Strong refers to as 'belonging to everybody' very often means finding the money to buy it back from those whose ancestors had appropriated and enclosed it in the first place.[36] The 'ordinary' public is in this sense paying twice over for its 'common' heritage: first in having been deprived of access to it, and then again in funding its restoration. The popular interest in this rural 'property' should in many ways, therefore, be the last to be reviled, since without it, it is almost certain that far more of the aristocrat's estate would have been handed over to the building speculator.

The Dialectics of Environmentalism

There has been a persistent tendency on the part of the Left to harp on the sentimental and elitist aspects of environmentalism, and to dismiss its nature aesthetic as always the voice of a (Not-in-my-backyard) form of self-interest. But if, as the economist Elmar Altvater has argued, the key ecological need is to minimize entropy increase (to keep energy use and the mixing of materials as low as possible),[37] then anything which 'freezes' an existing pattern of materials is good news from a resource preservation point of view. It is also likely to prove a better ally of the cause of social justice.

The right-wing neo-monetarist who pays little heed to the global consequences of the pursuit of First World affluence may reasonably deplore the 'anti-industrial' spirit of heritage and environmental preservation as a brake on 'progress' (or speak disdainfully of the impulse to 'sublimate' the force of economic appetites in 'higher pursuits').[38] But no one concerned with democracy and equality of distribution within a world of dwindling resources can subscribe to this rhetoric.

Here, as always, we have to attend not only to the socio-economic implications of successful acts of preservation, but also to the impact of the developments that would otherwise have taken place. Both environmental conservation and industrial development are inserted within the existing relations of production, and both will reflect the class structure and inequalities that these relations sustain and reproduce. In this sense, we cannot expect that the consequences of either will be wholly 'democratic'; but whereas the latter is dedicated only to the continued flourishing of the capitalist economy, the former, even as it is caught up in the market and its class conditioned system of need and desire, complicates its workings by its refusal to release space and resources back into the free-flow of materiality available to capital. A more dialectical approach to heritage and environmental preservation will recognize that, by contributing to the scarcity of materials over which capitalist enterprise can command a free hand, they are more allied than opposed to the aspirations of the socialist wing of the ecology movement.

This dialectical approach would not deny the patrician element in environmentalism, nor the extent to which it is caught up in the same mythologies about 'our' heritage and the 'common land' that have helped to sustain the property of those most directly responsible for ecological destruction. Even less will it deny the hypocrisy of those whose concern for 'nature' extends no further than the environs of the rural retreat to which they resort at weekends in order to refresh themselves for the Monday assault upon its resources.[39] It is, rather, to emphasize the importance of bringing a more discriminatory attitude to bear: the love of the countryside is by no means confined to those best placed to enjoy it, and the environmental movement includes within its ranks many whose 'backyard' is a strip of urban cement. It is also to assert, more fundamentally, that the sentiments that find expression in this movement are not a mere by-product of modernity but part of its dialectic. None of this complexity is registered by the simple dismissal of the preservationist impulse as 'elitist' or by treating it as an 'ideological' – and hence in principle dispensable – urge. What has made Williams's approach to the 'country and the city' of such seminal importance to the Left is the dual recognition it gives both to the ideological dimensions of rural nostalgia *and* to the sensibilities about time and placed expressed within it. Thus he can write that:

If there are any now ready to mourn the loss of country life, let them mourn the 'poachers' who were caught and savagely punished, until a different and urban conscience exerted some controls. Or if there are any who wish to attack those who destroyed country customs, let them attack the thieves who made the finding of food into theft.

And at the same time, he can question:

How many socialists, for example, have refused to pick up that settling archival sentence about the 'idiocy of rural life'? Until very recently, indeed until the peasant socialist revolutions in China and Cuba, this reflex was habitual among the metropolitan socialists of Europe. And behind it, all the time, was a more serious position, near the centre of historical argument. For it has been a commonplace since Marx to speak, in some contexts, of the progressive character of capitalism, and within it of urbanism and of social modernization . . . We hear again and again this brisk, impatient and as it is said realistic response: to the productive efficiency, the newly liberated forces, of the capitalist breakthrough; a simultaneous damnation and idealization of capitalism, in its specific forms of urban and industrial development; an unreflecting celebration of mastery – power, yield, production, man's mastery over nature – as if the exploitation of natural resources could be separated from the accompanying exploitation of men . . . Against this powerful tendency, in which forms of socialism offer to complete the capitalist enterprise, even the old, sad, retrospective radicalism seems to bear and to embody a human concern.

And then again, in a dialectical move beyond either the 'simple backward look' or the 'simple progressive thrust', he reminds us that we can begin from neither, but must look instead to 'the history to which they are only partial and misleading responses'.⁴⁰

Nature Love and Self-Love

Moving beyond these dual, but equally over-simple responses, means recognizing the ways they have shaped divisions within the ecological movement itself. For while 'shallow' environmentalists and some currents of 'deep' ecology have been moved primarily by a nature-centred aesthetic or ethic (it is to be preserved primarily because of its beauties or its 'intrinsic' value), eco-socialism and more 'anthropocentric' approaches have been primarily concerned with the consequences of the exploitation of natural resources for human beings, both now and in the future. Hence the emphasis they have placed on justice in ecological distribution and the sustainability of the eco-system. In the most abstract sense, then, one might be tempted to distinguish between those who would preserve nature for its own sake and those who would do so for 'our' sake: between the party of nature and the party of humanity.

Yet this tendency to construct an opposition between more and less 'anthropocentric' approaches is very misleading, and falsely collectivizes across political divisions that need to be exposed. Both the eco-socialist and the new-right critic may be said to be of the 'party of humanity', but their 'anthropocentric' priorities are very different. Where the latter sees nature-idolatry only as an obstacle to the entrepreneurial activities of an already favoured section of humanity, socialists are concerned with its impact on the emancipation and consumption of the most oppressed and deprived. Both the right and the left, therefore, have been critical of the effects of the 'simple backward look' on human progress, but from directly opposing allegiances, and nothing is to be gained by conflating these within the general charge of 'anthropocentrism'. On the contrary, it would be better to recognize that left criticism of and within the Green Movement has been focused on tensions between the advance of social justice ('love of humanity') and the cause of nature that the 'lovers of nature' have often shown themselves too casual about. Environmentalists should accept that when we are talking about 'nature' we are not simply talking about a collection of beauty spots or endangered species, but about the resources through which alone human needs both now and in the indefinite future can be met; and that in preserving the countryside we are preserving the inscription of a very unequal access to these. Ecocentric critics of 'instrumental' attitudes to nature should, for their part, accept that a simplistic anti-human speciesism that treats all human beings as equal 'enemies' of nature covers over the social relations responsible for the abuse of nature even as it recommends policies on its disabuse that are likely to hit hardest at that sector of humanity that is least to blame. All the 'parties of nature' need to recognize, moreover, the element of human self-interest that underlies their preservationist concerns. Environmentalists clearly want the beauties of nature saved for the sake of the pleasure and solace that human beings find in them. But even ecocentric arguments tacitly rely in their defence of the 'instrinsic' value of nature on the appeal to human aesthetic and moral sensibilities. For when they call upon us to value nature 'for its own sake', they are also implicitly suggesting that the correct environmental ethic for human beings to adopt is one that values nature for its independence and without concern for its utility.[41]

The cause of ecology is therefore best advanced through a readiness to confront the tensions between the two types of evaluation it brings into play. On the one hand, there is the value we place on nature either intrinsically or as

domain of aesthetic pleasure and source of sensual gratification. On the other hand, there is its utilitarian value
as a set of life-preserving, life-enhancing resources. Neither can be thought independently of the value we place
on the human community both now and in the future,
and both imply a concern with human moral well-being.
To ask about our responsibilities to nature is necessarily
therefore to ask about our responsibilities to ourselves.
What premium is to be placed on the respective needs
of different sectors of humanity? What premium is to be
placed on the satisfaction of the aesthetic need for nature
even if this will necessarily have some consequences on the
provisioning for other needs, and involves accommodating
a demand for a 'positional' good that can only be met by
constraining the individual's access to it? What obligations
do we have to future generations, and for how long, and
at what level of resource consumption? Should human
needs be sacrificed to those of other species, and if so,
which needs and which human beings should be the first
to suffer?

I shall discuss the tensions between the value priorities
that have guided the different responses to these questions
within the spectrum of ecological politics more fully in
chapter 8. Suffice it to say here that, while these do
in certain respects have very divergent implications for
policies on the use of nature, we should not overlook the
aspects in which they may be said to be complementary. I
have argued here, for example, that there is no reason to
view the environmental concern with preservation as being
opposed to the interest in the conservation of resources,
since what tends to preserve nature as a site of beauty will
also help to fetter industrial exploitation and thus restrict
the increase in entropy. Using nature in sustainable ways
is also, for its part, likely to enhance its aesthetic attraction. But if this is so, both these wings of the ecological
movement should appreciate the interdependency of the

respective values to which they appeal for legitimation. A community too sorely deprived of the joys of nature may come to care less for long term human survival and well-being. Encouragement must therefore be given to whatever promotes the enjoyment of nature in the interests of conserving its resources for future generations. Conversely, a community that sacrifices too much of human well-being in the interests of nature may so restrict the appreciation of its beauty or value that this becomes too narrowly experienced for it to function as a legitimating basis for the preservation of the environment.

Let us accept, then, that the appeal of eco-politics and the grounds for any confidence in its ultimate success is both aesthetic and moral, that it invokes both the delight in nature and the obligation to the future. But these appeals are likely to prove more powerful, so it seems to me, the more scrupulous the movement is in considering their validity, and the implications of the discourses in which they have been promoted. Particularly in the case of the appeal to nature as a source of aesthetic pleasure and consolation, we need to proceed in awareness of just how problematic it may be to offer a universalist discourse on the needs or responses of humanity, and it is to a consideration of this issue that the next chapter is devoted.

Notes

1 I use these terms in line with a general distinction that is drawn within the ecological movement between the *conservation* of natural resources for future consumption, and the *preservation* of the surface environment and non-human species. Cf. John Passmore, *Man's Responsibility for Nature*, 2nd edn (Duckworth, London, 1980), pp. 73, 101.

2 T. Adorno, *Aesthetic Theory* (Routledge, Kegan Paul, London, 1984), p. 104. But he also makes the point (p. 97) that the

appreciation of natural beauty 'focuses exclusively on nature as appearance, never on nature as the stuff of work and material reproduction of life, let alone on the substratum of science'. Cf. the discussion in chapter 7.

3 This is a term borrowed by geographers from the German, where *Kulturlandschaft* refers to humanly worked environments that include artefacts within them. Adorno tells us that 'probably at some point in the nineteenth century, the whole domain of what the Germans call *Kulturlandschaft* came to be subsumed under the beautiful in nature, although on the face of it cultural landscape or culturescape would seem to resist such subsumption, consisting primarily as it does of artefacts.' *Aesthetic Theory*, pp. 94–5; cf. Jay Appleton, *The Experience of Landscape* (John Wiley, London, 1975), p. 6.

4 David Harvey, 'The Nature of the Environment: the Dialectics of Social and Environmental Change', *Socialist Register* (1993). Many others have, of course, emphasized the culturality of the natural, cf. chapter 5, pp. 152–5, and note 4.

5 Raymond Williams, *The Country and the City* (Hogarth Press, London, 1993), p. 289.

6 Cf. Appleton, *The Experience of Landscape*, p. 4.

7 Henri Lefebvre, *The Production of Space*, trans. D. Nicholson-Smith (Blackwell, Oxford, 1991), p. 83.

8 Ibid., pp. 83–4.

9 Williams, *The Country and the City*, p. 9. A similar point has been made in respect of the American pastoral tradition by Leo Marx, *The Machine in the Garden* (Oxford University Press, Oxford, 1964), pp. 18–19.

10 Williams, *The Country and the City*, p. 11.

11 Ibid., pp. 26–32.

12 Ibid., p. 257. For some scrupulous discussion of the 'archaizing' tendencies and rural ideology at work in Heidegger's treatment of the Van Gogh painting (to be found in 'The Origin of the Work of Art' in David Farrell Krell, *Basic Writings* (Routledge, Kegan Paul, London, 1978) see Jay Bernstein, *The Fate of Art* (Polity, Oxford, 1992), pp. 132–5; on the romanticization of the 'humble life' in eighteenth century English poetry, see Williams, *The Country and the City*, pp. 72–5, and on Thomas's 'indiscriminate enfolding' of history in the figure of Lob, pp. 257–9. See also Peter Brooker and Peter Widdowson, 'A Literature for England' in Robert Colls and Philip Dodd (eds), *Englishness: Politics and Culture 1880–1920* (Croom Helm, Beckenham,

1987), pp. 116–63 (esp. pp. 126–33); John Barrell, *The Dark Side of the Landscape* (Cambridge University Press, Cambridge, 1980).

13 Martin Wiener, *English Culture and the Decline of the Industrial Spirit 1850–1980* (Cambridge University Press, Cambridge, 1982), pp. 52–4; cf. Williams, *The Country and the City*, ch. 18.

14 T. S. Eliot, *The Idea of a Christian Society* (London, 1939), p. 61; cf. Raymond Williams, *Culture and Society* (Hogarth, London, 1987), p. 229f.

15 Used as a frontispiece to Lucien Oldershawe, *England and the Nation* (1904), cited in Martin Wiener, *English Culture*, p. 61.

16 Speech of 1924, cited in Bill Schwarz, 'Conservatism, nationalism and imperialism' in *Politics and Ideology*, ed. James Donald and Stuart Hall (Open University Press, Milton Keynes, 1986), pp. 154–86. (One might note that with the inimitable logic of the politician, Baldwin proceeds to invoke the love of these 'eternal sights' as that which prompts 'our race' to seek new homes in the overseas Dominions, where 'they have room to see things like this that they can no more see at home'!)

17 Speech of 1934, cited in Wiener, *English Culture*, pp. 122–3.

18 Cf. Wiener, *English Culture*, p 177. The image of England as essentially 'rural' was also, of course, of paramount importance in generating and sustaining patriotic feeling up to and during the period of the First World War, and found continuous expression in the culture and political discourse of the time. On what they describe as 'the collusion of aestheticism and literary pastoral with patriotism and the construction of a myth of rural England' see Brooker and Widdowson, 'A Literature for England', esp. p. 133f; see also Alun Howkins, 'The Discovery of Rural England' (in Colls and Dodd, *Englishness*, pp. 62–88) who traces the popularization of the 'myth' and emphasizes the specifically 'southern England' quality of its imagery.

19 Alexander Wilson, *The Culture of Nature* (Blackwell, Oxford, 1992), p. 99.

20 Williams, *The Country and the City*, p. 248.

21 Nor does Wiener appear to perceive the tension between his claims within the space of a paragraph that 'commercialisation had already eroded much of Old England' and that the metaphor of Britain as romantic, traditional and aristocratic 'was triumphing in the realm of the tangible, as it had in that of the intangible'. See *English Culture*, p. 42.

22   No imputation of 'sneering' is here intended to Williams himself, who has done more than anyone to alert us to the 'dialectic' of environmentalism. See the penultimate section of this chapter.

23   Elmar Altvater, *The Future of the Market*, trans. Patrick Camiller (Verso, London, 1993), p. 187; cf. pp. 182–3. Altvater is here drawing on recent German research on human energy use.

24   John Urry, *The Tourist Gaze* (Sage, London, 1990), p. 96; cf. Robert Hewison, *The Heritage Industry: Britain in a Climate of Decline* (Methuen, London, 1987), p. 24.

25   Hewison, *The Heritage Industry*, p. 46.

26   Urry, *The Tourist Gaze*, pp. 94–5.

27   Hewison, *The Heritage Industry*, pp. 53, 72. Cf. Wiener, *English Culture*, p. 50.

28   Hewison, *The Heritage Industry*, p. 53. Cf. Patrick Wright *On Living in an Old Country* (Verso, London, 1985), esp. ch. 2.

29   Hewison, *The Heritage Industry*, p. 59. Hewison argues, moreover, that the bargain is one which very often cedes the public very minimal access to the estates they are funding. But see also Urry's response to the criticism of Hewison and Wright of the National Trust, *The Tourist Gaze*, p. 110f.

30   Hewison, *The Heritage Industry*, pp. 94–5, 98.

31   Urry, *The Tourist Gaze*, pp. 110–12.

32   Williams, *The Country and the City*, p. 289.

33   Wiener, *English Culture*, p. 61.

34   Adorno, *Aesthetic Theory*, pp. 95–6.

35   Williams, *The Country and the City*, p. 262.

36   As is evident from John Sheail's account of the struggles of local councils in his work on *Rural Conservation in Inter-War Britain* (Clarendon Press, Oxford, 1981). See esp. ch. 2, pp. 11–20 on the efforts of the Surrey council.

37   Altvater, *The Future of the Market*, pp. 193–8.

38   Clearly the *real* driving force of all of us! See Wiener, *English Culture*, p. 81.

39   Cf. Williams, *Problems in Materialism and Culture* (Verso, London, 1980), p. 81.

40   Williams, *The Country and the City*, p. 184, pp. 36–7.

41   For further discussion of this ecocentric argument on the value of nature, see chapter 8.

7

LOVING NATURE

Twilight combined with the scenery of Egdon Heath to evolve a thing majestic without severity, impressive without showiness, emphatic in its admonitions, grand in its simplicity. The qualifications which frequently invest the facade of a prison with far more dignity than is found in the facade of a palace double its size lent the heath a sublimity in which spots renowned for beauty of the accepted kind are utterly wanting. Fair prospects wed happily with fair times; but alas, if times be not fair! Men have oftener suffered from the mockery of a place too smiling for their reason than from the oppression of surroundings oversadly tinged. Haggard Egdon appealed to a subtler and scarcer instinct, to a more recently learnt emotion, than that which responds to the sort of beauty called charming and fair.

Indeed, it is a question if the exclusive reign of this orthodox beauty is not approaching its last quarter. The new Vale of Tempe may be a gaunt waste in Thule: human souls may find themselves in closer and closer harmony with external things wearing a sombreness distasteful to our race when it was young. The time seems near, if it has not actually arrived, when the chastened sublimity of a moor, a sea, or a mountain will be all of nature that is absolutely in keeping with the moods of the more thinking among mankind. And ultimately, to the commonest tourist, spots like Iceland may become what the vineyards and myrtle-gardens of South Europe are to him now; and Heidelberg and Baden be passed unheeded as he hastens from the Alps to the sand-dunes of Scheveningen.[1]

Justly famed for its depiction of 'nature' Hardy's commentary on Egdon Heath is also interesting testimony to the difficulties of writing about the aesthetic experience of it. Raymond Williams, we may recall, would have us recognize both the permanence of the need for the countryside and the cultural relativity of its expression. Hardy, in this passage, illustrates how difficult the spirit of this compact may be to observe in the letter. For even as he is disposed to offer a general reflection on the emotional responses of 'our race', Hardy reveals many of the reasons why it may be illegitimate to do so. Pulled as his text is, in certain respects, towards a discourse of 'man' and 'nature', it is as constantly pulled out of that framework of thinking by its acknowledgement of the factors that disqualify so abstract an approach. No sooner has it offered some universalist observation about the 'men' who have 'oftener suffered from the mockery of a place' than these 'men' have yielded to the more particular community of those of a 'scarcer instinct', and 'instinct' itself even more rapidly to the idea of 'recently learnt emotion'.

The 'human souls' of the opening of the second paragraph have been transmuted to the 'more thinking among mankind' by its mid-point, who have then in turn relayed their aesthetic to the 'commonest tourist' by its end. The reference to an 'accepted' landscape as if it were indeed a general preference is in itself belied by the generality of the claim about the demise of orthodoxy: the attractions of the sublime are, we are given to believe, in some general sense replacing those of the pastoral. Nor is it a question here of simply recognizing that in some epochal way the fashion in 'nature' can change; even as Hardy pits the reign of some supposedly general aesthetic against another, as if it *were* the mood of the culture at large, the qualifications that disturb the universal humanism of the social reference invite us also to think about which part of 'our race' has dictated the vogue either in the beauty called 'charming and fair', or in the more sombre attractions of the 'sublime'.

His equivocal discourse is an index of his sensitivity to that which must check the impulse to speak in any universal terms about human responses to nature. Even as Hardy is inclined to attribute some common aesthetic feeling to us all, he is alert to those factors that detract from confident pronouncements on its quality, and demand a more relativist appraisal. He thus registers a tension between the more universal and the more particular commentary that it is important to sustain in any exploration of humanity's 'love of nature'.

At one level, it is certainly unjustifiable to speak of what 'everyone' feels (or has felt) for nature, since we have the evidence here only of the sentiments recorded by a particular part of 'our race'. On the other hand, it may be equally presumptuous to suppose that the feelings which have been voiced are exclusive to that fraction of the human community that gave expression to them, or that the absence of a cultural record bespeaks an absence of sentiment. It may, in other words, be as complacent to assume that it is only the 'more thinking among mankind' who have felt the headiest inspiration in nature, or that their tastes have always cued those of the 'less thinking', as to overlook their hegemonic role in the creation of a supposedly 'common' aesthetic. In short, there could be as much elitism in refusing to credit any talk of 'human souls' in general as there is in ignoring the favoured position of those who do the talking. Yet we should clearly be cautious about accepting anyone's claim to knowledge in this area.

Though I shall here not be centrally concerned with the claims made within the Green Movement concerning human feelings for nature, I see the issues I shall be exploring as relevant to eco-politics on two main grounds. In the first place, those environmentalists whose primary

concern is with the preservation of the countryside and
an existing order of rural space do presuppose a general
aesthetic, as opposed to utilitarian, interest in the preservation of nature, and must appeal to this if they would
have their political activities viewed as representing the
collective concerns of the community. In other words, to
the extent that environmentalists regard their campaigning
as legitimated not by reference to minority tastes, but by
reference to a collective appreciation of 'nature', they
seek democratic credentials that require them to be as
open as possible to the problems of speaking on behalf
of a 'common aesthetic'. But, secondly, there are also
a number of ecologists whose primary concern is not
with preserving nature as a source of delight for human
beings, but with saving it (particularly wilderness) from
human intrusion, in other words, with conserving it as
an 'intrinsic value'. Yet it is not uncommon to find those
arguing this case doing so by way of appeal to the seemingly timeless and universal responses that nature elicits in
'humanity'. 'Visiting the Grand Canyon,' writes Holmes
Rolston, 'we intrinsically value the rock strata with their
color bands. Visiting Kentucky, we value Mammoth cave,
with its stalactites;'[2] and he and others defending the
'intrinsic value' of nature frequently write as if there were
a universal human capacity to 'love' nature, revere wilderness, simply to feel and respond to its absolute and
independent worth. The appeal, it would seem, is very
often to a common core of sensibility that we can and
should collectively experience. Now maybe this is the case,
and I do not want to suggest that there are no grounds
for defending it, but here too it seems that the argument
might be more persuasive were it to show itself more
troubled by historical considerations, more ready to look
at the role that specific cultural conditions have played
in constructing tastes and feelings for nature, including
the responses that are presented within the ecological

movement as those that 'humans' have or can be called upon to have.

Even, then, as environmental and ecological politics presumes common forms of appreciation of landscape or capacities to value nature, it should acknowledge how problematic it may be to imply that all human beings are as united in their aesthetic responses to nature as they are in their reliance upon it as a utility and means of satisfying material needs. At any rate, a reliance, which is obviously cross-cultural and universal in the one instance, is much less clearly so in the other. The specific 'satisfiers' of material needs (for food, shelter and the like) do indeed differ enormously across time and between (and within) given human societies, but natural resources are essential to every form of their provision. It is far more debatable whether there is any common structure of aesthetic need discernible within the variety of human affective responses to nature; or whether, if we insist that there is, we are not treating the aesthetic response itself as a merely elaborated form of the physical need, and thus mistaking its particular quality. Some, as we shall see, have offered an analysis of the attractions of nature in terms of human reliance on the means of survival supplied by the environment, but it is questionable whether this does full justice to a less instrumentally motivated, more specifically aesthetic, appreciation of it. The 'abnegation of the purpose of self-preservation,' argues Adorno, 'is just as crucial to the aesthetic perception of nature as it is to that of art. In this respect they hardly differ.'[3]

Indeed, it may be said that in treating aesthetic feeling as if it were comparable to a physical need or dependency, which persists even where it is not directly recognized or given expression,[4] we are in some sense failing to respect its status as an *experienced* response. To attribute a universal 'love' of nature, 'delight' in its beauty, 'awe' for its grandeur, and so forth, is precisely to attribute to the human collectivity at large a set of subjectively acknowledged feelings, and the claim can appeal to nothing more objective for support than the consensus about the experience itself. As an empirical claim, in fact, any statement to the effect that all human beings have an appreciation or aesthetic 'need' for nature is as open to refutation through the failure of the experience in question as is the claim that everyone likes wine or cheese.

It may be objected that claims about human aesthetic feeling for nature are not intended to be construed in that way, but are rather to be viewed as judgements on its value or attractions that are made with a demand for universal assent. What is being articulated is not an empirical claim to the effect that everyone does in fact revere or love nature, but a Kantian 'pure' aesthetic judgement to the effect that nature is 'awesome' or 'beautiful' (where the implication is that everyone ought to find it so – and, since 'ought' implies 'can', is possessed of the sensibility allowing them in principle to do so).[5]

But it is doubtful, to say the least, whether a judgement of this kind could lay claim to being 'pure', and hence universal, since this would require the aesthetic experience in question to be conceptually unmediated, and it is not at all clear how 'nature' as such, as opposed to particular instances of it, could be the object of an unmediated phenomenological response. An experience of, say, a rose or a sunset as beautiful is, we might agree, simply an experience of delight in that particular thing, and hence the object of a pure aesthetic judgement. We feel, and pronounce, this sunset or rose to be beautiful, and the experience and judgement upon it, is, as Kant argues, to be differentiated from the experience and judgement that it is beautiful *qua* rose or sunset (where what is intended is that it is a beautiful instance *of* a rose or sunset, and the judgement is mediated through the concept of 'rose' or 'sunset' and hence not pure). In judging 'nature' to be beautiful, however, it would seem that we are necessarily judging it beautiful *qua* nature, and that the aesthetic experience in question is therefore dependant on possession of what is arguably a culture-bound concept of nature as a totality and form of 'otherness' (it is that, for example, which is *not* the product of art or culture and to be valued for that reason). We may allow that there is an aesthetic experience mediated through the concept of nature that is universal to Western culture, where nature has generally been appreciated *as nature* (because it is 'natural' rather than a work of human artifice). But how far this is universal to *humanity* would depend, it would seem, on the degree of universality attaching to such a conception of nature.

There is, moreover, a tendency for environmentalist discussions of 'human' feelings for nature to overlook their historicity and dependency on culturally specific systems of belief. Even those evaluations of nature that may reasonably be said to be common to a given epoch of Western culture have shifted quite dramatically with such changes of cognition. The transformations that have marked our attitudes to animals are clearly a case in point. To view animals as a separate creation, specifically provided by God for the purpose of meeting human needs, is to bring a moral and aesthetic sensibility to them that will differ in significant ways from that of a culture generally committed to the correctness of evolutionary theory and sceptical about the idea that it is the possession of a 'soul' that distinguishes humanity from other living creatures. To regard other animals as creatures kindred to ourselves is to invite a rather different appraisal of them than is invited by the Cartesian view of them as insensate 'machines'. The point here is not that we have 'obviously' over time, and through such shifts of thinking, become less cruel or hypocritical in our attitudes to non-human creatures, that we now 'love' them more than in earlier epochs, or have a more profound understanding or aesthetic appreciation of them. None of these things is obviously true. Against the general abandonment of some practices (bear-baiting, cock-fighting, bird-stoning, horse-flogging) must be set the introduction of others (battery farming, vivisection, animal experimentation and use as human surrogates). Against the 'irrationality' of the canonization of a greyhound (France, thirteenth century); of rejecting a Bill in the House of Commons because of the flight of a jackdaw through the Chamber (England, 1604); of resistance to the idea of a Queen (as opposed to a King) bee (Aristotle to the mid-eighteenth century); of the claim that crows had been seen planting a grove of oaks to serve as future nesting (England, early eighteenth century),[6] must be set the more contemporary 'irrationalities' of the surrogate monkey-mother studies;[7] of animal beauty parlours; of Jurassic Park; of chicken-flavour injected chicken. Against the arrogant human speciesism of the theological cosmology must be set the racist and eugenical applications that have been made of evolutionary theory. Despite some rather muddled claims to the contrary, it is not clear that Western culture has become either more 'humane', or more intelligent, or more aesthetically sensitive towards other living creatures.

To make these points about the differing rationalities that have guided human feelings for animals is not to suppose that we do not also find good evidence of a trans-historical continuity in this. One is struck more by the similarities in the affections and interests informing the descriptions of animals in Homer and Joyce, Chaucer and Tolstoy, Buffon and Hardy than by the differences. The cat affrighted by the visitation of the Archangel Gabriel in Lotto's *Annunciation* is registered with the same empathy we have for the cat alarmed by the vacuum cleaner. There has been a remarkable stability in the animals that have been chosen as objects of human admiration or revulsion. But if we can detect the signs of a common sentiment across epochs and cultures, we need also to recognize, and account for, considerable differences of temper and treatment We are not, it would seem, dealing simply here with the presence or absence of a simple affective response ('love' or 'respect'), but with the ways in which the patterning and distribution of that response is structured by different interpretations of the world. The feelings elicited by animals may indeed guide our ideas about the kind of creatures they are, and thus inform our theories about them – or prompt a distrust of the theories that are offered. (As Bolingbroke commented apropos Descartes' hypotheses about animals: 'The plain man would persist in thinking that there was a difference between the town bull and the parish clock').[8] But the feelings are themselves in turn shaped by the theories. We did not, in fact, learn whether animals were or were not machines by treating them as if they were, and to that extent it may be said that a primary affective response has determined our comportment towards them as objects of knowledge. But the knowledge we gain of them is also an influence on the feelings we subsequently experience for them.

The Sublime and the Beautiful

Similarly, in respect of the aesthetic of landscape, we may argue that there are separate, if interlocking, registers of feeling of which we need to take account. Western culture has so persistently expressed a tension between the environment in its more awesome and in its more charming aspects that it is difficult to resist the idea that this does indeed speak to some permanent structure of response rooted in universal features of human psychology. Yet at the same time, there is no doubt that this tension has been differently experienced over time, and that changes of the kind that Hardy notes require us to recognize the historical mediations at work in their formation. From Homer to our own time, nature has been represented as both wild and pastoral, a site of exalting terror as well as of comforting serenity. To the 'sublime' of the Sirens, the Wandering Rocks, Scylla and Charybdis, and other terrors encountered by Odysseus, we have the 'beautiful' images of the well-tended flocks and cultivated lands that provide him hospitality on his travels, and to whose 'home' he eventually returns. Against the abysmal wastes of Dante's or Milton's hell is set the idyllic space of Paradise. Against the 'sublime' of Caliban in *The Tempest* or the 'heath' in *King Lear*, the charm of Ariel and the comforts of accommodated man. Yet this perennial abstract contrast, in which an antithetical topology is as often functioning as moral metaphor as describing any actual landscape and its respective attractions, must clearly be distinguished from that movement in thought, which from the mid-eighteenth century theorizes the response to the natural environment in terms of the 'beautiful' and the 'sublime', and cultivates the latter as a distinct aesthetic experience. It is one thing for nature as a chaotic or demonic instance of cosmic power to be opposed to nature as harmony and good order. It is another for chaos to be endowed with its own aesthetic appeal: the appeal of a certain limitlessness encountered in the landscape itself. The abyss, the whirlpool, the mountain range, the unbounded celestial space may have proved fearsome to earlier cultures, but it is only in the age of modernity that they begin to be celebrated as the source of a peculiar pleasure. Prior to the eighteenth century the 'sublime' is seldom used of landscape, but retains the sense given it by Longinus as a term of literary style or rhetoric, and it is only fully theorized as a nature aesthetic in the argument of Burke and Kant.[9] Even, then, as we recognize that this aesthetic development is only possible in virtue of some more fundamental and trans-cultural properties of ourselves and nature, we also need to pay due heed to those factors responsible for the specific quality and influence of its manifestation as a cultural movement or fashion.

It is a limitation, one may argue, of naturalistic attempts to account for the pleasure we take in landscape in terms of biological need that they fail sufficiently to distinguish and observe these different registers. One of the more developed of these is that of Jay Appleton, who offers it in response to the lack he diagnoses of 'any universally accepted general theory by which landscape and emotions may be connected.' We do not have, he argues, 'the same understanding of those emotional reactions which arise from our experience of our inanimate environment as we have of grief, anger, joy, etc. resulting from our relations with other people.'[10] Drawing on Dewey's aesthetics and ethological studies, Appleton attempts to remedy this with a 'habitat' and 'prospect-refuge' theory, which explains the aesthetic appeal of different types of landscape in terms ultimately of our appreciation of their strategic role in human survival:

> Habitat theory postulates that aesthetic pleasure in land-scape derives from the observer experiencing an environment favourable to the satisfaction of his biological needs. Prospect-refuge theory postulates that because the ability to see without being seen is an intermediate step in the satisfaction of many of those needs, the capacity of an environment to ensure the achievement of *this* becomes a more immediate source of aesthetic attraction.[11]

We respond to landscape (as also, it is claimed, to its representation in painting) intuitively on the basis of its ability to offer us both 'prospects' – commanding vantage points – and 'refuges' – places of concealment from which we may command the view without being viewable ourselves. Open landscapes attract because they offer a clear vista, secluded areas (woods, caves, sombre or shadowed reaches, etc.), because of what they promise in the way of possible retreats and look-out posts. An instinctual, 'animal' structure of responses is thus said to underlie aesthetic experience even when the instincts themselves are no longer essential to survival. What we like and dislike about 'nature' is in the end an effect of our assessment of its potential as habitat.

But how far does this inform us about a distinctively aesthetic as opposed to more instrumental reaction to landscape? Anyone who goes in for 'wild' camping will appreciate the truth in the argument that 'habitats' (in this case, tent-sites) are selected with a view to their combined prospect-refuge potential, and are found variously attractive in the light of it. But the landscape we choose simply to gaze upon as an object of aesthetic pleasure is often very different from that we would choose to inhabit, and it is the abstraction from consideration of how it might serve any other needs that seems more relevant to the pleasure we take in it than any vestigial and unconscious role these needs might play in determining our admiration for it. In many cases, moreover, most noticeably in the frisson felt for the sublime, it is the defiance of rather than the obedience to, these considerations that appears to be of the essence of the aesthetic appeal.

There is, in any case, the more general problem that such an account cannot do justice either to the complexity and shifting character of what is found attractive in the *representation* of landscape, or to the impact of this cultural representation on the preferences experienced for *actual* landscape. If we explain, for example, the aesthetic appreciation of landscape art in terms of a prospect-refuge 'aesthetic' experience of actual landscape, we shall overlook the extent to which the representation of landscape has been a vehicle of political ideologies, and cannot be adequately accounted for in abstraction from its social semiotics; but in the same process, we shall also overlook the extent to which the experience of actual landscape has been mediated historically by its artistic depiction. One relevant instance here would be the way in which a distinction between different types of landscape, and the taste in them, served in the 'civic humanist' aesthetic of the eighteenth century to map – and hence politically legitimate – a supposed difference between social strata. A distinction between the 'panoramic', ideal landscape and representations of occluded, enclosed landscapes without much depth of field, figured a difference between a refined capacity for thinking in general terms and a vulgar (and supposedly also female) incapacity to do so, with the taste in the former being associated with the powers of abstraction essential to the exercise of political authority.[12] In such a case, a habitat theory approach can offer no persuasive explanation of the advocacy of the 'prospect' over the 'refuge' landscape, and will remain blind to the political functions it is serving. Some of the issues raised here will be more fully explored at a later stage, but suffice it to note here that the relationship between the aesthetic experience of landscape and its cultural representation is not one-way but mutually determining; and that the political meanings embedded in the latter are both reflective of the actual inscription of social relations within the environment and refracted back into the aesthetic responses to it. Whatever insights are shed by 'habitat' theory on the fundamental motivations for discriminating between different types of landscape, it cannot accommodate the historical complexity of this dialectic.

Aesthetic theories that emerge in response to a particular fashion in nature may also be too little conscious of this historical complexity. Both Burke and Kant, for example, offer universalist explanations of the appreciation of the sublime in nature (Burke in terms of a common physiology of sensations, Kant in terms of the properties and functions of the human mind);[13] but this focus on the enabling conditions in human nature necessarily abstracts from the political dimensions of the sublime aesthetic, and from the particular social conditions responsible for its emergence. Neither Kant nor Burke appreciates the extent to which the aesthetic of the sublime must be related to the revolutionizing ferments within human society at the time, or the ways in which it is functioning as a register of the social transformations of the period and the conflictual responses to them. Yet the celebration of the sublime in nature cannot be understood in isolation from the bourgeois challenge to the aristocratic order, and the latter's support for an Arcadian aesthetic; nor from the way in which the 'sublime' becomes a problematic and contested image of its political struggles, where it figures the individual striving, energy and self-mastery necessary to their success, but only at the cost of intimating the more dangerously 'sublime' potential of its emphasis on individual autonomy. Thus, it has been suggested that the sublime 'functions as an aesthetic means through which bourgeois thought established itself as the locus of individual effort and virtue in face of the charges of "luxury" brought against it by traditional writers'; but that this project is also subject to the political hijacking of the 'radical sublime' of the more subversive representations of the Revolution.[14] Moreover, even if we abstract from these political inflections and focus simply on this aesthetic as a landscape preference, we may argue that neither Kant nor Burke shows much awareness of the need to link the fascination with the sublime to scientific Enlightenment, the growth of industry and the increasing domestication of nature. Even less do they consider the extent to which their theorization of the aesthetic of the sublime may be reliant on attitudes to nature engendered by those developments.

Yet the interest in the sublime and the Romantic movement into which it subsequently feeds, clearly do not come out of nowhere, but must be viewed as complex reactions to the Promethean achievements of the day in knowing and subduing a 'chaotic' nature. It is only, we may say, a culture that has commenced, in some sense, to experience its alienation from nature as the negative consequence of its industrial achievement that will be inclined to 'return' to the wilderness or to aestheticize its terrors as a form of foreboding against further encroachment on its territory. We may therefore argue in a general way that the cultivation of the sublime is the expression of anxiety, but also the aesthetic 'luxury', of a culture that has begun to experience its power over nature as a form of severance from it, while Romanticism only finds expression against the background of a certain mastery of its forces and a consequent concern for the alienation it entails. The romanticization of nature in its sublimer reaches is in this sense a manifestation of those same human powers over nature whose destructive effects it laments; or, as Neil Smith has rather bluntly put it, 'one does not pet a rattlesnake until it has been defanged.'[15] Where the nature at your doorstep is not a pastoral green, but rude, rugged and tempestuous, and you are still in the midst of the 'struggle against' its encroachment on *your* space, it is the aesthetic of the cultivated landscape that tends to prevail – as was the case in the North American preference well into the nineteenth century for a Concordian rather than a sublime aesthetic.[16] It is only, by contrast, where there is rather less wilderness left 'unfanged' that a landscape designer could promote the virtues of the 'sublime' garden replete with gibbets, crosses, poisonous weeds and 'scenes of terror' as did Sir William Chambers, the designer of Kew Gardens.[17]

The vogue for the sublime thus has its specific conditions of possibility that are overlooked by Burke and Kant even as they speak to these conditions in their own analyses of it. For we may note here that they both offer accounts of it that relate the particularity of the experience to an element of human transcendence. In Burke's empirical account, the frisson of confronting nature in its most 'delightfully horrible' aspects depends very much on our capacity to observe it without quailing, in other words to place ourselves at the brink of danger while nonetheless preserving a certain distance from it. As he puts it:

> When danger or pain presses too nearly, they are incapable of giving any delight, and are simply terrible; but at a certain distance, and with certain modifications, they may be, and they are, delightful, as we every day experience.[18]

Such 'modifications' and the 'distancing' required to convert terror into a form of delight are clearly deemed exclusive to humanity. The experience of the sublime is not pure 'animal' fear, but subtly differentiated from it in virtue of our ability to feel secure in the midst of danger. Burke does not question the source of this capacity, but his whole account clearly presupposes that, unlike other animals, we are in a position to court, rather than simply to take flight from, the terrors of nature.

Kant, by contrast, is very explicit about the reliance of the aesthetic of the sublime on our transcendence over nature, but roots it, not in external mastery, but in the internal power of human reason. Nature, he tells us, is sublime 'in such of its phenomena as in their intuition convey the idea of infinity.'[19] But since this idea is conveyed in such a way that it recalls us to the impossibility of imagining this magnitude in nature (we cannot think what it would be to experience sensorily what we can conceptualize only mathematically), the aesthetic experience which it provokes turns on an appreciation of the sublimity of the mind rather than of nature itself:

Where the size of a natural object is such that the imagination spends its whole faculty of comprehension upon
it in vain, it must carry our concept of nature to a
supersensible substrate (underlying both nature and our
faculty of thought) which is great beyond every standard
of sense. Thus, instead of the object, it is rather the cast
of mind in appreciating it that we have to estimate as
sublime.[20]

The sublime is thus an oxymoronic feeling combining dis-
pleasure in the inadequacy of our imagination to encompass the greatness of nature with pleasure at the evidence
it provides of the excess of our powers of rational understanding over anything offered to sensory experience. The
sublime is appalling because we cannot accommodate the
immensity with which it confronts us, and wonderful
because this failure itself indicates the superior power
of human reason to anything encountered in the natural
world.

Bold, overhanging, and, as it were, threatening rocks,
thunderclouds piled up the vault of heaven, borne along
with flashes and peals, volcanoes in all their violence of
destruction, hurricanes leaving desolation in their track,
the boundless ocean rising with rebellious force, the high
waterfall of some mighty river, and the like, make our
power of resistance of trifling moment in comparison
with their might. But, provided our own position is secure,
their aspect is all the more attractive for its fearfulness;
and we can readily call these objects sublime, because
they raise the forces of the soul above the height of vulgar
commonplace, and discover within us power of resistance
of quite another kind, which gives us courage to be able
to measure ourselves against the seeming omnipotence of
nature.[21]

In similar fashion, the infinite space of the heavens may
(as Pascal claimed) affright us, but for Kant the fear itself
invites us to consider the littleness or insignificance of

nature by comparison with an imagination that advances outwards in proportionately ever greater units as it encompasses the indefiniteness of the cosmos.[22] In the self-same moment, moreover, nature's immensity challenges us to forgo our own pettiness in favour of those highest principles over which it can exercise no 'rude dominion'. In inviting us to regard as nothing all those things over which it does hold this crude sway (wordly goods, health and life), it at the same time reveals to us all those transcendent qualities in ourselves that make it inappropriate to 'bow down before it'.[23] Nature, then, precisely in its most fearsome aspects, reveals our human dominion over it. As noumenal, rational and moral selves, we are not of this world; yet it is only in virtue of the aesthetic hold of the phenomenal world upon the imagination that we grasp this otherness in ourselves.

In Burke's theory, and even more explicitly in Kant's, then, the explanation of our awe of nature draws on the idea of an inherent human mastery or transcendence of it. Yet this very idea, we may argue, must be viewed as the cultural product of an age that, relative to earlier epochs, had de-deified nature and overcome a more directly 'animal' fear of its environment. Kant comes close to acknowledging this in his rejection of fear of nature as ignoble superstition, but he still fails to consider how far this freedom is the concrete social effect of Enlightenment as opposed to something achieved through an individual work of mastery upon the self.

One may also argue that the Kantian account of the sublime as that which reveals our human autonomy paved the way for the focus on art at the cost of nature in the aesthetic theory of the high bourgeois period. Though Kant himself remained committed to the eighteenth century view of the superiority of natural over artificial beauty, he was, suggests Adorno, one of the last philosophers to retain suspicions of artefactuality and the 'fallibility of making'; and in the subsequent idealist aesthetics inspired by his emphasis on human freedom and dignity art comes to be valued precisely as the work of the autonomous individual:

> Natural beauty vanished from aesthetics thanks to the expanding supremacy of the concept of human freedom and dignity inaugurated by Kant but fully realised in Schiller and Hegel, who transplanted these ethical concepts into aesthetics, with the result that in art, like everywhere else, nothing deserved respect unless it owed its existence to the autonomous subject. (. . .) If one were to start appellate proceedings on behalf of natural beauty, the latter would be acquitted, whereas dignity would be convicted as the real culprit for its prideful elevation of the animal 'man' above the animal realm.[24]

In Hegel's aesthetic theory, for example, nature is regarded as deficient and 'prosaic' relative to art precisely in virtue of its immanence or lack of affirmative purpose: its failure to produce beauty for the sake of a beautiful appearance. But it is this very 'deficiency', its 'meaningful silence' or lack of conceptual definition which, so Adorno argues, is the essence of its beauty.[25] Moreover, there is a deep paradox in the attempt to sever art from nature, and to assert or realize its autonomy, since this represents a striving within art to attain the immanence and non-conceptual language of nature itself. Thus the more art distances itself from nature and the imitation of nature, the more it can be viewed as attempting to approximate to the spontaneous, self-generating and non-intentional aesthetic mode of being of nature itself.[26]

Yet there is also a paradox – though perhaps a necessary and irresoluble one – in Adorno's own position given that he suggests both that the essence of the beauty of nature is occluded or denied in the idealist aesthetics of the bourgeois order, and that an appreciation of nature *as* beautiful comes only in the wake and as a consequence of its human mastery:

> ... There is no room for natural beauty in periods when nature has an overpowering presence for man, as seems to be the case with peasant populations, which are known to be insensitive to the aesthetic qualities of natural scenery because to them nature is merely an immediate object to be acted upon. The allegedly ahistorical beauty of nature does have a historical core, and it is this core which both legitimates and detracts from natural beauty.[27]

The suggestion here would seem to be that insofar as nature is beautiful, or comes to be aesthetically valued, it is only in a culture whose dominion over nature is pre-emptive of a 'true' or 'proper' appreciation of that beauty. We might add that there is also an element of paradox in Adorno's confidence about the 'insensitivity' of peasant populations; for his own argument might appear to imply the difficulty of finally pronouncing on this. At any rate, it is surely important to consider whose 'word' we are going by in these matters, and whether it can be trusted.

Whose Tastes in Nature?

This brings us to a further set of questions raised by Kant's account and of relevance to any commentary on the aesthetic of nature. For to put it in Hardy's terms, had we not better recognize that when the philosopher or writer or critic is speaking of the tastes of 'human' souls, what they often implicitly have in mind as a standard for their discussion is the tastes of 'the more thinking part of mankind' or of the 'cultivated' soul? So that even where the aesthetic commentary is not explicitly elitist, as it is in all those cases where the 'unthinking men' are simply ruled

out as possible subjects of aesthetic experience at all, there
is an uneasy hypothetical ascription at work in the text: we
are talking here at best of what the collectivity of human
souls would feel had they been given the leisure and
education essential to a lofty and refined taste. Now, as
far as Kant himself is concerned, it would be a little unfair
to accuse him of any conscious elitism. His argument for
the universality of human aesthetic responses to nature
may be open to the objection – particularly in regard
to his account of the sublime – that it is informed by
culturally specific conditions of which it is unaware. And
in a more fundamental sense, we may argue that it is compromised by a culture bound assumption of the concept
of nature. But the intentions of his theory are certainly
democratic, and this is particularly true of his treatment
of every individual judgement of taste (eg. regarding what
is beautiful or sublime in nature) as equal in normative
force. Each judger in these matters is to be regarded, and
to regard himself or herself, as exemplary of humanity
at large. Moreover, Kant is ready to admit in the case
of the appreciation for the sublime, that, although the
foundations for this are laid in human nature, and we
may expect of everyone the moral feeling requisite to the
experience, nonetheless a measure of culture may be an
essential precondition of this aesthetic response.[28] Even if
it is marked by a certain 'privileging' of the preferences
of the more thinking part of mankind, Kant's argument
may be said to be more alert than many to the ways
in which differences of culture or education determine
aesthetic responses to nature.

Rather than pursue the issue further, therefore, in respect
of Kant's philosophy, let us simply recognize here the need
further to complicate any general discourse about the aesthetic of nature by allowing not only that tastes in nature
are conditioned by the general ideas and fashions of their
period, but also that the ideas and fashions are themselves

for the most part dictated by a privileged minority within the culture. In other words, when we speak of 'fashions' in nature, of shifts in taste in landscape design, of movements or moments in its pictorial or literary representation, we are almost always speaking of concepts and experiences whose influence within the culture is indissolubly linked to the socio-economic power of the trend-setters themselves. We need, in short, to insert a class dimension into any account of ourselves as nature lovers, since relations of class are not only inscribed physically within the landscape itself, but have also had major impact on the production and consumption of its cultural representation. For this reason, as it has been said, landscape is an ideological concept:

> It represents a way in which certain people have signified themselves and their world through their imagined relationship with nature and through which they have underlined and communicated their own social role and that of others with respect to external nature.[29]

The portrayal of landscape can therefore never be received as an index of majority feelings, nor even as evidence of how nature actually appeared to those who produced and consumed this art. Certainly, it speaks to us of the preferences of those in a position to be the arbiters of taste within their culture, but, since these tastes have been so coloured by considerations of social role and self-esteem, the depiction has often more to tell us about a desired environment than about the feelings evoked by the encounter with the reality itself. Or, at any rate, if it does tell us about the latter, it does so only in the form of allowing a sense of what needed to be occluded or obscured from its imaging. Cultural representations are in this sense 'realist' testimony to a certain fantasy or projection of nature, but not necessarily documents of the kind of affection that the ecologists would recall us to. Just as a landscape painting is never simply painting the landscape, nor country writing ever simply description, so they can never be approached as reflecting a universal human feeling for nature or a common experience of it.

As John Barrell has shown in his study of the painting of Gainsborough, Morland and Constable, this element of ideological distortion affects the realism of even the more 'realist' renderings of landscape. In the work of these painters, as Barrell suggests, the indolent, bucolic shepherd, living in the responsive, servile nature of Pope's *Eclogues*, is exchanged for the working ploughmen of England in a representation that is both more plausible and more in tune with the prevailing concern and approval for human industry. In this sense, landscape painting from the mid-eighteenth century (reflecting the earlier shift to the Georgic mode in poetry) offers an altogether more actualized image of rural life. Yet, as Barrell convincingly argues, this more 'realist' portrayal remains marked by a profound tension. The real truth of rural existence is still too uncomfortable to be candidly displayed, and this results in a 'continual struggle at once to reveal more and more of the actuality of the life of the poor, and to find more effective ways of concealing that actuality.' The true harshness of rural existence – the reality of the 'dark side' of the landscape – could, as it were, be only half-imaged:

> As the figures become less and less the shepherds of French or Italian Pastoral, they become more and more ragged, but remain inexplicably cheerful. The effort is always to claim that the rural poor are as contented, the rural society as harmonious, as it is possible to claim them to be, in the face of the threatening awareness that all was not as well as it must have been in Arcadia. This jolly imagery of Merry England, which replaced the frankly

artificial imagery of classical Pastoral, was in turn replaced
when it had to be by an image of a cheerful, sober,
domestic peasantry, more industrious than before; this
gave way in turn to a picturesque image of the poor,
whereby their raggedness became of aesthetic interest,
and they become the objects of our pity; and when that
image would serve no longer, it was in turn replaced
by a romantic image of harmony with nature whereby
the labourers were merged as far as possible with their
surroundings too far away from us for the questions about
how contented or how ragged they were to arise.[30]

Barrell admits that the development was not quite as neat
and consecutive as this suggests, but the essential point is
surely valid: even as the depiction of landscape gains in
'realism' by comparison with an earlier pastoral tradition,
it perpetuates something of the same illusion, albeit by
subtler means, regarding the essential order and harmony
of man with nature. Or to put it more bluntly, the patrons
and consumers of this art are still to be spared any too
direct and unequivocal confrontation with the more pain-
fully divisive dimensions of their social pre-eminence and
its associated forms of control over 'nature'.

Democratizing the Nature Aesthetic

Much representation of landscape must for these reasons
be viewed as a partial documentation of 'human' aesthetic
responses to 'nature' , and neither the more blatantly delu-
sory neo-classical pastoral nor the more plausible imagings
of landscape that supplant it can be read as evidence
of the feelings of those whose relations to nature they
depict. The playful shepherd, the picturesque peasant,
the merry haymakers or the more obviously toiling, yet
basically contented ploughmen: none of these penned or
painted their own harmony with nature, or delight in its

charms; nor was it they who were destined to enjoy these representations of their responses to their environment.

Indeed, we can argue that there is a persistent tendency to *deny* any popular aesthetic of landscape in the presentation of the peasant or labourer as so closely in harmony with it that they become a party to it, and are thus – like the rest of nature – incapable of any evaluative relationship to it at all. The real feelings of the rural workers are refused or repressed through an idealization of their condition as one that is freed from alienation. Being so immanently part of their surroundings, they are spared the existential angst of cognitive separation from them, and in this guise, not infrequently, become the object of philosophic or poetic esteem and envy.

Heidegger's presentation of a mute and earthy peasantry, as embodying the 'pre-understanding' that is lost to technological wisdom, has proved inspirational as a rallying call to the establishment of 'authentic' relations with nature, but it functions only by denying to this 'peasantry' a Heideggerian consciousness of its own participation in Being. Wordsworth's celebration of rural wisdom may show more empathy for the actual travails of the 'peasant', yet in poems such as *Michael, Resolution and Independence, Old Man Travelling* or *Animal Tranquillity and Decay*, the argument turns on the contrast between the relative alienation of the poet-narrator and the more immanent 'being' of the workers.

The simple labourer in *Animal Tranquillity and Decay* is so unintrusive upon nature that birds of the hedge-row 'regard him not' and the young behold 'With envy, what the old man hardly feels'.[31] In *Resolution and Independence*, the silence or inarticulacy of the leech gatherer (whose voice 'was like a stream/ Scarce heard: nor word from word could I divide') is presented in idealized contrast to the voluble angst of the poet: 'I could have laughed myself to scorn to find/ In that decrepit Man so firm a mind.'[32]

Yet the fact remains, of course, that only the poet can tell us of his own comparative failure of gravity or philosophic insight.[33] However well-intentioned and sympathetic the writer or painter, there is an element of needed alienation, even a privileging of it, in the very attempt to give cultural expression to this form of intellectual self-deprecation. For this is essentially an ascription of feeling, knowledge or 'being' to those who are defined as incapable of giving voice to it themselves; or were they to prove capable of it, they would no longer be viewed as enjoying their envied harmony or closeness to their natural environment. (There is a curious contemporary ecological inversion of this tension, we might note, in Robert Goodin's objection that those who 'slavishly' adhere to green personal life-style recommendations 'will be living their lives so much in harmony with natural processes as to be wholly subsumed within them.'[34] Is this, we may wonder, because it is inappropriate for those who 'think' about nature to be 'subsumed' within it?)

Of course, there have been poets and painters who 'belonged' to the land, but their very exceptionality confirms the point. Had all country workers offered us poetry comparable to that of John Clare, we may be sure that poetry written about them would itself have been very different. As it is, 'their' closeness to nature can only be affirmed through 'our' distance; their philosophy only in 'our' philosophy; their truth only in the profundity of 'our' appreciation of it. (And this problem continues to afflict, of course, the 'intellectual' discourse which draws attention to it).[35]

The intellectual, then, who speaks to a 'peasant aesthetic' has obviously broken with a patrician humanism, and with any explicitly registered appeal to the 'man of culture' as the touchstone of good taste in nature. Yet the romanticization of rural immanence remains caught nonetheless in the paradox of its own implicit aesthetic transcendence. This paradox, one may argue, continues to vex contemporary ecological pronouncements about the ways 'we' value nature (or fail to do so), about 'our' alienation from nature, and about the attitudes 'we'should adopt in order to heal the rift. For here, too, the temptation is to speak on behalf of all from a position of understanding and sensibility to nature that is itself, at least in part, the product of the theorist's specific positioning within society.

In this connection, we may note a further paradox of much writing on the environment: that of the feared democratization of the nature aesthetic. This is most frequently voiced in the form of an anxiety lest the 'solitary's' appreciation of nature prove in the end to be more of a common property than is compatible with its continued enjoyment.

This anxiety comes fully into play only at the point where urbanization undermines the basis for treating the rural worker as emblematic of a popular 'sense' of nature or communion with it. Clearly the steady removal of the mass of the people to the town as steadily removed the ground for any romanticization of their special affinity with rusticity, and there is a consequent shift of focus in the perception of their relations to nature. What begins to find expression is a fear lest these new found urbanites (and sub-urbanites) come to resort *en masse* to the forms of solace in nature that had hitherto been deemed appealing only to the more poetic soul or thinking man. Thus, in the frequently expressed regrets for the 'tourist' invasion of nature, we may discern a tacit recognition that the taste for even its more recondite attractions is not, after all, the exclusive preserve of the discriminating 'soul'. Wordsworth may here again serve as an illustration. For alongside his appreciation of the 'old man's' depth of understanding (and perhaps it is no accident that it tends to be a dying order that has most to teach the poet), he registers clear anxieties about the encroachment of 'artisans and labourers, and the humbler classes' upon his cherished Lakes. Such persons, he recommends, should 'make little excursions with their wives and children among the neighbouring fields', rather than take the train to the Lakes themselves.[36]

From the point of view of our concern here with what can be claimed to be universal in the appeal of nature, what is interesting about these anxieties (and they are by no means exclusive to Wordsworth, but have been voiced continuously since his day) is the sense they betray that the nature so dear to the poetic spirit could also entrance the 'simple' or 'humble' masses.

Yet so far from being celebrated as a progress in human refinement, this provokes a certain alarm. There is, in this sense, a profound tension between the professed humanism of the discourse on 'our' love of nature, and the response to the evidence of its universal applicability. A cultivated taste that is generally recommended and applauded as the mark of the 'good' soul is regretted if it shows itself too actively among the masses at large. The aesthetic preference of the choicer spirit is fine, it would seem, when presented abstractly as a universal desideratum, but becomes a more problematic intrusion on the pleasures of the choicer spirit if concretized in actual popular desire. This tension needs to be appreciated wherever eco-politics draws on the support of the aesthetic of nature voiced by the 'more thinking part of mankind' in support of conservation. For the problem here, as Martin Ryle has noted, in challenging Jonathan Bate's presentation of Wordsworth as an uncomplicated ally of environmental politics, is that:

> Cultural appropriations of landscape can inflect, unhelp-fully, the difficult quest for a democratic ecological language. Alongside the hope that the poet might speak to and for everyone, we find in Wordsworth an insistent valorization of a more educated and special sensibility. The poet is not just 'a man speaking to men', and such a formulation is not problematic only for the gender of

its 'universal subject', for the same text (the 'Preface' to the *Lyrical Ballads*) also says much about what makes the poet different. We can agree that poets are different, in their expressive talents, while sensing that a 'Nature' constructed as the guardian and touchstone of aesthetic distinction makes a problematic reference point for ecological and environmental politics.[37]

More generally, we may argue that environmentalism needs to be aware of the double-edged quality of an eco-lect that both invokes a universal human aesthetic need for nature, and appeals to that 'rarer' sensibility which would preserve it from the negative effects of its mass enjoyment. Such appeals, of course, do not necessarily take so explicit a form. They may merely be implicit in the objections that are made to the 'opening up' of nature to a tourist influx. They may also, even more tacitly, be at work in the tendency to suppose a contrast between the 'artificial' and 'constructed' quality of the popular taste in nature, and the more 'natural' and spontaneous responses of the 'genuine' nature lover. But as we have seen, even the more refined spirits have changed their taste in nature fairly regularly, and to that extent may be said to have been culturally 'constructed' in their desires. Has there ever been a community, we may reasonably ask, whose reactions to nature have simply been 'natural'?

This is not to deny the extent to which nature in our own times has been constructed, and indeed spoilt, through the accommodation to a mass interest in easy access to 'human' amenities. Beauty spots have, one might concede, been made both less beautiful and more attractive to many of their visitors because of the toilets, cafeterias, signed trails, eco-centres, museums and tourist shops with which they have been 'enhanced'. Above all, it is undeniable that the general preference for travelling through 'nature' by car, rather than going on foot (or by bike) has both profoundly altered the non-urban landscape and shaped the appreciation of it. As Alexander Wilson has pointed out, the creation of 'scenic' routes is itself responsible for the promotion of a certain nature aesthetic – one that is essentially visual and has ruled out taste, touch and smell; for which landscape becomes an event in 'automotive space', and is comparable in its one-dimensionality to the view of it had in aerial photography. The designers of the great national parkways of North America have quite literally instructed their users in the 'beauties' of nature, he argues, by promoting some landscapes at the expense of others, by removing whatever bits of it were deemed unsightly, and by restricting all activities incompatible with the parkway aesthetic. The overriding strategy:

> is the production of nature itself. All of the road's design features organize our experience of nature. The result is that nature appears to produce itself with no apparent relation to the cultures that inhabit it or use it. Magnificent vistas now happily present themselves to us without the clutter of human work and settlement. The seasons begin to be synchronized with the tourist calendar: June is Rhododendron Time, autumn is Fall Foliage Time, winter is Wonderland.[38]

In this accommodation to a 'motorist's' aesthetic, and in many other instances, 'nature' has indisputably been tailored to modern needs, and a mass conception of its attractions shaped accordingly. It would be pointless to deny either these manipulations of nature in the process, or the offence they have caused to more minority tastes. My point here is only that the conundrum which this presents to the development of a democratic eco-politics must be fairly and squarely faced. An argument that appeals to the idea of a common structure of feeling and aesthetic dependency on nature cannot rationally employ a vocabulary that relies on a distinction between an 'inauthentic' (and destructive) 'popular' taste in nature and the more 'genuine' feelings for nature of the 'choicer spirit'. Even less can it lend itself to a position which implies that a difference in taste can justify an unequal distribution of the benefits of nature.

The beauties of the landscape, and the forms of solace it affords, cannot, of course, be preserved except by restricting human access to them, and we must recognize the extent to which human destruction of the environment has made it absolutely scarce as a source of gratification. But it is important that the forms of abstemiousness in its enjoyment that this imposes are equally distributed. The fact that the attractions of nature are destroyed by the demand for them is no reason for implying that it is only some – whose tastes are not those of the vulgar tourist, but more properly appreciative of its charm – who should be allowed to enjoy them. If we would develop a more democratic ecological language, then it is important to avoid a discourse on the aesthetic of nature which suggests that it is always some 'less thinking' part of humanity that is responsible for its popularity. It is a displacement of the problem of the scarcity of nature to attribute the blame for the destruction of its charms to the 'mass' demand for them; and there can be no egalitarian solution to this problem which pretends that, in virtue of their superior aesthetic endowment, some have more rights to enjoyment than others.

On Behalf of a Shared Aesthetic: Some Concluding Qualifications

Much of the foregoing discussion has been intended to disturb a too complacently humanist approach to the aesthetic of nature, and to highlight those factors that render claims about 'humanity's responses extremely problematic. However, I would be sympathetic to anyone suggesting that I may have bent the stick too far in the direction of a relativist account and not given due regard to the evidence or the arguments that might be adduced in defence of a more universalist position on the issue. In conclusion, then, let me simply note some of the factors that do need to be weighed in the balance here.

In the first place, though it may be presumptuous to speak of 'evidence' in any conclusive sense, it is indeed difficult not to feel that there has been a continuous and very extensively shared appreciation of natural phenomena – of flora and fauna, rivers and lakes, glades and forests, the sounds of bird-song, the colours and mutations of sea and sky, the heavens at night. Myth and epic poetry, religious imagery and the forms of public art all give us reason to suppose that nature, in at least certain of its aspects, has been a pervasive and perduring source of inspiration and delight, and that this speaks to some relatively direct and unmediated responses to the environment. Nor does it seem theoretically plausible to suppose otherwise. Cultural forces may mould preferences in landscape, and to some extent fashion even our tastes in roses or sunsets, but its mediations would not be possible were it not for the existence of certain phenomenological responses upon which they go to work and by which they are themselves informed and circumscribed. Moreover, the very extent to which art has been inspired by nature, and its standards, achievements and purposes considered in the light of the model provided by nature, is indicative of the importance of the latter as a primary or fundamental site of aesthetic judgement. Whether art is deemed inferior or superior to nature; whether it is applauded for imitating nature or for its abstraction from it; for its creative revelation of nature or autonomous transcendence of it: all such movements in art and shifts in the appraisal of its function in relation to nature speak to the significant role of the latter in providing the criteria of aesthetic judgement.

To this we might add that the very fact that tastes in landscape have changed is indicative of some underlying communality in human responses given the extent to which these changes – most notably the shift from the concordian to the sublime aesthetic – have come in reaction to the human encroachment upon nature and reflect a concern with what is lost to us in the very process of progressive dominion over it. That the new Vale of Tempe, as Hardy puts it, may be a gaunt waste in Thule; that it is now the parts which pre-industrial society reviled as 'nature's pudenda', that are now acclaimed as the most beautiful: this does not necessarily suggest, I think, that our affective responses to nature are at a profound level different from those of pre-industrial culture. What it suggests, rather, is the extent to which the history of the aesthetic of nature has to be thought in relation to the history of human domination: what we have come to prefer now is itself the effect of human transformations of the landscape and the particular forms of loss and destruction involved in these. But if that is the case, it also in a sense unites us across time with those in the past who, it may be said, did not esteem what we do now precisely because they had yet to experience its demise. What they valued less because of its abundance we now value more because of its progressive erosion. In this sense, one might claim that the very shifts of the aesthetic taste in nature speak to something more universal in the patterning of our responses to it.

Notes

1 Thomas Hardy, *The Return of the Native* (Macmillan, London, 1965), pp. 12–13.
2 Holmes Rolston 111, 'Value in Nature and the Nature of Value' in *Philosophy and the Natural Environment*, ed. Robin Attfield and Andrew Belsey (Cambridge University Press, Cambridge, 1994). Cf. *Philosophy Gone Wild* (Prometheus Books, Buffalo, 1989).

3 Adorno, *Aesthetic Theory* (Routledge, Kegan Paul, London, 1984), p. 97.

4 I am not supposing here that this claim is entirely uncontroversial, or that the legitimacy of imputing unrecognized or 'objective' needs to persons is not very much at issue in the disputes between relativist and universalist theories of need and welfare. For a sense of these debates, see Len Doyal and Ian Gough, *A Theory of Human Need* (Macmillan, London, 1991), my comment on that work in *New Left Review* 197 (January–February 1993), pp. 113–28, and Doyal's response, *New Left Review* 200 (July–August 1993); Martha Nussbaum, 'Human Functioning and Social Justice: in Defence of Aristotelian Essentialism', *Political Theory* 20, 2 (May 1992); Glenn Drover and Patrick Kerans (eds), *New Approaches to Welfare Theory* (Edward Elgar, Aldershot and Vermont, 1993). My point here is only that these debates cannot have the same purchase in respect of aesthetic response, given its necessarily subjectively experienced character.

5 Immanuel Kant, *The Critique of Judgement*, trans. J. C. Meredith (Clarendon Press, Oxford, 1952) Book I, esp. sects. 6–8, pp. 50–7. For an exposition and very illuminating discussion of the argument of *The Critique of Judgement*, see Jay Bernstein, *The Fate of Art* (Polity, Oxford, 1992); cf. Terry Eagleton, *The Ideology of the Aesthetic* (Blackwell, Oxford, 1990), pp. 70–101.

6 All recorded in Keith Thomas, *Man and the Natural World* (Allen Lane, London, 1983), see pp. 106, 78, 62, 126.

7 Donna Haraway, *Primate Visions* (Routledge, London, 1989), pp. 226–40.

8 Thomas, *Man and the Natural World*, p. 35,

9 For a useful, brief discussion of the use of the 'sublime' as a rhetorical term, and of the development of its application to landscape in Burke and Kant's precursors (notably in the writing of John Dennis, Addison and John Baillie), see James Boulton's introduction to Edmund Burke, *A Philosophical Enquiry into the Origins of our Ideas of the Sublime and the Beautiful* (Routledge, Kegan Paul, London, 1958), pp. xliv–lxxii, and cf. the discussion of Kant, pp. cxxv–cxxvii. For an insightful account of Burke and Kant's argument and the literary sublime, see Thomas Weiskel, *The Romantic Sublime* (Baltimore and London, 1976).

10 Jay Appleton, *The Experience of Landscape* (John Wiley, London, 1975), pp. 20–1.

11   Ibid., p. 73.

12   John Barrell, 'The Public Prospect and the Private View' in *Landscape, Natural Beauty and the Arts*, ed. Salim Kemal and Ivan Gaskell (Cambridge University Press, Cambridge, 1993), pp. 81–102.

13   Though Kant, we might note, is critical of Burke's sensationalism for treating aesthetic judgements as if they were a matter of personal, subjective feeling, since this, he argues, offers no justification for their claim to universality, *Critique of Judgement*, pp. 130–3, sects 277–9.

14   See Tom Furniss, 'Bourgeois Revolutionary in a Radical Crisis', in Peter Osborne (ed.), *Socialism and the Limits of Liberalism* (Verso, London, 1991), p. 33; cf. p. 39. Furniss here offers a very interesting exploration of the ideological impasse to which Burke's argument on the sublime is subject in consequence of this tension between its 'individualizing' and its 'democratizing' impulses.

15   Neil Smith, *Uneven Development* (Blackwell, Oxford, 1990), p. 13.

16   The Hudson River School in the early nineteenth century draws heavily on sublime imagery, but remains a minority taste opposed to the dominant Concordian sympathies. See Appleton, *Experience of Landscape*, p. 40f; cf. Annette Kolodny's discussion of Philip Freneau's poem, 'American Village' where the praise is for the soil which 'Now reft of trees, admits the cheerful light', and for a landscape from which wild animals have been eradicated, *The Lay of the Land* (University of North Carolina Press, Chapel Hill, 1975), p. 34; Leo Marx's emphasis on the 'garden' image of the American pastoral ideal, *The Machine in the Garden* (Oxford University Press, Oxford, 1964), pp. 36–44, 75–88.

17   See James Boulton's accounts, in his edition of Burke's *Enquiry*, pp. ciii–civ, of Chambers' *Dissertation on Oriental Gardening* (1722), and of Thomas Whateley's advocacy of 'sublimity' in his *Observations on Modern Gardening* (1770).

18   Burke, *Enquiry*, p. 40.

19   Kant, *Critique of Judgement*, p. 103, sect. 255.

20   Ibid., p. 104, sect. 256.

21   Ibid., pp. 110–11, sect. 261; for some consideration of the possible implications of these Kantian arguments for our own times, see Arnold Berleant, 'The Aesthetics of Art and Nature' in *Landscape, Natural Beauty and the Arts*, ed. Kemal and Gaskell, pp. 228–43.

22   Kant, *Critique of Judgement*, p. 111, sect. 262.

23 Ibid., p. 105, sect. 257.
24 Adorno, *Aesthetic Theory*, p. 92.
25 Ibid., pp. 109–13.
26 Ibid., pp. 113–15.
27 Ibid., p. 96.
28 Kant, *Critique of Judgement*, p. 116, sect. 265.
29 D. E. Cosgrove, *Social Formation and Symbolic Landscape* (Croom Helm, London, 1984), p. 15.
30 John Barrell, *The Dark Side of the Landscape* (Cambridge University Press, Cambridge, 1980), p. 16; cf. pp. 6–10.
31 Roger Sharrock (ed.), *Selected Poems of William Wordsworth* (Heinemann, London 1958), p. 42.
32 Ibid., p. 85.
33 As we have seen (chapters 3 and 4) these same tendencies are notable in the presentation of women as closer to nature.
34 Robert E. Goodin, *Green Political Theory* (Polity, Oxford, 1992), pp. 81–2.
35 Cf. John Barrell's recognition of the recurring reflexivity of the intellectual critique of class bias in the representation of nature, *The Dark Side of the Landscape*, p. 5.
36 Wordsworth, 'Letter on the projected Windermere railway' in *The Illustrated Wordsworth's Guide to the Lakes*, ed. Peter Bicknell (Webbs Bower, Exeter, 1984), p. 191.
37 Martin Ryle, review of Jonathan Bate, *Romantic Ecology: Wordsworth and the Environment* (Routledge, London, 1991), in *Radical Philosophy* 62 (Autumn 1992), p. 42.
38 Alexander Wilson, *The Culture of Nature* (Blackwell, Oxford, 1992), p. 37, and passim, ch. 1.

8

ECOLOGY, NATURE
AND RESPONSIBILITY

The discussions in this book have been shaped by two concerns: firstly, to acknowledge and give due weight to those arguments that invite us to be suspicious of the concept of 'nature' because of the numerous ideological roles it has been called upon to play; and secondly, to endorse the ecologists' concern for human destruction of nature and the validity of their claims regarding the calamitous consequences of failure to respect the limits and conditions it imposes. The aim has been to admit – and hold in productive tension – the wisdom both of those who insist on the 'culturality' or 'constructed' nature of 'nature', and of those who would insist on the independent existence and specific determinations of that which is referred to through the concept of 'nature'. For while it is true that much of what we refer to as 'natural' is a 'cultural construct' in the sense that it has acquired its form as a consequence of human activity, that activity does not 'construct' the powers and processes upon which it is dependent for its operation. And while it is also true that our discourses on nature are constitutive of a series of conceptions and representations through which our policies on the environment are necessarily mediated, it is not the discourse of 'global warming' or 'industrial pollution' that has created the conditions of which it speaks.

Few, perhaps, would wish in the end to dispute these points. But if I have dwelt in this book on the tension between 'nature' and nature, it is because of the ways in which the emphasis on inverted commas 'nature' tends to a denial of nature, and the ways in which the emphasis on nature tends to ignore the reasons for the inverted commas. As we have seen, there are many reasons to be sceptical of those discourses that see no reason for the inverted commas. Western philosophy, for example, has shown too little awareness of the extent to which its distinction between humanity and nature is reflecting an ethnocentric bias in favour of 'civilized' humanity; nor has it properly registered the historicity of its concepts of nature and naturality, which insofar as they have been thought in opposition to the human have themselves been revised in the light of changing perceptions of who belongs within that community and what constitutes the distinguishing attributes of human 'being'. Indisputably, too, the discourse of 'nature' has served mystifying and oppressive ends, whether in legitimating divisions of class, race and gender, in encouraging intolerance of sexual minorities, or in promoting fictitious conceptions of national and tribal identity that have been all too destructive in their actual effect.

Yet none of these points about the constructed nature of 'nature', its pseudo or ideological status, can be registered without at least implicitly invoking the extra-discursive reality of the nature that is distorted or misrepresented through these cultural appropriations of the term. Moreover, much of the critique of the violence that has been done through the concept of nature is directed at the policing functions it has performed in sustaining ecologically destructive social relations. The nature that the ecologists are concerned to conserve is also the nature that has been dominated and destroyed in the name of the 'naturality' of a certain order of human relations, needs, rights of ownership and forms of exploitation. A postmodernist argument that fails to acknowledge these points cannot, I have argued, consistently present itself as a friend of the ecological cause. But this also means that adherents of that cause should avoid forms of political discourse that tend to conflate the reality of nature with its ideological representation. Such conflations, I have argued, occur whenever eco-politics valorizes a past 'harmony' with nature or rural order in ways that abstract from the divisive social relations responsible for the production of that 'order'; whenever it draws on the traditional genderization of the nature–culture opposition; and whenever, in inviting us to appreciate our kinship with other animal species, it overlooks those ways in which we profoundly differ from them, and are by comparison under-determined either by biology or by existing environmental conditions. It is an implication of this argument that green politics needs always to consider its prescriptions about nature in the light of its frequently professed commitments to feminism, anti-racism, respect for sexual minorities and the promotion of democracy and social justice. For many of the gains that have been made in advancing these emancipatory causes have come out of the refusal to accept that some set of behaviours is more in conformity to 'nature' than others, and they have in some case depended quite directly on our acquired powers to intervene in biology and divert the course it might otherwise have taken.

Plural Values

Relatedly, green politics needs to recognize that it is appealing not to a single, but to a plurality of values, the mutual compatibility of which is by no means obvious and certainly needs to be displayed rather than merely assumed.

We may briefly consider in this connection the relations among three of the more important types of argument that have been offered in support of ecological preservation and conservation and that have been continuously referred to in the course of this work. In the first place, there is the aesthetic argument, whose primary appeal is to the beauty of nature and to the pleasures and solace afforded by an unspoilt environment. According to this strand of environmentalist argument, nature should be preserved for much the same reasons we would want to preserve a work of art: because of the delight and inspiration it provides. Closely allied to this in some respects, though sharply distinguished from it in others, is the argument from the 'intrinsic worth' of nature. Nature should be preserved not as a means to any human end, whether aesthetic or utilitarian, but because it is inherently valuable *as* nature, and in itself, because, it has been said, its value cannot be regarded as 'reducible to its value to God or humanity'.[1] Those defending this position may differ in respect of the parts of nature that may be said to have value in themselves, whether, for example, value is inherent in both animate and inanimate nature, whether it extends to non-life supporting parts of the cosmos or is confined to planet earth; but there is essential agreement that nature has value independently of human purposes or perceptions, that this has to do with its autonomy of those purposes, and that this provides the compelling reason why human beings should revere it and as far as possible leave it be.[2] Thirdly, there is the argument from utility, which emphasizes the importance of nature as a means to the end of human survival and flourishing. We have a duty to conserve the resources of nature (in other words to make use of them in sustainable ways) because they are essential to all human life both now and in the indefinite future. Here the moral emphasis falls less on our responsibilities to other species or to nature in itself, and more on the duties we have towards it in virtue of the obligations we have towards future human generations.

Green politics frequently appeals to all these reasons conjointly, though we may distinguish here between the more prominent role played by arguments from the aesthetic and intrinsic worth of nature in the case for *preservation* (for the maintenance of wilderness, wildlife and unspoilt countryside), and the more prominent role played by utilitarian argument in the case for *conservation* (for the maintenance of resources).[3] Arguments for the preservation of landscape, however, do also frequently appeal to more utilitarian considerations (when they draw attention to its importance in providing a 'scientific laboratory' for naturalist studies, to the use of the countryside as a means of recreation and retreat, to the potential pharmacological value of its flora, or to the role it plays in maintaining genetic diversity).[4] The main emphasis may be on the aesthetic attractions or independent value of nature, but a case made on these grounds is often supplemented by a more instrumental appeal to the practical use that is made of the non-urban environment, or to the potential dangers of disturbing eco-balance and distraining on bio-diversity through destruction of natural habitats. I myself have argued that policies aimed at preserving the beauties of nature may also help to promote its sustainable use as a resource, and vice-versa, and that what practically serves to enhance the aesthetic attractions of the environment may also advance the conservationist cause. But there can certainly be clashes of interests at this level. Energy conversion programmes, such as the use of wind-power, are not necessarily guaranteed to beautify the landscape, and may well involve the siting of machinery in some of nature's most rugged and unspoilt reaches.[5] To observe the 'hands off' approach to the environment recommended by some deep ecologists would inevitably be to restrict even the most eco-benign attempts to conserve resources by means of technological interventions in nature. So while it would seem plausible to suppose that conservationary policies would on the whole advance rather than obstruct preservationist objectives, one can still recognize the possibilities for practical conflicts of interest, and the extent to which these reflect more fundamental, if less explicitly acknowledged, differences of moral outlook. The ecology movement, when viewed as a whole, draws its force from a range of arguments whose ethical underpinnings are really quite divergent and difficult to reconcile.

We might note here the normative tension between the appeal to the aesthetic attractions of nature and the appeal to its intrinsic worth. It may perhaps seem odd to some to speak of a tension here, given the regularity with which deep ecological claims about the independent value of nature refer us to its beauties and illustrate their argument by reference to aesthetically valued properties. Not only are many of the items revered by deep ecologists those *we* regard as beautiful (sunsets, waterfalls, mountains, rivers, lakes, trees etc.), but it is not uncommonly suggested that the value of some natural feature, such as a sun-set or volcano, resides precisely in its beauty.[6] Still, there is a significant difference between the position which insists that these things are admirable 'in themselves' and hence valuable regardless of their observer, and the aestheticist approach which sees the joys of nature as residing in their delight for us. The environmentalist who wants to preserve a beauty spot is precisely not suggesting that it be preserved whether or not it is aesthetically valued by human beings, but appealing to the pleasure and solace that it affords to them. Preservationists of this stamp may well argue that by preserving beauty spots we also advance the cause of other species and help in the maintenance of as rich and diverse an eco-system as possible; but the essential appeal of the argument is 'anthropocentric' in the sense that nature is being valued for the value it has for us. An argument from the intrinsic worth of nature (including its supposed intrinsic beauty) is, strictly speaking, not of this order, since its logic would seem to require us to preserve the environment and its wildlife whatever value it happened to have for us (and even if, one may surmise, they struck us as ugly, monotonous and worthless). To be asked to preserve nature for its own sake is to be asked to maintain it regardless of what merit or interest it might have in our eyes, and whatever its ravages upon human health and well-being.

Or so it might seem. But it is here that we encounter tensions within the argument of deep ecology itself. For while, on the one hand, there is a tendency to dismiss as 'anthropocentric' any attempt to bring human values and interests to bear in judging the claims of nature to preservation, there is also a pervasive inclination to point to humanly admired qualities – its diversity, richness, autonomy and beauty, for example – as those that endow it with 'intrinsic' value. Yet why invoke the qualities of nature at all, let alone these positive ones, unless to invite appraisal of it on a scale of human values? If nature does genuinely have value independently of human estimation of it, then, strictly speaking, we cannot know what it is, nor, a fortiori, applaud or condemn it and should refrain from pronouncing on its qualities. Either, then, the argument to value nature 'for its own sake' is self-defeating since, in the absence of knowledge of those ways in which nature might be an end in itself, we have no conceptual means of obeying an injunction to respect it for those ends; or it is intended to register the fact that nature is (or should be) valued for other than instrumental purposes, and thus to draw attention to those properties in nature which, in the eyes of human beings, make it worth salvaging even if the salvage operation has to proceed at the cost of other projects they also value, and even (such is the perspective of an extreme eco-centrism) if it means sacrificing their own species' well-being or survival. When construed in this latter sense, however, the ascription of 'intrinsic' value remains human-orientated both in the sense that the worth of nature is being judged and advocated by reference to human criteria of value (notably, the value placed on non-instrumental valuing), and in its assumption that human beings, unlike any other species in nature, could in principle subordinate their own interests to those of the 'rest of nature'. Indeed, it may be said that this latter assumption is incompatible with many of the claims that deep ecology is wont to make concerning human kinship with the 'rest of nature'. For we would not expect any other species to prioritize the needs of others over its own, and would regard it as profoundly unnatural were it to give evidence of doing so.

Of course, it may always be argued that human interests are themselves best served by enhancing the survival and flourishing of the rest of nature, and there are self-styled 'deep' ecologists who invite us to view the matter in this light. Thus, Arne Naess, who is usually credited with laying the foundations of a deep ecology perspective, defends his eco-centric and bio-centric argument by reference to a philosophy of human self-realization. Naess's 'ecosophy' (the term he has coined for a philosophical world-view inspired by the conditions of life in the eco-sphere)[7] justifies its call for the development of a 'deep identification of individuals with all life forms',[8] precisely in terms of its significance for the individual adopting such a perspective. But while it may well be true that an individual's life can only be enhanced by a deeper concern for other species and inorganic nature (and certainly true that the quality of all human species life both now and in the future can only be improved by rejecting a more consumerist interpretation of human interests), it is also clear that anyone arguing for preservation on this basis is operating within a value system that makes it extremely problematic to defend the equal value and rights to survival of all life forms. Naess's human self-realization thesis, which pays special attention to the gains for our species of respecting the intrinsic value of nature, is, in other words, difficult to reconcile with his bio-centric egalitarianism. Anyone inviting us to view all life as having equal intrinsic value, or deeply to identify with the mosquito or the locust, the streptococcus or the AIDS virus, cannot consistently place more weight on human self-realization than on the gains that will accrue thereby to any other participant in the eco-system. Either some parts of nature are more valuable (rich, complex, sentient, beautiful . . .), and hence to be more energetically preserved, or they are not. But if they are not, then we should take the measure of the value system involved, and not present bio-centrism as if were plainly in the interests of the species being called upon to adopt its values. We cannot both emphasize the importance of human self-realization and adopt a position on the value of nature which would, for example, problematize the use of anti-biotics in the prevention of childhood illness.

None of these arguments are meant to deny the role that eco-centric and bio-centric philosophies may play in inviting us to re-think our attitudes to nature, and thus in becoming more sensitive to wasteful, cruel or irrational dimensions of our treatment of it. In checking nonchalance and causing a more embarrassed sense of our relations to nature, these eco- or bio-centric perspectives are a valuable adjunct of green politics. But they may be most valuable, paradoxically, precisely because of the reflections they provoke about the limitations of their logic. Through their very insistence on the 'intrinsic' value of nature, they invite us to think more seriously about how nature may be said to have value, and about the incoherence of attempting to speak for this except by reference to human utilitarian, moral or aesthetic interests and predispositions. By insisting on the equal value of all life forms, they recall us to the absurdity of going to that extreme, to the actual dependency of life on the destruction of life, and thus to the compromised nature of all biotic relations to nature. The virtue of such moral recommendations, in other words, lies in the thought they provoke about the impossibility of following them to the letter, and about the immoralities into which we may be led by attempting to follow them in the spirit. They are useful not because we can observe them, but because they cause us to reflect on how we cannot, or why we do not want to. In this sense, they provide cautionary tales against the temptation to suppose that human relations to nature can be resolved from a position of moral absolutism.

For the most part, it should be said, those who insist on the 'intrinsic' value of nature do not go to the 'democratic' extreme of pressing the equal worth of all natural entities, but remain committed either explicitly or implicitly to the idea of a hierarchical ordering in nature. Those, for example, defending the cause of animal rights have challenged the Great Chain of Being conception of human superiority over other mortal creatures, and have entered into extensive debate about where exactly one draws the line between those non-humans who may be said to have rights (or, towards whom, at any rate, human beings have special duties), but there is a general consensus that we are here talking about rights or obligations that apply only to a restricted range of living beings – those who by virtue of their neuro-physiology are capable of a significant degree of sentience.[9] Such animals, whether or not we want to refer to them as 'higher' in virtue of their capacities for feeling (and hence to regard the epithets 'cruel' or 'insensitive' as appropriate descriptions of human maltreatment of them) are clearly being thought of as having claims to moral attention that are denied to less developed forms of life. Even, then, where arguments on the preservation of other species have been couched in terms strongly denunciatory of 'anthropocentric' attitudes to nature, they have very frequently recognized, at least implicitly, that there are logical limits and practical difficulties in pressing to the extreme the case against human perspectives and self-privileging.

Obligations to the Future?

Nonetheless, we should still note the extensive difference of moral bias between all those arguments that stress the 'intrinsic' and non-instrumental value of nature, and call upon us to preserve it as an *end* in itself, and those that emphasize the value of nature as an essential *means* of the preservation and enhancement of human life, and thus the duty we have to conserve its resources for future generations. Neither theoretically nor practically are these two positions easy to reconcile, and we should not suppose that they are. Nor should we make the 'anthropocentric' mistake of simply assuming that the argument from 'utility' is more obviously coherent and morally compelling than the arguments from the intrinsic merit of nature.

Both its presuppositions – that human beings *do* have obligations towards future generations, and that it is the sense of these that provides the primary source of moral legitimation for the cause of ecological conservation – could well be disputed: the first on the grounds that there is something altogether too vague, and maybe incoherent, about imputing such an indefinite form of obligation; the second on the grounds that any such possible obligation is simply not sufficiently widely felt to merit the confidence placed by the Green Movement in this motivation to adopt policies of ecological sustainability. In other words, whatever the limitations of the arguments which appeal to the aesthetic or intrinsic value of nature, might not the argument from utility be said to be an equally vulnerable form of legitimation of the cause of nature conservation?

It is certainly deeply problematic, and not least because of the difficulties of imputing any general obligation to a human species, many of whose members have been deprived the access to those utilities they are supposedly obliged to bequeath to the future. But even if we abstract from this aspect of the problem for the moment, and accept the terms in which discussions of this issue are commonly pursued, namely, as a question about 'human' obligations to the future, there are still a number of objections to the idea of any such duty of which we need to take account. The most nonchalant, and I think more readily dismissible, are those that appeal to the idea of future human ingenuity and technical mastery: humanity has never set itself historical problems that it has not found the means to resolve; it matters little what 'we' do now, 'they' of the future will find means to surmount the ecological problems they inherit from the past, and may even discover ways of turning to their own advantage what we regard as deficiencies. But this 'Promethean' objection simply evades the moral issue, since the obligation is one that arises in virtue of the *present* knowledge we have, firstly about the predictable consequences of current levels of resource use and forms of pollution, and secondly of the likely limits of human powers, technical or otherwise, to contain or adapt to those consequences. One would not think very highly of an argument to the effect that we need not bother very much about infant malnutrition *now* because medical science over the next couple of decades or so is almost bound to find some means of correcting its negative effects on the adult individual; and we should not use similar forms of argument to justify ecological irresponsibility.

A second set of objections also proceeds from the premise of our 'ignorance' about future eventuation, but argues to the rather differing, and more convincing effect, that the inherent limitations in the knowledge that any given generation can be expected to have about the most long term consequences of its environmental policies must also limit the obligations that it can be said to have towards those that will succeed it. As various commentators have pointed out, since we cannot predict all possible outcomes of our actions, and even those adopted for the best motives can have unintended adverse effects, the notion of human obligations to succeeding generations cannot be construed as extending into an unlimited future.[10] Just as the notion of a distinctively moral responsibility would begin to collapse were we to regard individuals as accountable for the entire concatenation of effects that might be causally traceable to any of their actions, so it does if attributions of a more collective or generational obligation are interpreted in those terms, as in effect they would have to be if viewed as indefinitely extending into the future.

But against this, it can also be said that the argument applies conversely, and on much the same grounds on which we do attribute individual responsibility for the more immediately foreseeable consequences of action, so it can be argued there is a more general and indefinitely relayed generational liability for the predictable consequences of the use, or misuse, of the environment and its resources. In this sense we might claim that the human species has a continuous intra-generational obligation to ensure ecological viability for those who are not yet born, although there will be definite limits on its liability at any point in time.

But it is at this point that the argument needs to address the implications of its universalist premises. For it would seem that the most compelling grounds for supposing that any given generation of occupants of the planet is ecologically answerable as a collective to all the members of the next lies in the assumption that these latter, too, in virtue of being humans possessed of certain needs for survival and self-fulfilment, have a right to avail themselves, as 'we' have done, of the natural resources essential to meeting those needs. But unless the 'we' of this argument does have the universal applicability it claims, then the attribution of a general species accountability cannot be sustained. If there are some of 'us' who *been deprived* of the resources whose supposed availability grounds this obligation, then the argument for a collective species responsibility to the future ceases to have the validity that is claimed for it. For the 'human species' to be obliged to the future on these lines is for it also to be obliged to the present: to all those of its members who are currently denied the means of survival, let alone of the means of self-realization or 'flourishing' that it is assumed, on this argument, are included within the 'legacy' that each generation has a duty to bequeath. In short, there can be no justifiable grounds for arguing that there is a commonly shared 'species' responsibility to ensure ecological sustainability, which does not also at the present time provide grounds for insisting that this is a responsibility that has to fall essentially on those sectors of the global community that have hitherto been most selfishly irresponsible and profligate in their use of global resources. Thus we can argue that although there *is* an obligation to future generations that is grounded in what is common to us as human beings and in the knowledge we have of ecology, it is precisely because there is that there is also an obligation on the more affluent nations to promote the conditions in the present that might allow it to be more universally assumed and efficaciously pursued: which might actualize what for the time being must remain a merely regulative ideal of 'collective' species responsibility.

This, of course, has direct bearing on the question of the extent to which the argument from utility can draw on an acknowledged and morally compelling sense of obligation to conserve nature as a future resource. For one answer we might give is that the obligation to future generations will be the more universally and compellingly felt, the more justice comes to prevail in the distribution of global resources in the present. Which means, in effect, that it will depend on the extent to which those who have been most privileged in the access they have had to the earth's resources come to feel obligated to constrain their own consumption and to provide for those who have hitherto been seriously deprived.

Green Politics

These implications of the 'utility' argument have, it should be said, been widely acknowledged within the Green Movement. In pressing the claims of future generations, the Green parties have consistently emphasized their commitment to a more equitable distribution of global resources and the alleviation of poverty, and their manifestos and programmes systematically link the cause of nature conservation with the promotion of democracy, the emancipation of oppressed groups, and the adoption of more egalitarian economic strategies.[11]

In this sense, green politics, though tending to eschew the vocabulary of socialism and capitalism in favour of that of social justice and anti-industrialism, adopts an integrated and essentially left-wing perspective on the resolution of ecological crisis: a perspective wherein – to invoke the tension I sketched at the end of chapter 6 – the cause of the 'party of humanity' and that of the 'party of nature' are seen to be intimately connected: promoting global equality will reduce over-population, thus alleviating the stress on nature and allowing for the development of more conservatory practices towards the environment and non-human forms of life.

Yet it is one thing to argue for an integral perspective, another to accept, or be able to act upon, its implications in practice, and we would have to recognize that there are very real difficulties in attempting to promote a green agenda of this kind within the existing economic context. We have already noted some of the ways in which heritage and rural preservation tends to confirm the ideologies of nature through which its exploitation has been legitimated and, in virtue of its insertion within the market economy, remains obedient to economic imperatives that serve neither social justice nor ecological good management. Other practical tensions relate to the socio-economic impact of successful acts of nature and wildlife conservation on the livelihood of human beings. One may certainly argue that there is no necessity for a conflict between nature and humanity at this level, and that conflicts arise only because of an economic system within which it is the imperatives of the accumulation of capital and maximization of profits that determine the allocation of human labour and the utilization of natural resources. An alternative economic system, in other words, could assert political control over production in ways that could in principle allow for a resolution of the competition between human and environmental interests. But there is no denying that within the existing economic order there must be a continuous contradiction between preserving nature and securing human employment, and that the one is very frequently achieved only at the cost to the other. It is, of course, precisely the argument of capitalism that human jobs will be placed on the line if we give too much priority to nature, and the workers who will have to pay the price if the costs of curbing pollution are set too high. It is an argument that can only be challenged by challenging the fundamental tenets of capitalist philosophy itself: that there can be no value placed on time and space that is not operational (and therefore reducible to monetary terms);[12] that human progress and well-being are to be judged by reference to rates of economic growth and GNP indices of living standards; that private consumer choice takes precedence over the provision of public goods; and that there should always be strict correlation between work performed and rewards received. Such challenges to the alienation, commodity fetishism and work ethic of capitalist logic have of course been central themes of ecological critique. But so long as this logic does determine the course of social life, it will also ensure the truth of its own predictions, and thus protract a situation in which it is rather easier to be green and to triumph in the successful preservation of the environment, if it is not one's own employment that is put at risk in consequence.

Or perhaps it would be fairer to say that one of the effects of the inegalitarian structure of the market economy is that it distributes the conflicts of interest between humanity and nature very unfairly, and renders them a more acute experience for some than for others. Required by the state conservation laws to leave standing a certain ratio of trees to spotted owls, the lumberjacks in some parts of Oregon, where the spotted owl is doing particularly well, have now come to an end of their permitted logging activities, and are facing unemployment in consequence. Do they resent the spotted owl, or wish it unprotected? Not exactly, and some, it seems, have spent their enforced idleness in perfecting suitable hoots whereby to communicate with them. But there is a certain envy of the owl's prosperity and self-realization; or, as one of them has wryly commented, maybe it was now up to the lumberjacks to see whether they couldn't flourish on a diet of mice.[13]

Of course, against episodes of this kind must be set numerous others where the workers in question display no such ironic affection for the species whose protection may be endangering their own viability, and many have been markedly hostile to attempts to restrict whaling, seal-culling and similar enforcements. Those dependent on defence and nuclear contracts or employed in other dangerous and highly polluting industries have also shown rather little sympathy for Greenpeace activities or the politics of the Green Movement. All the same, it would be a mistake for environmentalists to overlook the complexity of feeling that the ecological cause may engender in those whose means of life bring them most directly into conflict with it; and an even greater mistake to suppose that it is simply some failure of green sensibility on the part of the employees in these industries that accounts for their resistance to the ecological cause.

One implication of these tensions is that all of us who are critical of the destruction of nature may need to develop a stronger sense of our involvement in, and reliance upon, the industrial processes and means of communication whose effects we so deplore. Ecological writing offers many powerful descriptions of what it is like to be a *consumer* of pollution, a traveller through industrial wastelands, an observer of nature's spoilage, a victim of the poisons of its abuse; rather less attention gets drawn to the role played in the creation of these frightful scenarios by our most everyday needs (for electricity, house paint, medicine, glues, batteries, chemical cleaners, dyes, insecticides, etc.): for a whole range of commodities, that is, which we assume an easy access to and do not think twice about going to the nearest retailer to acquire. This is not to say that the contribution of consumer wants in precipitating ecological crisis is never targeted in this literature, and the role that individuals play at this level in its creation has come in for a good deal of criticism, notably in respect of the use of the private motor-car. But there is, all the same, a pervasive tendency to think in terms of a 'them' versus 'us', producers versus consumers, allocation of causes and consequences, which is not necessarily helpful in getting our moral bearings on the issue. To place all the blame on the indomitable forces of the modern industrial juggernaut, or to present its faceless agents and authorities as locked into a conspiracy to keep us from the truth of the toxins it daily insinuates into our blood and breast-milk, air and water, is itself a piece of mystification: a reification of social relations that may indeed be hugely difficult to transform, but do not have the natural intransigence of the law of gravity. If we are all of us locked into systems of work, modes of consumption, and forms of transport which make our individual acts daily involuntary agents of pollution, waste and ozone deficiency, and if there are indeed innumerable agencies and bureaucratic authorities bent on denying us accurate information of the risks we run in satisfying our most natural functions, this is in part because so many continue to give their mandate to a mode of production geared first to the production of profit, and only very secondarily to making good its negative by-products for nature and human welfare.

This, to my mind, is a limitation of Ulrich Beck's influential and powerful indictment of the environmental consequences of modern society: that it is so predominantly addressed to the victimization of its collective client-consumers and so little to their differential and in some cases very collusive roles in maintaining the system of production that creates their plight. This universal vulnerability is associated by Beck with a shift from the 'classical' (and class) society of industrialism to that of the 'risk' society, a shift, he argues, that has been accompanied by significant changes in economic structures and political agencies. 'What corresponds,' he writes, 'to the political subject of class society – the proletariat – in risk society is only the *victimisation of all of us by more or less tangible, massive dangers.*'[14] But while Beck is right to point to the ways in which the 'risk' and dangers of modernity's manipulations of nature cannot be class confined or finally kept at bay through property and personal wealth, it would surely be a mistake to overlook the vast inequalities in their distribution, both globally and within the nation state; or the extent to which their production is the consequence of a system that is still very much dependent on class and gender division and designed to sustain its inequalities of wealth, privilege and relative safety. The risk society may tend towards a consumer 'democratization' in the sense that it increasingly exposes everyone equally to its negative by-products; but one could hardly claim that its structures of *production* are tending towards any such 'democracy' of victimization. Hence when Beck assumes, as he tends to, that the resolution of the ecological problems of modernity will come through a 'collective' transcendence of its technocratic practice and its current modes of legitimation, he may be seriously underestimating the vested interests that the more privileged sectors of this 'collective' have in sustaining the existing relations of production and their divisive structure of wealth production.

Moreover, while it may be true, as Beck says, that the contemporary plea is 'I am afraid' where that of 'classical' industrial society was 'I am hungry',[15] this is in part, at least, because we expect so much more today than to 'live by bread alone', and because of the success of industrial society in meeting those expectancies. Victims we may be in many ways, and caught up unwillingly in the system that creates us such, but that system could not function without the cooperation and legitimation of certain desires, tolerances, and life priorities. Always to view the destruction of nature from the consumer end, as if it were a problem produced by others elsewhere beyond our powers of intervention, is, in a sense, to retain at the very heart of one's critique a misleading view of nature as an 'externality' rather than to see ourselves as permanently within its midst and determining of its context in all our acts of production and consumption. If we are serious about protecting nature (and hence ourselves from the risks incurred by its exploitation) we have also seriously to consider what we are willing to forego materially in order to achieve it. Or to put it more positively, we need to re-think hedonism itself: to consider whether we might not derive more pleasure by restraining those forms of consumption that place most stress on nature and most endanger ourselves in the process. Our experience of life might, after all, be altogether more heady and exotic were it to be less narrowly fixated on the acquisition of resource-hungry, cumbersome, short-lived, junk-creating commodities.

Advocates of a less materially orientated consumption are often presented as puritan ascetics bent on inculcating a more 'spiritual' sense of needs and pleasures. Yet this is in some ways quite misleading. Modern consumption, it could be said, is too little interested in the goods of the flesh, too unconcerned with sensory experience, too obsessed with a whole range of products that screen out or keep us at a sanitary distance from a more sensuous and erotic gratification. Many of the goods deemed essential to a high standard of living are more anaesthetizing than they are indulgent of sensual experience, more ascetic than profligate in what they offer in the way of the pleasures of conviviality, neighbourliness and relaxation, freedom from noise, stench and ugliness. An eco-friendly consumption would not involve a reduction of living standards, but rather an altered conception of the standard itself; nor would it depend on some mass conversion to other-worldliness. It might require only that far more people become more exorbitant in their demand for such goods as to walk where they want to, when they want to; to loiter talking on street corners; to travel slowly; to have solitude, space to play and time to be idle – and were willing to pay the price in terms of a more modest and less privatized structure of material satisfactions.[16]

One is inclined to think, in fact, that the ecological cause can be best served by turning some of the sensibility we bring to the appreciation of the value of nature back upon ourselves. Mark Sagoff is quite right to argue that cost-benefit analysis of environmental degradation fails to acknowledge, and cannot accommodate, the moral and aesthetic quality of the consumer concern for the preservation of nature and the risks run through pollution.[17] But if consumers are to be consistent on this issue, they ought also to consider the impact on the environment of the cost-benefit analysis that is so widely used in assessing the quality of their individual life-style and self-enhancement. The tendency for the value of nature to be represented only in monetary terms cannot in the end be entirely divorced from the tendency for individuals to assess the pleasures and potentials of their personal lives along similar lines.

I make these points not because I think they are the only ones that can be made about affluent consumption; nor because I think most Greens would disagree with them; but because of their bearing on the coherence of the 'utility' argument for nature conservation. For if this does entail, as it might appear to, some collective responsibility on the part of the more 'fearful' societies towards the more 'famished', then there are, to say the least, severe limits on the extent to which this obligation can be assumed within the existing order of capitalist relations; nor can one feel at all hopeful at the present time about the emergence of any extensive popular will to supersede those relations.

This has some bearing on the promotion of any eco socialist programme, since the prospects for its adoption in the West do, it would seem, look rather bleak if we are relying exclusively on some wholesale conversion to socialist morality. At any rate, one is not encouraged to think that the peoples of the affluent nations will readily forego their privileged modes of consumption in order to promote global equity now and to ensure the needs of future generations. This is not to deny the measure of support for these aims that does now exist – and the socialist case can, indeed, build on this through continuous exposure of the suffering and damage incurred by capitalist accumulation. Against the inherent tendency of global capitalism to 'contain' and 'manage' ecological scarcities in ever more unjust ways, it can emphasize the potential of an alternative economic order to reconcile the cause of nature with that of social justice and greater human well-being. But I think it also has to be accepted that had a concern for parity been predominant, we would not be facing the forms of ecological collapse and social barbarism we now are. Worried though people may be about ecological attrition, and alarmed though many are about the ways in which the pursuit of First World affluence protracts and exacerbates deprivation elsewhere, it is abundantly clear that these anxieties in themselves have not proved sufficient to prompt any radical transformation of consumer habits. This means, I suggest, that the appeal to altruism has to be complemented by an appeal to self-interest, where what is stressed is not simply the misery and risk to be alleviated, but the pleasures to be realized by breaking with current market-defined and capitalist promoted conceptions of the good life. In other words, it is only if sufficient numbers come to experience the enticement of the gratifications promised by less materially fixated life-styles that they will seriously consider mandating policies to constrain very resource-hungry and exploitative modes of consumption. If there is to be any chance of reversing the profound, and in many ways justified, scepticism about the viability of an alternative to the market, it will require the socialist argument to be backed not only by some very convincing blue-printing of the institutions that could realize an 'authentic' and genuinely democratic socialist order, but also by an alternative hedonist vision: by very different conceptions of consumption and human welfare from those promoted under capitalism, pursued under 'actual existing socialism' or hitherto associated with orthodox socialist theory. If socialists are genuinely concerned with the universal satisfaction of basic needs now and in the future, they must become advocates of an alternative utopia of wants.

Transforming Attitudes

But these points equally have bearing on the argument of those who would seek to promote the Green agenda simply by emphasizing the 'intrinsic' value of nature and insisting that it must be 'respected'. Robert Goodin's argument, for example, that Green politics is driven by a 'single moral vision' rooted in the primary, self-occurring value of nature, and that priority should always be given to the preservation of this value, seems absurdly voluntaristic in its supposition that 'people' could, or would ever wish, to cede such primacy to nature. Morover, given that Goodin's professed aim is to supply a theory of value for Green party politics, and that he is clearly committed to the democratic and humanly emancipatory aspects of the Green programme, his preparedness so to sever the question of agency from that of the protection of nature seems deeply problematic. There is, in fact, more of a tension between Goodin's Green theory of value and the interests expressed in justice, equality and human welfare in the Green party manifestos than Goodin himself seems prepared to acknowledge. When he claims that Green values should be given preference over a 'green theory of agency', and that it is therefore always more important that the right things be done to nature than that they be done in a particular way or through a particular agency;[18] or when, citing the Mediaeval English village in illustration, he tells us that 'living in harmony' with nature does not require egalitarian communities,[19] he is offering a moral foundation for Green politics that could in principle legitimate extremely reactionary policies on conservation. (We must, in any case, always ask what

exactly is meant by speaking of such communities as 'living
in harmony' with nature when their individual members
were so differentiated in their relations to it.)

Goodin is no doubt right that value and agency are
divorced in the sense that ecological crisis might be accommodated in a variety of political modes. But it is precisely
because a regard for the immediate interests of nature may
be consistent with the least democratic political forms and
the implementation of totalitarian methods of controlling
human consumption and population that a Green politics
that professes a concern for global equity and the emancipation of oppressed sectors of the human community must
eschew a theory of value of a simplistic kind. It must surely
also take issue with Goodin's suggestion that individuals
could 'depart from a green personal lifestyle in almost any
given respect' while still endorsing the Green theory of
value and its public policies.[20] It may be true that we do not
have to have 'silly beliefs about homoeopathic medicine
or tree spirits,'[21] in order to be ecologically responsible,
but we surely cannot consistently endorse Green policies
on transport or resource conservation while retaining the
'greyest' or 'brownest' habits of consumption at the level
of personal life-style.

There is, finally, a tension in offering a theory of value
which places such weight on the preservation of nature as
an *end* in itself to a Green party politics whose emphasis on
the needs of future generations only makes sense if nature
is viewed as a *means* to human preservation. At any rate,
it is difficult both to argue for a theory of natural value,
which implies that human beings distrain on the value of
nature when they harness it to the satisfaction of their
own interests, and to appeal to the obligations they have
(and should feel) to ensure the indefinite continuity and
flourishing of their species.

Goodin and other ecological writers, however, are quite
right to imply that a transformation of our attitudes to

nature, including a re-thinking of the ways in which we have (or have not) valued it, can have an important role to play in transforming modes of production and consumption along lines that can help to ensure the provisioning for future generations. I support Goodin's sense, too, that the revaluation process does not require us to become deeply spiritual about nature, and is unlikely to be advanced by adopting mystical and divining attitudes towards it.

At any rate, one can certainly argue that the calls for a new 'religion' of nature are confused and quixotic if they are based on the assumption that by re-inspiring a certain 'awe' of nature we shall protect it against its further exploitation. The theological idea of nature as the purposeful gift of God did, perhaps, help to protect it by encouraging a certain fear of retribution for its abuse.[22] It is true, too, that animistic beliefs about nature have generally gone together with fears and taboos constraining human relations with it. But we must dispute the idea that these forms of reverence or superstition played any significant *causal* role in inhibiting its technical mastery.

Pre-industrial cultures were not spared the ravages of 'instrumental rationality' because of their religious feelings for nature; they experienced those feelings in the absence of the scientific understanding of its 'cosmic forces' and the technical means to harness its powers. It may indeed be more difficult to sustain a sense of obligation towards the preservation of nature (or to argue for that obligation), in the absence of any belief in its divine origins or spiritual purpose. But it is a mistake to suppose that by re-instilling some such structure of belief, even if that were possible, one would stay the hand of technology.

We cannot seek to protect nature by pretending to forms of belief that have been exploded by the march of science and technology, however destructive that may have proved. Nor, one may argue, would it be desirable or appropriate to seek to rediscover in nature itself some quasi-divine authority compelling our obligations towards it. This is in part because of the implications of doing so for the conception of moral responsibility itself. The desanctification of nature has certainly gone together with, and in part encouraged, attitudes to its use that have had grave consequences from an ecological point of view; but the damage has proceeded correlatively with the development of modes of thinking that have conceived the morality of human actions to consist in their liberation from the coercion of fear and superstition.

It is this autonomous quality that arguably gives special value to those forms of obligation for the preservation of nature that we do happen to experience. The experience may, in a sense, come harder in a culture that has ceased to believe in a divinely ordained and supervised universe, but it is the more properly ethical for being motivated neither by irrational forms of superstition nor by any fear of divine retribution for the abuse of nature.

But there is also the further, and related, consideration that the holding of false beliefs about nature may be incompatible with the adoption of a properly moral regard for its preservation. As John O'Neill has put it:

> There is a necessary regulation between ethical concern for an object and true beliefs about it: proper concern for an object x presupposes the possession of a core set of true beliefs about x. This is not just because if one has false beliefs about x concerned actions for x are likely to be misplaced, true as this is. It is also that if one has systematically false beliefs about x, there is a sense in which x is not the object of one's concern

at all. Hence the justifiable complaint lovers sometimes make on parting: 'You never really loved me; you loved someone else you mistook me for.' A similar complaint can be made of those in green movements who insist on an anti-scientific, mythologized and personalized picture of the natural world: the natural world simply isn't the object of their concern.[23]

Of course, there are relativists who will dispute this whole picture on the grounds that it speaks to the prejudices of scientific culture itself in supposing that any one account of nature can be said to be 'truer' than any other. But those who seriously espouse this form of relativism should also refrain themselves from any confident pronouncements about the damage inflicted by science or the risks incurred by the adoption of its methods. For to condemn the effects of conventional medicine, to target the poisons or pollutants of modern industry, or to offer any similar critique of the negative impact of the 'technical fix' approach to nature, is implicitly to accept as 'true' the accounts of the workings of biological and physical nature that are offered by science itself.

It is a profound error to suppose that, in defending a secular view of nature, one is in some sense committed to an uncritical acceptance of the 'authority' of science or bound to endorse the rationality of the modes in which scientific knowledge has been put to use. To defend such a view is, on the contrary, to seek to further the rational disenchantment with those forms of scientific wisdom and technological 'expertise' that have proved so catastrophic in their impact on the environment. To pit a religious or mystical conception of nature against these forms of technological abuse is less to undermine than to collude in the myth of the omnipotence of science: it is to perpetuate precisely the supposition that needs to be challenged – that because science and technology *can* achieve results that magical interactions with nature cannot, they are always put to work to good effect. What is needed, in fact, is not more Green religion, but more Green science of the kind that the Green parties, Greenpeace, Friends of the Earth, Vertic, and numerous other agencies one might name, are continuously throwing in the way of the smooth running of the military-industrial complex. Government and industry and all those bent on confirming us in our 'greyer' or 'browner' habits would far sooner that the Green Movement *did* confine itself to mysticism than come to them, as it fortunately so often does, armed with incontrovertible statistics and scientific evidence on the damage and risks of current policy on the environment.

In any case, it is not clear that by becoming more mystical or religious about nature one necessarily overcomes the damaging forms of separation or loss of concern that have been the consequence of a secular and instrumental rationality. What is really needed, one might argue, is not so much new forms of awe and reverence of nature, but rather to extend to it some of the more painful forms of concern we have for ourselves. The sense of rupture and distance that has been encouraged by secular rationality may be better overcome, not by worshipping this 'other' to humanity, but through a process of re-sensitization to our combined separation from it and dependence upon it. We need, in other words, to feel something of the anxiety and pain we experience in our relations with other human beings in virtue of the necessity of death, loss and separation. We are inevitably compromised in our dealings with nature in the sense that we cannot hope to live in the world without distraining on its resources, without bringing preferences to it that are shaped by our own concerns and conceptions of worth, and hence without establishing a certain structure of priorities in regard to its use. Nor can we even begin to reconsider the ways in which we have been too nonchalant and callous in our attitudes to other life forms, except in the light of a certain privileging of our own sense of identity and value. All the same, we can certainly be more or less aware of the compromise, more or less pained by it, and more or less sensitive to the patterning of the bonds and separations that it imposes.

This, as I have argued throughout the book, precisely does not mean overlooking differences between ourselves and other creatures. It may on the contrary mean becoming more alert to what is problematic in the attempt to do so. To become more sensitive to nature may, in this sense, simply be to experience a little more regret than we have tended to in the past at the fact that the bonds cannot be indefinitely extended. We cannot be equally protective towards everything in nature; nor, one might argue, would it be any more appropriate to seek to be so than it is to attempt to protect one's child from every possible source of pain or damage. But our relations to the environment and its life forms could certainly benefit from something more of the angst experienced in the case of the child – whose exposure to risk we continue to feel very acutely in the very moment of appreciating the necessity for it. Rather than becoming more awe-struck by nature, we need perhaps to become more stricken by the ways in which our dependency upon its resources involves us irremediably in certain forms of detachment from it. To get 'closer' to nature is, in a sense, to experience more anxiety about all those ways in which we cannot finally identify with it nor it with us. But in that very process, of course, we would also be transforming our sense of human identity itself.

Notes

1   Cf. Robert Goodin, *Green Political Theory* (Polity Press, Oxford, 1992), p. 8. The ecology movement today, suggests Goodin, is to be distinguished from that of the 1970s, in terms of the greater emphasis it places on the independent value of nature, by comparison with the earlier, more instrumental quality of the arguments for nature preservation and conservation.

2   Important treatments of the idea are to be found in Paul Taylor, *Respect for Nature* (Princeton University Press, Princeton, 1986); Holmes Rolston, *Environmental Ethics* (Temple University Press, Philadelphia, 1988); Robin Attfield, *The Ethics of Environmental Concern* (The University of Georgia Press, London, 1991). See also the section on 'green philosophy' in *The Green Reader*, ed. Andrew Dobson (André Deutsche, London, 1994); A. Brennan, *Thinking about Nature* (Routledge, London, 1988); J. B. Callicott, *In Defence of the Land Ethic* (State University of New York Press, New York, 1989), part III; J. O'Neill, 'The Varieties of Intrinsic Value', *The Monist* 75 (1992); *Ecology, Policy and Politics* (Routledge, London, 1993), ch. 2.

3   Cf. John Passmore, *Man's Responsibility for Nature*, 2nd edn (Duckworth, London, 1980), p. 73. The quality of the distinction, and differential moral obligations to nature implied by it, are usefully illustrated in this work, esp. in chs 4 and 5.

4   Ibid., pp. 101–7.

5   Cf. *The Guardian*, pages on the environment, 5 November 1993. On the general question of the compatibility between the objectives of sustainability and the protection of the environment, see Bryan Norton, 'Sustainability, Human Welfare and Ecosystem Health', *Environmental Values* 1, 2 (1992), pp. 97–111.

6   See Robert Sylvan's discussion of 'deep' ecological conceptions of intrinsic value, *Radical Philosophy* 40 (Summer 1985), pp. 12, esp. pp. 8–9; Cf. Brennan, *Thinking About Nature*, chs 5–8.

7   Arne Naess, *Ecology, Community and Lifestyle*, trans. David Rothenberg (Cambridge University Press, Cambridge, 1989), p. 38; cf. pp. 34–67 passim.

8   Ibid., p. 85; cf. pp. 194–5 (where Naess makes clear a sympathy for Jainism).

9   The literature on animal rights is now vast. The more influential works include: Peter Singer, *Animal Liberation* (London, 1976); Tom Regan, *The Case for Animal Rights* (London, 1988); Tom Regan and Peter Singer (eds), *Animal Rights and Human Obligations* (Englewood Cliffs, 1976); Peter Singer (ed.), *In Defence of Animals* (Oxford, 1988); S. Clark, *The Moral Status of Animals* (Oxford University Press, Oxford, 1984); Mary Midgley, *Animals and Why They Matter* (The University of Georgia Press, Athens US, 1983); Keith Tester, *Animals and Society: the Humanity of Animal Rights* (London, 1991); M. P. T. Leahy, *Against Liberation: Putting Animals in Perspective* (London, 1991). For a superb discussion of the debates in this

field, and critique of liberal approaches, see Ted Benton, *Natural Relations* (Verso, London 1993); for an interesting appraisal of Benton's argument, see Bob Brecher, *Radical Philosophy* 67 (Summer 1994), pp. 43–5.

10 Passmore, *Man's Responsibility for Nature*, pp. 75–87; J. B. Cameron, 'Do Future Generations Matter?' in *Ethics and Environmental Responsibility*, ed. Nigel Dower (Gower Publishing, Aldershot, 1989) pp. 57–78, esp. part II; B. Barry, 'Justice Between the Generations' in *Law, Morality and Society* ed. P. M. S. Hacker and J. Raz (Clarendon Press, Oxford, 1977), pp. 268–84 (though Cameron and Barry both contest Passmore's conclusion that the basis for our obligations to posterity resides in the love experienced for immediate descendants, and cannot be expected to extend beyond that foundation). Commentators, in fact, diverge considerably in the view they take of the implications of the point about limited knowledge for the degree and grounds of responsibility. See also the discussions of Gregory Kavka, 'The Futurity Problem' in *Obligations to Future Generations*, ed. R. I. Sikora and B. Barry (Temple University Press, Philadelphia, 1978), pp. 186–203; Robin Attfield, *The Ethics of Environmental Concern*, pp. 88–114; R. and V. Routley, 'Nuclear Energy and Obligations to the Future' *Inquiry* 21 (1978), pp. 133–79; *Responsibilities to Future Generations*, ed. Ernest Partridge (Prometheus Books, New York, 1981).

11 Cf. The Manifesto of *Die Grünen* 1983 (which has been a model for other European Green parties). For further documentation and discussion of Green party policies, see Rudolf Bahro, *Building the Green Movement*, trans. Mary Tyler (Heretic Books, London, 1986); Andrew Dobson, *Green Political Thought* (Unwin Hyman, London, 1990); *Into the 21st Century: An Agenda for Political Realignment*, ed. Felix Dodds (Green Print, Basingstoke, 1988); European Greens 1989: *Common Statement of the European Greens for the 1989 Elections to the European Parliament* (European Greens, Brussels); Robert Goodin, *Green Political Theory*, chs 4, 5; Werner Hülsberg, *The German Greens* (Verso, London, 1988); André Gorz, *Ecology as Politics*, trans. P. Vigderman and J. Cloud (Pluto Press, London, 1987); Martin Ryle, *Ecology and Socialism* (Radius, London, 1988); Penny Kemp and Derek Wall, *A Green Manifesto for the 1990s* (Penguin, Harmondsworth, 1990); Jonathan Porritt, *Seeing Green* (Blackwell, Oxford, 1984); Jonathan Porritt and David Winner, *The Coming of the Greens* (Fontana, London,

1988); Charlene Spretnak and Fritjof Capra, *Green Politics: the Global Promise* (Hutchinson, London, 1984).

12 For an excellent recent critique of the short-comings of any attempt to value nature in monetary terms, see David Harvey, 'The Nature of the Environment: the Dialectics of Social and Environmental Change', *Socialist Register* (1993), part III; cf. Andrew Collier, 'Value, Rationality and the Environment', *Radical Philosophy* 66 (Spring 1994).

13 Report on *PM Programme*, Radio 4, 1992.

14 Ulrich Beck, *Risk Society: Towards a New Modernity*, trans. Mark Ritter (Sage, London, 1992), p. 45. It is impossible to do justice here to the richness of Beck's analysis of modernity, and my criticisms refer only to what I think is a problematic dimension of his account of the quality and political import of the public reaction to ecological dangers. For a much more adequate and considered analysis of Beck's overall argument, see Michael Rustin, *Radical Philosophy* 67 (Summer 1994), pp. 3–12.

15 Beck, *Risk Society*, see esp. part I.

16 The case for an 'alternative hedonism' is elaborated further in my *Troubled Pleasures* (Verso, London, 1990), pp. 23–86.

17 Mark Sagoff, *The Economy of the Earth* (Cambridge University Press, Cambridge, 1988), esp. ch. 6.

18 Goodin, *Green Political Theory*, pp. 24–83.

19 Ibid., pp. 119–20.

20 Ibid., p. 82.

21 Ibid., p. 83.

22 The claim that religion has acted as a deterrent to ecologically damaging practices is, indeed, controversial, and we must note that there are very diverging opinions of the extent to which theological teaching (particularly that of the Judaeo-Christian tradition) constrains, rather than licenses, instrumental rationality. Some argue that Christian scripture has significantly encouraged the abuse of nature, others that it advocates a caring ethic of human stewardship towards it. But this dispute is itself very much about the interpretation to be placed on teachings (notably the Book of Genesis) that are not clear-cut in their message, and tends to be conducted in the light of the secular rationalizations to which theology can always be made to lend itself. But whatever the interpretation placed on scripture, it remains disputable how far beliefs in the divine creation and pre-ordained order of the universe can be said to have acted as a curb on the spread of Enlightenment forms of

confidence in human powers to interfere in its natural order and to disturb its social hierarchy. For discussion of the scriptural tradition, and some sense of the disputes it has generated, see: C. J. Glacken, *Traces on the Rhodian Shore, Nature and Culture in Western Thought from Ancient Times to the End of the Eighteenth Century* (University of California Press, Berkeley and London, 1967), pp. 150–68; John Passmore, *Man's Responsibility for Nature*, pp. 3–27; Robin Attfield, *The Ethics of Environmental Concern*, pp. 20–50; cf. Carolyn Merchant, *The Death of Nature* (Wildwood House, London, 1982), pp. 29ff; Stephen Clark, *How to Think about the Earth* (Mowbray, London, 1993).

23 John O'Neill, 'Humanism and Nature', *Radical Philosophy* 66 (Spring 1994), p. 27.

INDEX

Addison, Joseph, 23
Adorno, Theodor, 181, 201,
    209–10n, 217, 230–2
Aesop, 83
aesthetics, 101, 231–2, 244,
    247n; aesthetic capacities/
    needs, 163–4, 174; aesthetic
    of nature, 11–12, 28–9, 38,
    48–9, 180–1, 202–3, 206,
    208–9, 214–45, 252–9;
    see also pastoral; sublime
agriculture, 102–3, 137,
    139, 184
alienation, 5, 29–30, 33–4,
    45–6, 48–9, 61, 66,
    86, 227, 237–9, 265;
    inter-subjective, 84–6
Alvater, Elmar, 203
Anderson, Benedict, 110, 118n
animals, animality, 10–12, 19,
    23–8, 38, 40, 42, 46–7,
    49–57, 60, 66, 74, 77–9,
    81, 84, 99, 115n, 125–6,
    131–2, 136, 143, 156,
    161, 163–6, 170–4, 181,
    219–21, 228, 277–8; animal
    rights, 54, 172–3, 179n,
    258, 279–80n; domestic,
    87–90; as pests, 84, 86; as
    pets, 84–5; and religion,
    89–90; symbolism of, 82–3,
    94–5, 114n
anthropocentricity, 5, 13, 23–4,
    40, 53, 73, 121, 123, 131,
    150, 170–2, 178n, 206–9,
    254–5, 258–9
anthropology, 62–5, 99–100
anthropomorphism, 71, 82–6
Appleton, Jay, 223, 247n
Ardener, E., 116n
Ardrey, Robert, 57
Aristophanes, 83
Aristotle, 52–3, 103
art, 17, 38, 100–1, 217, 219,
    230–1, 244; depiction of
    nature in, 85, 101, 114n,
    191, 220, 223–4
artifice, artificiality, 2, 15–19,
    37–8, 135–7, 150, 153,
    185–7, 200, 219, 231, 241
Attfield, Robin, 279–80n, 282n
Augustine, Saint, 75

Bacon, Francis, 103, 117n
Bahro, Rudolf, 280n
Bakhtin, Mikhail, 92, 94
Baldwin, Stanley, 193, 211n
Barrell, John, 211n, 235–6, 248n
Barry, Brian, 280n
Bartram, George, 193
Bataille, Georges, 89

Bate, Jonathan, 240
Baudelaire, Charles, 26, 32
Beauvoir, Simone de, 99
Beck, Ulrich, 267, 281n
Berger, John, 88, 114n
Bersani, Leo, 116n
Benton, Ted, 61, 115n, 117n,
    148n, 157–9, 162–6, 169,
    175n, 177–9, 280n
Berleant, Arnold, 247n
Bernal, Martin, 67
Bernstein, Jay, 210n, 246n
Bhaskar, Roy, 61, 157, 177n
Biehl, Janet, 146n
biology, 42, 50–3, 55–8, 60,
    99–100, 115n, 123–6,
    132–3, 138–40, 142–5, 156,
    174, 251–2, 276; biological
    determinism, 57–61
Birke, Linda, 70n
Blake, William, 31, 193
body: associated with nature,
    6, 10, 90–1; celebration of,
    92–4, 97–8; constructivist
    theories of, 127–30, 133–7,
    140; and 'grotesque realism',
    91–8; and mind, 31, 43,
    46–8, 90–2, 98, 115n;
    and reproduction, 74, 91,
    99–101, 133–4; repudiation
    of, 90–2
Bolingbroke, Henry, 24
Bordo, Susan, 129
Boulton, James, 246–7n
Brennan, A., 279n
Brooker, Peter, 210–11n
Bruno, Giordano, 96
Burke, Edmund, 222, 225–8,
    230
Butler, Judith, 128, 147–8n

Callicott, J. B., 279n

Cameron, J. B., 280n
Campanella, Tommaso, 96
Caplan, A. L., 69n
Capra, Fritjof, 281n
Carew, Thomas, 190
Cavalieri, Paola, 179n
Chambers, Sir William, 227
Chaucer, Geoffrey, 83, 220
Chomsky, Naom, 55–7, 62, 65
Clare, John, 189, 238
Clark, Stephen, 279n, 282n
Cicero, 152
Cobbett, William, 189, 197
Collier, Andrew, 177n, 281n
Collingwood, R. C., 37
convention, conventionalism,
    4, 15, 27, 32–40, 42, 55,
    72, 79, 121, 125, 129,
    138–9, 144
Cosgrove, D. E., 248n
cosmology, 21–5, 92, 94–8
Coughlan, Patricia, 111
countryside, 20, 153–4, 156,
    182–8, 191–3, 196–202,
    204–7, 253; see also
    landscape, rurality
Crabbe, George, 189, 197
culture, culturality 2–11, 15,
    28–34, 37–68, 85–6, 131,
    135–9, 142–5; and gender,
    99–102, 126–30, 138;
    naturalisation of 32–4, 58,
    91, 110–12, 121; and needs,
    163–4, 174

Davitt, Michael, 110
Dawkins, Richard, 69–70n
Delphy, Christine, 127–8
Derrida, Jacques, 6, 63–4, 68n
Descartes, René, 23, 30,
    43–4, 53–5
Dickens, Peter, 115n

Dobson, Andrew, 279–80n
Dollimore, Jonathan, 116n,
    119–21, 124, 145, 147n
Douglas, Mary, 89–90, 115n
Doyal, Len, 179n
Dupré, Louis, 68n

ecology, 2–12, 16, 24–5, 31,
    40–1, 49, 59, 61, 98, 107,
    112, 119–32, 137–8, 141–5,
    149–55, 157–60, 166–70,
    174–6, 178n, 197–8, 206–9,
    215–16, 238–43, 249–53,
    260–74, 278n; 'deep' 18,
    124, 146n, 206–7, 253–9
Eagleton, Terry, 92, 116n,
    177n, 246n
Eliot, T. S., 193
Empson, William, 27
ethnocentrism, 7, 10, 61–8, 250
Engels, Friedrich, 60
environment, natural, 1–2,
    10–12, 16–18, 20–1, 137,
    142, 144, 152, 154–6,
    159–60, 180–8, 202–6,
    242–5, 249, 253, 261, 263,
    270; built, 20, 153, 182–8
environmental ethics, 12–13,
    59–60, 251–78
environmentalism, 12, 160,
    162, 187, 197–206, 241,
    252–4, 264
Enlightenment, 5, 7, 23, 29–31,
    45, 76, 97, 103, 122, 226,
    230, 281–2n
evolution, evolutionary theory,
    50–3, 57–8, 60, 82, 174,
    219–20

feminism, 4–5, 10, 58, 99–102,
    121–2, 141–3, 251; eco-,
    122–5, 127, 146n

feminization of nature, 10, 71,
    74, 91, 98–107, 111–12,
    122–5, 127
Ficino, Marsile, 96
Foucault, Michel, 6, 32, 36n,
    56, 120, 127–9, 134–5,
    140, 146n
Frankfurt School, 30, 113n
Fraser, Nancy, 117n
Freud, Sigmund, 60, 91–2, 116n
Furniss, Tom, 247n
Friends of the Earth, 198, 277

Gellner, Ernest, 110, 118n
Geras, Norman, 115n
Gillison, C., 117n
Glacken, C. J., 68n, 282n
Goodin, Robert, 16–18, 35n,
    238, 272–4, 278n, 280n
Gorz, André, 113n, 280n
Gough, Ian, 179n, 246n
Gould, S. J., 69n
Great Chain of Being, 21–5,
    95–6, 258
Green Movement, 4–5, 9, 123,
    126, 176, 207, 215, 259,
    263, 272–4, 277
Greenberg, David, 145n
Greenblatt, Stephen, 76
Greenpeace, 266, 277; UK, 198
Grundmann, Reiner, 178n

Haraway, Donna, 70n, 85,
    246n
Hardy, Thomas, 189, 192, 214,
    220, 232, 246
Harris, Olivia, 99
Harrison, Fraser, 87, 114n
Harvey, David, 177n, 182, 281n
Hayward, Tim, 162, 164, 166,
    175, 178n
Hazlitt, William, 193

Heaney, Seamus, 111
Hegel, G. W. F., 45–6, 85, 109
Heidegger, Martin, 47–9, 181,
   191, 210n, 237
heritage, 12, 150, 192, 196–9,
   204, 264
Hesiod, 189, 197
Hewison, Robert, 200
Hirst, Paul, 56
Homer, 220, 222
Horigan, Stephen, 113–14n
Howkins, Alun, 211n
Hulme, T. E., 32
Hülsberg, Werner, 280n
human nature, 2, 10, 25–34,
   49, 55–6, 86, 119, 145,
   168–9, 178n
human needs, 145, 163–70,
   173–4, 184, 207–8, 217–19,
   246n, 261–2, 266, 269–70

Ireland, 108, 110–12

Jefferson, Thomas, 103
Jeffreys, Sheila, 145n
Johnson, Samuel, 151
Jonson, Ben, 88, 94, 190, 192
Joyce, James, 110–11, 220

Kamin, L., 69n
Kant, Immanuel, 23, 30, 38,
   44–5, 54, 171, 173, 218,
   222, 225–33, 247n
Kemp, Penny, 280n
Kitzinger, Celia, 145n
Kolodny, Annette, 80, 106–7,
   247n

landscape, 103–5, 137, 142,
   152–3, 156, 180–2, 187,
   197, 210n, 234–45, 246n
Lansbury, George, 194

language, 50–7, 62, 76, 85–6,
   125, 131, 139, 151, 174
Las Casas, Bartolomé de, 77
Leach, E. R., 70n
Leahy, M. P. T., 279n
Lefebvre, Henri, 177n, 185–6
Leibniz, G. W., 23
Lévi-Strauss, Claude, 51,
   62–4, 68–9n
Lewontin, R. C., 69n
Lichtman, Richard, 178n
Linnaeus, 82
Lloyd, Genevieve, 117–18n
Locke, John, 23, 30
Longinus, 222
Lorenz, Konrad, 57
Lovejoy, A. O., 35n

MacCormack, C., 116n
Mahon, Derek, 173
Mandeville, Bernard, 83
Marcuse, Herbert, 113n
Marvell, Andrew, 192, 197
Massey, Doreen, 118n, 177n
Marx, Karl, 18, 30, 38, 46, 60,
   68n, 91–2, 102, 178n, 205
Marx, Leo, 210n, 247n
Marxism, 4, 47, 113n, 162
materialism, 43, 91–2,
   97–8, 115n
Merchant, Caroline, 282n
Midgley, Mary, 83, 279n
Mill, John Stuart, 26, 34n
Miller, James, 36n
Monboddo, Lord J. B., 82, 114n
Montague, John, 104, 111
More, Thomas, 189, 197
Morris, Desmond, 57
Morton, Thomas, 106

Naess, Arne, 256–7, 279n
nationalism, 32, 46, 107–12

National Trust, 198, 202, 212n
naturalism, 6–7, 11, 41–3,
  47, 49–61, 81, 119, 124,
  127–32, 150, 161–70,
  174–6, 178n; in aesthetics,
  223–5; reductive, 57–61,
  165–6, 170–1, 174
nature: aesthetic of, 11–12,
  28–9, 38, 48–7, 180–1,
  202–3, 206, 208–9, 214–45,
  252–4, 259; and art, 38, 85,
  217–9, 230–2; and artifice,
  2, 15–19, 37–8, 135–7,
  150, 153, 185–7, 200,
  219, 231, 241; alienation
  from, 5, 29–30, 33–4, 45–6,
  48–9, 61, 66, 86, 227,
  237–9; conservation and
  preservation of, 4, 7–9, 12,
  34, 60, 112, 123, 150–1,
  153, 156, 158–60, 175–6,
  180, 202–9, 240–5, 253–65,
  272–8; and convention,
  4, 15, 27, 37–40; and
  corporeality, 2, 10, 74,
  90–8, 127–45; and culture,
  2, 8–9, 11–15, 28–34,
  37–61, 81, 149–76, 187–8;
  cultural construction of, 4,
  6–8, 33–4, 110–11, 126–30,
  152–5, 177n, 182–8,
  241–3, 249–50; dualist and
  anti-dualist conceptions
  of, 10–11, 49–61, 81–9,
  131–2, 161–3, 165, 170,
  174–5 (see also naturalism);
  endorsement of, 4, 8, 34,
  78–81, 120–1, 150 (see also
  romanticism); evaluation
  of, 7, 11–13, 16–19, 145,
  150–4, 160, 176, 180,
  206–9, 245, 252–9, 269–78;
  as externality, 10, 16, 21,
  38, 40–9, 268, 72 and
  the feminine, 10, 71, 91,
  98–107, 111–12, 122–7,
  248n; human communality
  with, 15, 39–41, 81, 125–6,
  131, 161, 175, 252, 256,
  278; 'lay' concepts of,
  11–12, 155–8, 160, 180–1,
  metaphysical concepts
  of, 38–40, 61–8, 130–2,
  155–6, 160–70, 174–6;
  and primitivity, 10, 29,
  61, 66–8, 74–81; realist
  concepts of, 4, 7–10, 130,
  132–7, 141–2, 151–2,
  155–60 (see also realism);
  redemption through, 29–32;
  representation/symbolism
  of, 4, 8–9, 10–12, 71–107,
  126–7, 220, 224–5, 234–44
  (see also aesthetic of nature);
  scepticism 4–5, 8, 34,
  120–1; and sexuality, 3, 5–7,
  11, 92, 98, 103–7, 119–48,
  251 (see also sex, sexuality);
  utilitarian attitudes to, 11,
  29–30, 126, 252–3
Nietzsche, Friedrich, 91–2
norms, normativity, 3, 28,
  33, 42, 55, 66–8, 129–30,
  133–4, 138, 141–5
  (see also convention,
  conventionalism)
Nussbaum, Martha, 246n

O'Neill, John, 178n, 275, 279n
Ortner, Sherry, 99–100,
  116–17n
Orwell, George, 83

Parker, Rozsika, 101

Passmore, John, 16–17, 153, 279–80n, 282n
pastoral, the, 71, 106–7, 114n, 188–96, 202, 210–11n, 214, 222, 235–7
Pico della Mirandola, 96
pigs, piggishness, 87–90, 92, 94
Plumwood, Val, 146n
Pollock, Griselda, 101
Poole, Ross, 109
Pope, Alexander, 22, 235
Porritt, Jonathan, 280n
Porta, Giambattisto, 96
postmodernism, 4–5, 9, 13–14, 251
post-structuralism, 54–5, 138
primatology, 85–6
primitivity, 10, 29, 61, 66–8
Prometheanism, 5, 23–4, 30, 143, 162, 227, 260; paradox of, 94–8
psychoanalysis, 106–7; Lacanian, 60, 85

Rabelais, François, 92–8
racism, 31–2, 58, 62, 220
Raleigh, Sir Walter, 76
realism, 4, 7–11, 34, 39, 130, 132–7, 141–2, 151–2, 155–60; 'critical', 61, 157–60
Rée, Jonathan, 118n
Regan, Tom, 279n
Reid, Michael, 179n
religion, 89–90, 95, 97, 281–2n, Christian 95–7; of nature; 98, 274–8
Rich, Adrienne, 145n
Ricoeur, Paul, 116n
Rieff, Paul, 116n
Rolston, Holmes, 216, 245n, 279n

romanticism, 26, 29–32, 126–7, 150, 197, 238–9; Romantic Movement, 26, 29–32, 226–8
Rosaldo, M. Z., 116n
Ross, Andrew, 70n, 146n
Rousseau, Jean-Jacques, 29–32, 79–80, 82
Royal Society for Nature Conservancy, 198
rurality, 12, 108, 110, 156, 182–3, 187–8, 191–7, 211n, 238–40 see also countryside
Ryle, Martin H., 240, 280n

Sagoff, Mark, 269
Sahlins, Marshall 51, 69n
Sartre, J-P., 85
Sayers, Janet, 70n
sex, sexuality, 3, 5–7, 11, 31–2, 57–9, 89–90, 102, 108, 112, 119–45; hetero-, 128, 142–3; homo-, 112, 119–21, 142–3, 146n, 251
Sheail, John 212n
Shelley, P. B., 31, 193
Singer, Peter, 179n, 279n
Smith, Neil, 35n, 227
socialism, 4, 113n, 119, 169, 192, 205, 271; eco-, 162, 206, 263–4, 270–2
Society for the Protection of Birds, 198
sociobiology, 57–9
Soja, Ed., 177n
Sperber, Dan, 70n
Spinoza, Baruch, 23
Spretnak, Charlene, 281n
Stallybrass, Peter, 94, 116n
Strathern, M., 116n
Strawson, Peter, 171
Strong, Roy, 199, 202

structuralism, 54–5, 62–3
Sturt, George, 188–9
sublime, the, 71, 213–15, 221–2,
    225–30, 245, 246–7n
Sylvan, Robert, 146n, 279n
Synge, J. M., 110

taboos: animal, 88–9; dietary,
    89–90, 115n; incest, 51,
    57–8, 62–4, 105
Taylor, Charles, 36n
Taylor, Paul, 279n
theology, 22–5, 98, 274–5
Tester, Keith, 279n
Thomas, Keith, 23, 35n
Timpanaro, Sebastiano, 115n
Trivers, R. L., 70n

Urry, John, 199–200

Virgil, 188–9, 197
Vertic, 277

Wall, Derek, 280n
Watson, G. J., 110, 118n

Weeks, Jeffrey, 145–6n
Weiskel, Thomas, 246n
White, Allon, 94, 116n
Widdowson, Peter, 210–11n
Wiener, Martin, 197, 211n
Wilde, Oscar, 32
Williams, Raymond, 1, 13,
    177n, 182, 188, 196–7,
    200, 202, 204–5, 210n,
    212n, 214
Wilson, Alexander, 107,
    177n, 242
Wilson, E. O. 69n
Winner, David, 280n
Wittgenstein, Ludwig, 20
Wittig, Monique, 127–8
Wittkower, R., 112n
Wollstonecraft, Mary, 79
Woolley, Penny, 56
Wordsworth, William, 104, 107,
    117n, 237, 239–41

Yeats, W. B., 110

Zizek, Slovoj, 110, 118n